Eschatology and Ethics
in the Teaching
of Jesus

Eschatology and Ethics in the Teaching of Jesus

REVISED EDITION

AMOS N. WILDER

GREENWOOD PRESS, PUBLISHERS

WESTPORT, CONNECTICUT

Library of Congress Cataloging in Publication Data

Wilder, Amos Niven, 1895-
   Eschatology and ethics in the teaching of Jesus.

   Reprint of the ed. published by Harper, New York.
   Bibliography: p.
   Includes index.
   1. Jesus Christ--Teachings. 2. Eschatology--
Biblical teaching. 3. Kingdom of God--Biblical teach-
ing. 4. Jesus Christ--Ethics. I. Title.
[BS2417.E7W5 1978]   236   78-16425
ISBN 0-313-20585-X

Reprinted with the permission of Harper & Row, Publishers, Inc.

Reprinted in 1978 by Greenwood Press
A division of Congressional Information Service
88 Post Road West, Westport, Connecticut 06881

Library of Congress Catalog Card Number 78-16425

ISBN 0-313-20585-X

Printed in the United States of America

10 9 8 7 6 5 4 3 2

TO MY FATHER

AMOS PARKER WILDER

Contents

7

8   *Contents*

Preface

THERE is increasingly general consent among biblical scholars today that when Jesus announced the coming of the Kingdom of God he envisaged an imminent divine intervention in the world or dramatic judgment and world-renewal similar in nature to the phenomena of the end-time pictured in the Jewish apocalyptic writings. This at least was the implication of the terms and imagery which he used. The reign of God in this future aspect meant to his hearers, as George Foot Moore has defined it, "the undisputed supremacy of God throughout his creation." This was "at hand," a consummation involving both catastrophic judgment and the inauguration of the new age through the agency of the heavenly Son of Man. Jesus used these and cognate terms and images familiar to the men of his time without feeling the need to define them anew, though he may have wished to correct certain misunderstandings bearing especially on their moral implications.

Recognition of this eschatological outlook of Jesus has disturbed men in their estimate of him. At this point particularly the results of modern scholarship have not passed over into the churches but have rather met a continuing resistance. It has not been realized that the gain is greater than the loss. For Jesus' message so understood not only fits more satisfactorily into its context in the Old Testament and Jewish background and in the New Testament sequel so that it is illuminated by its background and illuminates the beginnings of the church. More significant still, the intensity of the hope and its universality and ultimacy are better grasped when the good news is seen as couched in these transcendental symbols.

But special difficulty arises here also in connection with the authority of Jesus as a moral teacher for modern times. A bewildering diversity of views exists in any case as to his ethic. Tolstoy is only the most notable of those who have held that his imperatives should be taken as obligatory in the most literal sense. Nietzsche saw in the requirements of love and meekness a slave-morality incompatible with the heroic temper. Many Christians have been honestly puzzled as to the relevance of his moral attitudes to the problems of organized social and political institutions. Lutheran moral theology has often held that the demands of Jesus represented an impossible counsel of perfection, so framed as to drive the despairing conscience back upon grace. Modern liberal interpreters have tended to accommodate the requirements to the secular code of the day. Yet the resulting confusion has not undermined the authority of the teaching to any such degree as the conclusion that Jesus' ethical demands were intended alone for an emergency situation, an interim, with which our historical outlook and situation have little or nothing in common. Such a conclusion has tempted men to surrender up in despair the question of the historical Jesus, his significance, his authority.

Such a despair is by no means justified. It would be above all regrettable if the great and revolutionary advances of New Testament studies should lead to disillusionment when, on the contrary, they are achieving great positive results. We may have had to abandon jealously guarded dogmatic preconceptions as to Jesus. We may have had to recognize the cultural and psychological conditioning of his outlook. This only means, perhaps, that we accept in a more thoroughgoing way the implications of the doctrine of the Incarnation. Or, to put it in other terms, it means that we situate the founder of Christianity more persuasively in his own actual circumstance without thereby denying his uniqueness but rather bringing it more clearly into focus. Moreover there is clearly one advantage in recognizing the eschatological conditioning of Jesus' ethic. As far as the content of the ethic is concerned a great simplification results: we no longer strain to apply literally in new generations those things spoken in the terms of a particular situation. Yet the relevance can be defined and without evasion.

In what concerns admission of the eschatological outlook of Jesus, and the sway in his thought of this strain so alien to us, we are only going one step further along the way we have already gone in recognizing that Jesus shared in his own way the ideas of his time. We have already applied a process of historically sympathetic appreciation to the phenomena of demonology in the gospels and no longer find a scandal in Jesus' acquiescence in the views of his time at this point. We need to do the same now as regards his use of the apocalyptic ideas of his day. "The inference is clear. If not today then in the easily forseeable future Christianity will be constrained for its very life to apply a similar process of historically sympathetic appreciation to the whole domain of New Testament eschatology."[1]

The first step, certainly, towards understanding the ethical teaching of Jesus in its general bearing or in its present application is to understand it in its relation to its original occasion. More than one element went to make up the original antecedents and circumstances of this teaching, of which the most important were the standing ethical norms of the time, the Torah and the tradition and their practice. Strains of ethical teaching cognate with one or other element in Jesus' own can be found in the ethics of the prophets, of the wisdom teachers, of the apocalyptists and of the rabbis. All study of the teaching of Jesus must have these relationships in mind. Any other factors bearing on the sayings must be held in mind, particularly the immediate circumstances under which they were spoken, if such can be established. When all such matters are noted it still remains that a most significant factor in the presentation, if not in the content, of the ethical teaching was the eschatological expectation. It is difficult to deny that Jesus' whole call to repentance and his urgent summons to the righteousness he preached were set against a background of vivid eschatological rewards and punishments which he saw as imminent. And it is difficult to deny that some of his demands, certainly as laid on certain individuals, were extraordinary demands conditioned by an extraordinary situation.

The task of stating what the original teaching of Jesus himself was, either as regards eschatology or ethics, not to mention their mutual relation, is one beset with immense obstacles. Scholarship

[1] B. W. Bacon, *Studies in Matthew* (New York, 1930), p. 429.

is ever more aware of the difficulty of drawing a line between the *ipsissima verba* and the sayings ascribed to Jesus in the gospels but bearing the stamp of later formulation. The Jesus of the synoptic gospels, even the Jesus of our oldest sources, is a figure whose outline has already been modified unconsciously in the thinking of the church. In any case an effort must be made and has been made with good results to distinguish some of the clearer modifications which the tradition has undergone, by the use of all the criteria open to us. On the basis of these a working hypothesis as to the historical Jesus and his teaching can be presented. Such a hypothesis must underlie a study of this kind. While the detailed argument of this hypothesis is not included in the present form of this inquiry, its main points will appear.

But for the central issues we are here concerned with, we have one great advantage. Even supposing we err in some degree in confusing the Jesus of the gospels with the Jesus of history we may well, none the less, in our final findings reach conclusions of real value. For one thing we may have some confidence that our discriminations in the tradition will have eliminated from the picture all really late and flagrant distortions. And in the second place our findings will in any case throw light on the central problem in the thinking of the earliest Christian community. For it is our firm conviction that at bottom, in its essential meaning, the relation of eschatology to ethics was much the same for this community as it was for Jesus himself. The distortion has affected not the essence of the matter but the externals. Even supposing that our best hypothesis only presents us with a Jesus created by the tradition, the value of the study of the topic still remains for the light it throws on the motivation of the primitive church. Bultmann has this to say with regard to the view of some that the eschatological features were added to the teaching of Jesus by the Christian community: "Even so, the meaning of the eschatological announcement would at bottom remain the same, and the question would still remain, whether or how this announcement was related to the preaching of the will of God in the community. Instead of the message of Jesus, it would be the message of the community that needed exposition, and since

it finally comes down to the substance, meaning and claim of the
evangelical tradition, the question as to how much the historical
Jesus and how much others contributed thereto would be a secondary matter."[2]

In presenting this revised edition of the book it is timely to note
the changing situation of studies in this field with special reference
to the interrelation of scholarship and the general influences of our
time, especially the changing theological outlook. Each generation
has its own special needs and orientation and these affect the approach made to our subject matter and the questions asked of it.
Nineteenth century liberal Christianity from Ritschl to Harnack
envisaged the meaning of the Kingdom of God in a certain way
and its historical study of the matter received both incentive and
limitations from the theological outlook and cultural assumptions
of the period. The rise of the social gospel in this country carried
with it a powerful motive to new historical study. Together with
the contemporaneous development of social historical method, it
opened the eyes of the historian to a better understanding of Jesus'
message. At the same time there was in this phase of scholarship a
degree of modernization which subsequent investigation has sought
to obviate. The emergence of the theology of crisis and kindred
emphases on the transcendent aspects of the primitive gospel have
motivated in their turn an intensive study of the idea of the Kingdom, again not without its own unconscious modernization. Reaction to this movement characterizes the present situation.

But concern with the topic does not arise alone today out of
scholarly pursuits and changing theological views. Pressing problems of social ethics and public order, and of the proper message
of the church with regard to them, create a responsibility for biblical
scholarship in this field. The best evidence for this is found in the
particular topics set for world-wide examination by the Study Department of the World Council of Churches. These topics, brought
specifically before the Amsterdam Assembly but subject to con-

---

[2] Rudolf Bultmann, *Jesus*, (Berlin, 1929), p. 114; English translation: *Jesus and the Word*, translated by Louise Pettibone Smith and Erminie Huntress (New York, 1934), p. 123 and cf. pp. 12–14.

tinuing discussion, concern the church's message for the social and political problems of our time. Underlying these inquiries is the basic question of "The Biblical Authority for the Church's Social and Political Message Today." In preparation for a volume dealing with this question a series of ecumenical study conferences have been held and participation of scholars in various countries has been enlisted. Examination of the preliminary reports of these consultations indicates how significant a place is taken by the questions with which the present book is concerned.[3]

From many sides, therefore, we observe that the concerns of the church and of scholarship today lead to the study of the early Christian message and in particular to the study of Jesus' message of the Kingdom. It is not surprising that college curricula in religion, seminary courses and seminars, as well as programs in religious education and lay study constantly return to this subject matter.

On the other hand, the continued work in technical scholarship has been a contributing factor in keeping the eschatological question to the fore in theological circles. The labors of Johannes Weiss, Loisy and Albert Schweitzer provided an essential base for and played into the hands of dialectical or neo-orthodox interpretations of the gospel, though this development was entirely uncongenial to the scholars named. Their thoroughgoing eschatological interpretation of Jesus' message and work implied an otherworldly outlook and a transcendental view of the Kingdom which could easily find a place in the theology of crisis. Again, the work of Bultmann and Dibelius in form criticism had theological implications. The radical criticism of Bultmann and his historical skepticism are commonly felt to have an immediate relation to his form of dialectical theology. Some similar relation no doubt exists between Dibelius' *Die Formgeschichte des Evangeliums* (1919) and his *Geschichtliche und übergeschichtliche Religion im Christentum* (1925). Contrariwise, religious-historical investigation, especially that of Rudolf Otto, has contributed to the reaction against dialectical views of Jesus' mes-

---

[3] See *From the Bible to the Modern World: Two Conference Reports.* Edited by The Study Department of the World Council of Churches; 17 route de Malagnou, Geneva, 1947.

sage. More considered views with regard to form criticism and tradition criticism and more judicious conclusions as to the apocalyptic literature and outlook have had their repercussions in biblical theology, though they have by no means led to agreement on the eschatological question among scholars today.

Thus historical-exegetical study must continue and with it consideration of the larger question of the relevance of New Testament eschatology to the modern world. In English, we have, among others, comparatively recent works on these matters by C. H. Dodd, T. W. Manson, C. J. Cadoux, F. C. Grant, J. W. Bowman, and translations of volumes by Bultmann, Dibelius and Otto. In this country of late attempts at synthesis are unfortunately largely confined to single chapters in general studies of the career of Jesus or in works on biblical theology. Several of our best treatments of any length available in English are written from a rather special viewpoint, such as Dodd's *Parables of the Kingdom,* Bultmann's *Jesus the Word,* and F. C. Grant's *Gospel of the Kingdom.* In general, moreover, the eschatology or the ethics are treated alone rather than in relation to each other, at least in any systematic way. In these circumstances it appears worth while to bring the present work up to date and to republish it with revisions.

The chief revisions in the present edition are the following: The second chapter dealing with the eschatological teaching of Jesus has been enlarged and brought up to date. To the summary there of the contributions of Schweitzer, Dodd and Otto has been added a review of the work of other and more recent scholars both as regards their critical findings and the theological implications of their results. The discussion in the third chapter of the historical and transcendental elements in Jesus' view of the future has likewise been enlarged with special reference to the issue today as to their bearing on the Christian understanding of history. In Part I changes are not made in the text apart from minor corrections and clarifications. In Part II, however, numerous modifications have been made in the text and in the approach, especially in what concerns the relation of Jesus' person to the formulation of his demands. A chapter has been added at the end of the book supplementing the conclusions of the whole discussion and entitled, "The Kingdom of God and the Moral Life." Here we venture to broaden somewhat the area considered and to relate our conclusions to certain contemporary issues, especially to the dangers of moralism in the interpretation of the Christian faith. The bibliography has been greatly expanded and brought up to date. In view of this bibliography abbreviated titles are given in the references except in the first citation of a work. We wish again to acknowledge our debt to the International Council of Religious Education for permission to cite as we do in almost all cases from the American Standard Edition of the Revised Bible.

We are indebted to certain reviewers for suggestions. Part II connects certain of the most drastic of Jesus' ethical demands with the critical situation that arose in his ministry. Is this interpretation, then, a return to "interim ethics" which is earlier rejected? It would not seem so. It does indeed constitute an emergency ethic, but the emergency is not that of Schweitzer's interim, rather it is that of Jesus' mission. This does occasion a particular kind of demand, but it is shown that no double standard of conduct is involved, and that such emergency ethics or "mission ethics" are often relevant on later occasions.

A more difficult issue raised in the same part is the question of Jesus' person and its relation to the ethics. If it be granted that the ethics of Jesus can be characterized as ethics of the messianic age or new covenant ethics, can we speak of it also as "discipleship ethics"? We believe that it can be so presented in view of the fact that Jesus and the cause of the Kingdom are so inseparable. Nevertheless, we have modified our position on this matter. What is said on this point is admittedly problematic since the whole question of the messianic claim of Jesus is involved. But at least a thesis is proposed to the reader.

It will be noted that the distinction between the eschatology of the individual and the eschatology of the world is referred to at various points. Quite apart from the message of the imminent new age, the Jews envisaged rewards and penalties for the individual after death. Jesus sometimes speaks in this vein; the Dives' and

Lazarus' saying if authentic would be an example. But in Jesus' preaching such compensations usually merge with the compensations at the Judgment. A further matter of terminology may also be noted. Eschatology is understood as the teaching with regard to last things and there are various forms of it in the Bible, not to mention non-biblical writings. Apocalyptic eschatology is one kind of eschatology and refers to the more dualistic and transcendental kind usually found in the apocalyptic literature. The adjective "eschatological," however, is very commonly used in the latter more restricted sense (i.e., for "apocalyptic eschatological") and this is admissible if the context safeguards the distinction.

Amos N. Wilder

Chicago Theological Seminary and
Federated Theological Faculty
of the University of Chicago
June 20, 1949

Introduction

CHAPTER ONE

The Nature of Jewish Eschatology[1]

CERTAIN general questions of interpretation and valuation underlie a study of this kind. The features and detail of the doctrine of the future found in the Gospels cannot be properly understood without a picture of their antecedents and a just idea of the world-outlook from which they proceed. The inspiration, nature and quality of Jewish eschatology are of the first importance here. There has been much misconception of it through overemphasis upon certain adventitious apocalyptic strains and through the drawing of a false contrast with the prophetic writings. Until it is seen in its true light and assigned its proper ethical and spiritual significance it will be impossible to give a true reading to the movements of the Baptist and of Jesus, or to understand the eschatology of the Gospels. Our introduction will therefore treat of these matters and place the eschatology of Jesus in such a way as to illuminate the later analysis.

Eschatology is myth. But whereas most myth represents the unknown past and gives a symbolic picture of unknown origins, eschatology is that form of myth which represents the unknown future. Men walk in a here and now whose extent, indeed, varies with the accuracy of their historical and geographical observation. Beyond the relatively limited bounds of that here and now, in any stage of science or culture, they must fall back on an imaginative picture of what preceded the known and what is to follow it. They

[1] Compare the writer's briefer study, "The Nature of Jewish Eschatology," *The Journal of Biblical Literature,* L (1931), 201–206.

foreshorten the disappearing continuity of past and future into
dogmatic representations which serve to focus in themselves all the
past and all the future, and which become the termini of temporal
experience. Behind any people in its march in history is, as it were,
a painted backdrop representing their belief as to their past and
their origins, and before them a like scenery representing their belief as to the future.

We are not to think that more enlightened or modern epochs are
free of this necessity. Our myth will differ, but our representations
of origins and of the future will still partake of the nature of myth.[2]
Prophecies of the ideal community, a world-wide communist order,
the superman, are of the nature of eschatological myth as were those
of the millennium. Nor is properly transcendental eschatology today confined to adventists. The destruction of life on the earth is,
indeed, referred to so far distant a date by science as perhaps to be
deprived of eschatological significance. But the evolutionary view
expressed in terms of mutations—successive new creations or altera-
tions of human nature—represents a series of real eschatological
ends and renewals. The school that calls its teaching the "theology of
crisis" anticipates similar transcendental incursions in history from
time to time in crises whose issue is especially seen in judgment on
elements not worthy to abide.

If eschatology is of the nature of myth, we must look in it for

[2] Speaking of the apocalyptic anticipations of the Massachusetts colonists, Herbert
W. Schneider says, "the great gulf which separates their minds from ours lies not
so much in their habits of thinking as in the body of so-called facts or data out of
which thinking proceeds. For us, human history begins with the anthropoid apes
and is organized about the idea of the gradual development of modern civilization
out of the life of primitive man, a process which we sometimes call progress, sometimes merely evolution, and which we believe will continue until human life
disappears from this cooling planet. No doubt there is more myth and imagination
in this picture of history than we are conscious of; future generations may soon
be entertained by it, regarding it as another of those pretty myths and epics on
which the human mind feeds. On the whole, however, it is constructed out of the
facts and records of experience in so far as these have been discovered to us. But
the so-called facts and records which were available in the seventeenth century were
radically different, and the resultant picture of history was also radically different."
The Puritan Mind (Studies in Religion and Culture, American Religion Series, I)
(New York, 1930), pp. 10–11.

similar value. The world's greatest myths have always been summary and symbolic representations of essential truths. They have
sprung anonymously from the folk-soul subject to the shaping and
correction of long periods. Certain myths, indeed, represent only a
personification of natural phenomena, but others objectify the profoundest experience of a people or the race. The story of the Fall
in Genesis is such a myth and has a truth as to the origin and nature of the moral sense which is unaffected by later views of social development. Similarly with the more significant of the Greek
myths.[3]

Now Jewish eschatology, minor accretions apart, is such a myth
and carries a weight of spiritual truth such as only the greatest art
can convey. It is an artificial schema, indeed; it became a dogma
with fixed detail. But it had behind it as creative and shaping and
inspiring force a profound and true intuition with regard to the
future, a wealth of obscure religious intimations and presentiment,
which charged the projection with truth and made it a dogma so
correspondent with psychological reality that Jesus could employ it
from within as vehicle for the effecting of his work and the fulfilment of its own essential prophecy. The properly spiritual experience of Judaism persuaded them of coming creative change in human nature and society. Like Dante they felt the stupor of unknown
things to come:

> quand' io senti a me gravar la fronte
> allo splendore assai piu che di prima,
> e stupor m' eran le cose non conte:[4]

With their antecedents this sense of what was to come formulated
itself in the eschatological scheme and dogma. This dogma was with
its human limitations and the particular scientific limitations of the
age only an utterly imperfect forecast of world-history and destiny,

[3] N. Berdiaeff, *Esprit et Liberté* (Paris, 1933), deals with the significance of the
myth of Prometheus, pp. 90, 241–42, and with the myth of the Fall, pp. 90–91, in a
highly illuminating way.

[4] "When I felt my brow weighed down by the splendor far more than before,
and I was struck with consternation and amazement at the unknown things."
Purg. XV: 10–12.

but like all myth with its limitation it yet wonderfully and truly represented the essential intuition. And in any case it became necessarily the context and presupposition and dogma in which men lived, at least those of deeper religious experience, and by which they made their contribution. Thus with Jesus it became not a mere borrowed imagery and terminology, but the very rationale of his purpose and destiny. Thus are dogmas and ideals creative in the psychological, the spiritual history of mankind.

Eschatologies will vary with the power and truth of the religious intuitions that create them. These imaginative tableaux will be vivid or sober, imminent or remote, ethical or unethical, universal or particularist, transcendental or earthly, according as they spring from a religious apprehension that is immediate and elevated or not. As a man's faith, so is his eschatology. This same holds for a people or for an age.

The imminence of the eschatological event is a particular problem. In general it seems to be in proportion to the intensity of faith. It seems a natural corollary of faith's immediate grasp on the unseen that in the category of time also the apprehended object should be sensed as close. This is in any case true of a people like the Jews with their conception of history. Even a modern finds an inseparable connection between his hours of profoundest insight and his sense of the immediate and present and continuous divine assize and sifting in human affairs. Times of great stress and sacrifice such as the Cromwellian period or the years of the first World War had as their accompaniment a vivid and close-up picture of the future Kingdom of the Saints or a regenerated world to follow on the time of affliction. In time of effort and faith men have always foreshortened the future after this fashion.

A remarkable parallel to the Jewish apocalyptic ardor in times of stress is found in the case of the English Puritans. They sustained themselves in their costly struggle against what seemed to them to be the later Babylon of heathenish tyranny or against the rigors of exile and the wilderness by the conviction that upon them all the ends of the world had come, and that the brief hour of suffering would give place to the realized Kingdom of Christ. "The poem of

Milton (*Paradise Lost*) was the epic of a fallen cause. The broken hope, which had seen the Kingdom of the Saints pass like a dream away, spoke in its very name."[5] The colonists in New England maintained their hopes longer and built the Holy Commonwealth into the realities of the state. "These are the times drawing on, wherein prophecies are to attain to performances: . . . These are the times, when the knowledge of the Lord shall cover the earth as the waters the sea; . . . These are the times when people shall be fitted for such privileges, fit I say to obtain them, and fit to use them. . . . Now the Lord will write his law in their hearts, and put it into their inward parts, and they shall teach no more every man his neighbor, for they shall all know me, from the least of them, to the greatest of them. . . . This being the season, when all the kingdoms of the world, are becoming the Lord's and his Christ's; and to this purpose he is taking to himself his great might, which heretofore he seemed to lay aside . . ."[6]

This imminent feature characterized Jewish eschatology at various periods. The Jewish view of the future presents us with a unique study in the psychology of faith. Faith under certain circumstances, discouraging circumstances, looks to the compensations of God. Oppression, martyrdom, the sway of evil, these demand a divine reversal provided the sense of divine actuality and holiness is sufficiently alive. It is true that we get this anticipation on different ethical levels. A lower view of Jahweh and his purposes with Israel and the world will lead to an unethical nationalist eschatology. But it is probable that the main spring of Jewish eschatology and certainly its most dynamic and obstinate strain was a purer demand for the destruction of all evil and the fulfilment of Israel's larger mission. The roots of this appear in Isaiah but probably go farther back. The later Isaiah is of supreme importance for shaping the hope and giving it its ethical content. The later Judaism saw the issue presented ever more and more sharply. On the one hand the sanctity of

[5] John Richard Green, *A Short History of the English People* (London, 1875), p. 586 (closing page of chap. VIII).

[6] Thomas Hooker, *Survey of the Summe of Church Discipline* (London, 1648), Preface, cited in Schneider, *op. cit.,* p. 28.

God and his universal rule. On the other, the prolonged oppression of his people or of the true core and remnant of his people, and the clearer realization of the power and perversion of the Gentile nations. The insight of faith saw that transformation of the earthly situation was inevitable, so flagrant was the discrepancy. It also saw that such a reversal would necessarily be a work of power, a transcendent act. The power of Rome, the inveterate perversity of Israel, its present worldliness, these challenged divine intervention, that divine act which had come to be a commonplace of Jewish expectation. For not only were earthly conditions to be transformed, but accompanying it there must be the overthrow of the demonic powers in the spiritual world. Faith demanded nothing less than a palingenesis of all things, and it was absurd to look elsewhere than to God for such a work. In all this the best of the Jewish apocalyptists were only putting in what conceptions were available to them their assurance that the unique insight of Israel, the oracles of God, would not be frustrated but would be given free course in the life of the future.

It is probable that we lend a false concreteness to their anticipations. It is a very real problem here to know just what they really expected when they used apocalyptic imagery. The Son of Man coming "with the clouds of heaven," the onset of Gog and Magog, such traits of the eschatological event and a hundred others we probably are quite unable to understand as they understood them. No doubt we take them too literally and ignore the poetical mentality of the race and the age. On the other hand we make a mistake if we think of them as merely symbol and poetry as a modern would understand these. The eschatological event was their picture of the asserted sovereignty of God. This certainly did not have the same crassness and literalness as modern premillenarian expectations. The modern naïve second-adventist travesties Jewish and Christian apocalyptic. Though he may have the identical scheme and features, these taken out of their original world-view have a totally different significance. We must remember that the Jews of that age had a less scientific or rather non-scientific frame of mind, for which revery, imagination, myth, dream and ideal were less distinguished from the sensible external world and event. Men looked for the enactment of long-prophesied roles in the persons and events of the day. The invisible world with its angels and demons and other figures mingled in the throng of the living and took part in their strifes. We should make a real effort to enter into this spiritual *Weltanschauung* for without it we can never do justice to the significant phases of later Judaism and the rise of Christianity. This view of the world and of life, these presumptions both by what they included and by what they excluded, constituted a very extraordinary setting, and as such conditioned certain ranges of extraordinary events in the actual world of happenings. We may say that the Jewish eschatological program was "symbolic" only, provided we bear in mind that the distinction between historical and suprahistorical events was not clear cut to them.

The lack of consistency in the various main features of the eschatological program, as well as the fantastic quality of many, should warn us against too literal an interpretation of these expectations. Speaking of the inconsistent "periodization" of the hereafter, G. F. Moore says, "There is in this sphere not merely an indefiniteness of terminology but an indistinctness of conception."[7] Also, "It is probable that these stages of the future were not so sharply distinguished in thought as we should like to have them."[8] Such variety is only partly due to the fact that the various ingredients of the total program came from different stages of a historical development. Rabbis contemporary with each other could hold opposite opinions on major features. Speaking of one such disagreement Moore says, "The diverse opinions of these two distinguished teachers of the third century is further evidence that there was not only no orthodoxy, but no attempt to secure uniformity in such matters."[9] Lake and Jackson in their discussion of apocalyptic thought and literature in *The Beginnings of Christianity* point out especially three features of the eschatological program which are extremely variable in the liter-

[7] *Judaism in the First Centuries of the Christian Era. The Age of the Tannaim* (Cambridge, 1927), II, 378.

[8] *Ibid.*, p. 391.

[9] *Ibid.*, p. 379.

ature: the figure of the Messiah, the agent in the Judgment, and the portrayal of the "last effort of the powers of evil."[10]

We have two things to bear in mind here with regard to the Jewish mind and its imaginative expression. On the one hand it gives expression to spiritual experience in extremely realistic, detailed, precise imagery. There is no indefiniteness or ambiguity in any one unit or tableau, though it may be exceedingly bizarre. There is no effort to move the reader by the prestige of abstract conceptions, or by impressionism or vague suggestion. The visions of Ezekiel, the apocalyptic detail, are very concrete and precise, and the art of the Jewish visionary here resembles that of the Italian or the Flemish primitives.

But in the second place we need to remember that such minute exactness of portrayal does not, by any means, require of the reader a crass literalness of understanding. Ezekiel's visions with their recognizable literary elaboration should not be received as a literal picture of what the prophet saw; the realism and detail are there to emphasize the reality of the prophet's central experience. So with the apocalyptic tableaux. To the detail natural to the naïve picture-faculty of the Jew at that time came to be added the detail accumulating as a legacy of the apocalyptic tradition. But the eschatological prophecies were not meant to be received as literal pictures either of what the seer saw in heaven or of what events were to transpire in the future. Again, the realism is there to emphasize the reality of the prophet's central experience.

While any one unit of apocalyptic vision will form a consistent if sometimes a bizarre picture, an apocalyptic writing may include numerous inconsistent separate pictures, and the apocalyptic literature as a whole will include many such. "Any attempt to systematize the Jewish notions of the hereafter imposes upon them an order and consistency which does not exist in them."[11] But this only demonstrates that the eschatological program belonged for the Jewish mind to the category of imaginative forecast rather than literal prophecy,

---

[10] *The Beginnings of Christianity*. Part I, The Acts of the Apostles (London, 1920), I, 133–34.

[11] Moore, *op. cit.*, I, 389.

for this acquiescence in the inconsistency (common to Jew and Christian) would not otherwise have persisted.

Apart from the inconsistency of the features, their fantastic character also speaks against the literal interpretation. As Moore says of parts of Revelation, "the visions are frequently unvisualizable,"[12] or of the visions of Esdras and Baruch, "the whole drama moves on a fantastic stage, like the last conflict with the hordes that gather to war upon him (the Messiah) in 4 Esdras 13, and the Messiah is a symbol, not a hero."[13] The vision-convention itself renders suspect the literal sense of the content of the revelations. Moore analyzes the whole issue exactly when he asks concerning the seer's treatment of typical features of the future Event, the Messiah waiting in heaven, the New Jerusalem descending: "What else could he do? Did he, therefore, imagine that the Messiah was really existent in heaven, waiting for God's hour to be revealed, or his new Jerusalem as a real city built in heaven, one day to be let down to earth? Or rather, was this the original conception; for after this manner of representation became an apocalyptic convention, writers may have taken thus realistically the imagery of their predecessors, and the common man was sure to do so."[14]

This is the key to the matter. The visions at first and in their later creative examples were imaginative in intention. But in varying measure they were taken realistically and imitated realistically. Against the intention and protests of such men as Paul among the Christians and Maimonides among the Jews, the common Christian and Jewish imagination has literalized eschatology. In the Gospels as in all the literature having eschatological elements the tendency is at work.[15]

We can see the genesis of properly transcendental apocalyptic in the Old Testament. The biblical messianism that grew up in the

[12] Moore, *op. cit.*, I, 343.

[13] *Ibid.*, I, 338.

[14] *Ibid.*, I, 343–44.

[15] "Does not religion teach by parables; and have not the profoundest intuitions of faith been often wrapped up in poetical myths and symbols, which dogmatism turns into flat historical narratives, and rationalism as ponderously rejects?" W. R. Inge, *The Platonic Tradition in English Religious Thought* (London, 1926), p. 71.

vicissitudes of the kingdom with its ideal of a perfect or restored kingdom more and more decked itself out with the use of transcendental features. These were but the legitimate hyperbole of the poet. In the second Isaiah the whole conception passed farther into the realm of the supernatural. Still later came the clearer dogma of the transcendental world where spiritual events control and precede or parallel earthly events. Apocalyptic, however, is really only a natural extension of the older messianism with the added use of transcendental symbolism in the larger place given to vision-properties. In those expressions of the apocalyptic hope which are genuinely spiritual, the impulse to the transcendental development was ethical and prophetic. It was the ethical consciousness asserting its faith, its vision, its certainty.

There is a fallacy in the common reading of apocalyptic as a discouraged abandonment of an impossible task to divine intervention. There are, no doubt, strains in the literature where this is the case. As there were inferior prophets so there were inferior visionaries of the later school. Political and military victory over oppressors would really require supernatural intervention and an effort the Jews who looked this way must have largely counted hopeless. The Zealots probably only hoped to occasion the intervention, not to make it unnecessary. But ethical and spiritual achievement in the world did not wait on a divine intrusion of such a type. The true apocalyptists whose aim was the vindication of good irrespective of Israel did not renounce effort but multiplied it in sacrifice and martyrdom.[16] In any case, it was good orthodox teaching since the time of

[16] Such fidelity to the faith and such heroism on the part of the apocalyptist is well reflected in the first six chapters of Daniel. See also the characterization of the ethics of the apocalyptist in Gerhard Sevenster, *Ethiek en Eschatologie in de Synoptische Evangeliën, Een Studie over het Typische in Jezus' Zedeleer* (Leiden, 1929), chap. I. Lake and Jackson point out that while for the apocalyptists history has a determined plan, yet such determinism is not extended to individuals. They quote Akiba: "All is foreseen by God, and the power of choice is given to man" (Aboth, 3:19). Cf. Hanina, "All is in the power of Heaven, except the fear of God" (Berachoth, 33b). *Op. cit.*, I, 128–29. Volz in his pages that point out the value of eschatology shows that its true root was in the hearts of the pious, and that its object was to sustain them in their fidelity to God. "The apocalyptists took themselves and their fellow Jews to the heights of the Beyond and of the outlook upon

the prophets that God was the ruler of all peoples and had his own plan with them to be followed to its preordained conclusion. We should not indict the true apocalyptic hope which without relinquishing its task asserted the divine action which it sensed as imminent. Its vision was of God overcoming evil in "the heavenly places" as guarantee of the same on earth. If it extended the personal intervention of God to this world it was but a corollary of this last, and consciously symbolic of coming human regeneration that it was beyond them to describe otherwise. How could the Jews envisage two thousand or two hundred thousand years of continuing history? They lacked completely our view of time and development, and for them the whole conscious spiritual age of man was but a very few generations.[17]

Those who waited for redemption in Israel, the humble in the land, the persecuted, the martyrs, those who lived on the word of the prophets, the second Isaiah, the Psalms, looked indeed for vindication which must somehow involve confusion to all thisworldly power and military display. But this process they only symbolically represented. The main thing this community saw was the victorious divine will and power waiting at the door of the times, and its action they foresaw as both the annulment of worldly power and, chiefly, the fulfilment of the promises of righteousness and salvation to all peoples. The apocalyptist often unduly stresses the former under persecution and because of pardonable nationalist preconceptions, but the heart of the whole is ethical and spiritual vision and demand.

Again, when we read the frequent opinion that in contrast with the prophets the apocalyptists diverged farther and farther from actual historical events and conditions, we must be on our guard.

the future in order that they should not cease to battle for the faith or that at least they might forget the melancholy present." *Jüdische Eschatologie* (Tübingen und Leipzig, 1903), p. 152. See pp. 150–52. Its doctrine of the value of suffering and loss encouraged heroism, *Ibid.*, pp. 156–58.

[17] It is remarkable how the Jews foreshortened even their own past, at least that part that did not belong to the sphere of pure legend. Thus they so telescoped the Persian period as to allow only thirty-four years from the rebuilding of the temple to the overthrow of the Persian monarchy by Alexander. G. F. Moore, *op. cit.*, I, 6.

Whereas Isaiah or Jeremiah referred to a particular foe or a particular campaign, the apocalyptists, it is said, left the ground of history, introducing, for example a great host from the north attached to no definite historical conjuncture. It is true that apocalyptic writers did not preach specifically on foreign policy. They were poets rather than statesmen. Their use of features like the onset of Gog and Magog was a borrowing from unfulfilled prophecy for the purposes of imaginative symbolism. But in another sense they were in close touch with their times, in lending courage, consolation, hope to the necessities of the suffering righteous in very definite crises and disasters. They spoke to the suffering righteous; the prophets to a blinded nation: this difference is sufficient to account for the contrast in their messages. Ethical and religious insight were the inspiration of both groups. Montefiore has shown us[18] that in this late period the ethical teaching of the prophets had been to a great extent assimilated into the religion and society of the Second Temple, and the prophetic impulse would inevitably take a different channel. Ethics was inextricably implied in the best apocalyptic, it was assumed. The eschatological hope was only for those who were righteous. And it was the ethical consciousness which in the first place demanded the Kingdom. From first to last we should draw our contrasts not between ethics and apocalyptic, for all Israel's prophecy partook of apocalyptic in the sense that some dualism was presupposed. But we should draw our contrast between an ethical and a non-ethical apocalyptic. Similarly in the case of Jesus himself, we are to acknowledge his apocalyptic eschatology, but to set it over against the inferior eschatology of many of his contemporaries.

We have said that eschatology partakes of the nature of myth. An interpretation of eschatology in terms of a value philosophy may be ventured as follows. Each individual experience of values, of the religious object, will dramatize itself in some form appropriate to the ideas and circumstances of those concerned. "Eschatology is a temporal representation of essence and value (*Seins- und Wertvor-*

---

[18] *Lectures on the Origin and Growth of Religion as Illustrated by the Religion of the Ancient Hebrews* (Hibbert Lectures, 1892) (London, 1897). Cf. Moore, *op. cit.,* I, 15–16.

stellung); a naïvely represented 'last' which is to be seen as an eternal and temporal and continually pressing 'now.' "[19] The essential thing is the personal or group discovery of extraordinary psychical and spiritual fact. These discoveries witness to a realm or a reality which must be their ground. *It is part of such experience to anticipate its greater fulfilment.* The picturing of this realm and of the attainment of its greatest enjoyment is a dramatizing or myth-building process of which the eschatology of the Jews is an outstanding example. We can find other examples where we will.[20] The conception of the future Kingdom of God was the way by which the Jews dramatized their experience of values. We get it in its purest form, because proceeding from the supreme sense of values, in the eschatology of Jesus himself: the benevolent will of the Father bringing in a transformed world. A modern like Carlyle can give expression to his experience of values by saying that the constellations themselves are but porch lights to something greater and more majestic behind, which man shall enjoy. The doctrine of progress is a contemporary expression of our experience of values, and in its superficial nature testifies to a superficial experience.[21] Our proneness to build distorted and misconceived schemes upon our fragmentary experience is well evidenced here in this doctrine of inevitable progress, as it was in seventh-century Judah's deduction of the inviolability of Jerusalem. At every stage of religious thinking the same process may be observed at work; in the picturing of forces and spiritual beings, and in the myriad eschatologies dictated by the myriad circumstances of human society.[22]

[19] Hans Windisch, *Der Sinn der Bergpredigt, Ein Beitrag zum Problem der Richtigen Exegese* (Leipzig, 1929), p. 8.

[20] Compare Nichiren's doctrine of the Buddha-land as an example in Japanese Buddhism; Masaharu Anesaki, *Nichiren, The Buddhist Prophet* (Harvard University Press, 1916), pp. 37, 101 ff., 108, 110.

[21] See discussion by Inge, *op. cit.*, pp. 113–19.

[22] An example from a more primitive stratum of culture is afforded by the prophecy in 1889 of Wovoka ("Jack Wilson") of the Paviotso tribe of American Indians of Nevada. "It seems that at the time of a solar eclipse, probably on January 1, 1889, Wovoka fell asleep during the daytime and was taken up to the other world, where he saw God and all the dead of long ago who were happy and young, playing at their old games and engaged in their old occupations in a land

The danger always is that men deduce from their experience of values a false assurance of inferior goods: security, material blessings, vengeance, indulgence in respect of evil-doing. The story of Jewish eschatology is full of such degenerate Utopias. The eschatology of Jesus is pure at this point. It has no place for pictures of a new age like those of a sensuous Paradise, or like those of apocryphal books where chief stress is laid on the miraculous fruitfulness of the land. Again, Jesus rejects the particularist strain of Jewish eschatology. With him, belonging to the Jews is no claim on the Kingdom. Nor is there talk of revenge on the foes of Israel. In Jesus' conception, moreover, there is no indulgence of sin. The stern presence of the judgment feature, judgment impartial to all the nations and judgment based on purely ethical standards, this sets the eschatology of Jesus in a place by itself. But in addition we have to note the uniqueness of the very presentation of his scheme if it can be called a scheme. It could almost be called unapocalyptic. If we eliminate the apocalyptic chapter and the Matthean elaborations of the vigilance motif, we find that Jesus' sayings are very "spiritual" and symbolic in nature. They are the utterances of a

---

of joy and plenty. After showing him everything, God bade him return with a message of peace, good will and moral exhortation. If the people obeyed instructions, they were to be reunited with their dead friends. They were to practice the dance revealed to Wovoka in his vision. 'By performing this dance at intervals, for five consecutive days each time, they would secure this happiness to themselves and hasten the event.' " An early Cheyenne delegate also reported: " 'He told us that all our dead were to be resurrected; that they were all to come back to earth. . . . He spoke to us about fighting and said that that was bad and we must all keep from it; that the earth was to be all good hereafter, and we must all be friends with one another. . . . He told us not to fight or quarrel or strike each other, or shoot one another; that the whites and Indians were to be all one people.' " R. H. Lowie, *Primitive Religion* (New York, 1924), pp. 191–92.

This prophecy was the main antecedent of the Ghost Dance of the Teton or Sioux reservations of Western Dakota. Among this people the prophecy was transformed into an expectation of the defeat of the whites and a return of the old conditions with abundance of game, in accordance with the bitter grievances of this people at this time. It is a good illustration of the submerging of ethical prophecy and cult by particularist loyalties. In both cases *the conditioning of the prophecy and eschatology by the social circumstance is clear,* as well as the original experience of values.

great poet and seer rather than of a fantasist. As Bultmann says, he rejects the entire wisdom of curious apocalyptic speculation, along with the calculation of the end and scrutiny of the signs.[23] He spoke of the Kingdom and of the coming of the Son of Man and of the banquet of the Kingdom and of the Judgment as a poet would speak—but, indeed, as a poet speaking true things. He did not speak in childish naïveté nor in a crass concrete way. He foresaw beyond all doubt the imminent action of the Father in transforming the moral and spiritual condition of men, and that in a way closely related to his own person and fate; and he expressed this in a great way as a great seer would, in terms of the conceptions of his own age. He used the conception of the Son of Man coming on the clouds of heaven to judgment, and related himself to that figure in his own thought and before men at his trial. Thereby he was representing in the only terms he could the spiritual significance of his work in history. Jesus, in his eschatology, cast into the form of myth the epoch-making, world-transforming significance of his own life, in Jewish terms. An inevitable part of the picture was the foreshortening of the time. Jesus naturally envisaged only his own generation and related the supernatural event to the imminent destruction of Jerusalem.

All this has been well put by J. A. McCulloch. "Intense convictions loom large on the mental horizon and assume a nearness of fulfilment which is illusory. In times of intense thought we 'can crowd eternity into an hour.' This was true of many prophetic utterances and it was much more true of Apocalyptic convictions, which frequently speak of the nearness of the last things, as if they could not otherwise be conceived of . . . Still, what is emphatic is less the thought of nearness than the absolute certainty of the reality of the things of the end. For these reasons Christ's deeper knowledge and conviction of his position as Judge . . . took shape in his surface thoughts, mainly, though not always, in intense eschatological convictions, which . . . then assume the form of an imminent and catastrophic Parousia. We must, therefore, search

[23] See R. Bultmann, *Jesus* (Berlin, 1929), p. 39; *Jesus and the Word*, p. 39.

for the rich meaning of which Christ's eschatology is full, and which its associations with the past already connotes."[24]

The elaboration of the Gospels, either as relating to the historical situation of the early church,[25] or as relating to the homiletical application of the warnings, does not essentially debase the ethical quality of the eschatology of Jesus. They carry farther the process of myth-building; give a more pictorial representation of the warnings and blessings; assign to Jesus himself a more definite role than he had assigned himself. All this proceeded from the circumstances of the church; the demand for practical apologetic and pedagogy, the greater variety, simplicity, no doubt ignorance, of the faithful, and the intensity bred by conditions of stress and persecution. But the essential inspiration of the eschatology remains what it was with Jesus, what it was in Jewish eschatology at its best: the appeal of the ethical consciousness against things as they are, and the incontrovertible assurance of faith that God will act.

[24] Art., *Eschatology*, in Hastings, *Encyclopædia of Religion and Ethics* (New York, 1912), V, 390.
[25] Mk, 13 and its parallels, etc.

CHAPTER TWO

The Eschatological Teaching of Jesus

I T IS not possible within the scope of the present treatment to take up in detail the issues raised by this topic. Such a study has been made and underlies the present chapter and the whole work. It will suffice here to state the classical view of Albert Schweitzer, to note what significant corrections are proposed by more recent study of the topic, and to conclude with a summary of the views held by the present writer. A critical discussion of many points will be found in the sequel.

The consistent eschatological view of Schweitzer may be briefly stated as follows. Jesus began his ministry proclaiming the near advent of the catastrophic Judgment and the Kingdom of God, and calling upon men to repent in view of them. He was already conscious of his Messiahship, a humble and unrecognized Messiahship, a mystery that only a few were called to recognize. But he anticipated his own metamorphosis with the coming of the Kingdom, and his manifestation to all as Son of Man at that time. He sent out the disciples to the lost sheep of the house of Israel to broaden the work of proclamation of the Kingdom. So soon was the Son of Man to appear that Jesus could tell them that they would not have passed through the cities of Israel before that event. When their preaching tour had taken place and they had returned, all things continuing as they had, Jesus was led to revise his outlook. Whereas in sending out the Twelve he had anticipated that they like himself would have to endure the immediate messianic woes, he now sees that he himself shall bear those woes alone, "for many," that is, for the predestined elect. It is now that there comes to Jesus the daring thought that since the Kingdom delays its coming, he will precipitate it. He will take hold of the great wheel of destiny, of the eschatological train of events, and fling it around, even if he be crushed in his venture. The "dogmatic history" of the eschatological outlook Jesus will introduce by faith into real history. His astounding act of faith issued in despair on the cross. But from him have flowed streams of spiritual power in the life of humanity.

Schweitzer presented his sketch of Jesus in a particular conjuncture of New Testament criticism which went far to condition it. So-called liberal criticism had been led by its own preconceptions to desperate measures with the records, both arbitrary and mutually contradictory. Schweitzer took Wrede as his foil. The latter's radicalism, especially in the excision of all eschatological "dogma" from the record of Mark, and in the reduced portrait of Jesus as a prophet, seemed to Schweitzer the inevitable outcome of such irresponsibility with the sources, and a proper rebuke to the modernizing tendencies of the liberal criticism. But Schweitzer validated the eschatological elements. For him it was, indeed, "dogma," but instead of having been read into the record by the later church, as Wrede believed, he held that it was read in by Jesus himself.

Jesus, then, according to Schweitzer, announced an imminent Judgment and world renovation. This left no room for a continuing historical order. All ethics were interim ethics. Jesus' indifference to family, state and property resulted from the acute sense of tension as the present age confronted its Judge. Thus Schweitzer abolished the modernized Jesus and restored him to the alien, largely unknowable categories of his own time and people. In so doing he felt that he had vindicated the records as against Wrede, and vindicated the true greatness of Jesus as against the liberal school.

Today there are few to disagree with Schweitzer among New Testament critics as regards the main point. Almost all feel that a flood of light is thrown upon him and his teaching and the early church by recognizing that he expected the end of the age and the last word of God upon human history, the coming of the Son of Man, the harvest, in his own generation, if not in the very year of his ministry. It is interesting to find von Hügel, a Roman Catholic writer, already in 1919 accepting the position, stressing the fact that the Incarnation "could not, even by Himself (i.e. God), be made other than the entering into, and possession of, a human mind and will endowed with special racial dispositions and particular racial categories of thought." Among these categories, permeating the Bible from cover to cover, is the view that, "Everywhere the divine action is, as such, conceived to be instantaneous . . . If then Jesus held that the world's present order would be terminated by an act of God, He could not image and propound this act other than as sudden and rapid."[1]

But if most scholars have accepted the main point in Schweitzer's view, one can say that the subsequent development of New Testament study has placed that emphasis in a somewhat different light. Schweitzer's work on the life of Jesus was done at a time when the study of the gospel tradition fell very far short of what it has since become. The first German edition of *Das Messianitäts und Leidensgeheimnis, Eine Skizze des Lebens Jesu* was published in 1901 and all of Schweitzer's leading ideas later to be found in *Von Reimarus zu Wrede* (1906), translated under the title, *The Quest of the Historical Jesus* (1910), are there. For instance, Schweitzer took at face value the discourse of Jesus at the sending out of the Twelve in Mt. 10, and naturally saw in it a delineation of the immediate messianic woes which the disciples should endure and of the coming of the Son of Man before the completion of their tour. It must be said that Goguel today assigns this view to Jesus on this occasion at least in so far as the coming of the Son of Man is concerned. But most scholars today, with Bacon, assign this saying to Palestinian Christians, perhaps when fleeing from Jerusalem before the great siege and making their way from city to city: a word of prophecy granted by Christ to his church through some Christian prophet.

[1] F. von Hügel, *Essays and Addresses on the Philosophy of Religion* (London, 1921), pp. 125, 126.

In general our clearer understanding of the character of the Gospel of Matthew relieves us of the obligation of taking its tenth chapter as spoken *in toto* by Jesus on the occasion supposed.[2]

Again, Schweitzer went to great pains to deny all reference by Jesus to a present Kingdom or a present aspect of the Kingdom. Not only the "parables of the Kingdom" like those of the leaven and the mustard seed, but the sayings about the Kingdom suffering violence and the Kingdom "in your midst," were turned into references to the future catastrophic Kingdom. Guignebert does the same thing verse by verse in his *Jesus*. The Kingdom is in your midst can mean: it *will* be suddenly in your midst; or, the evidence of its future coming is in your midst; or, the possibility of entering it (when it comes) is within you. But on the whole the later study has shown that Jesus taught a present aspect of the Kingdom. The parables of the leaven and the mustard seed can no longer be taken as the liberal school took them, thanks to Schweitzer. We must see in them the mystery of the divine operation, not an evolutionary growth of the Kingdom. But they do also bear witness to a present unrecognized phase of the Kingdom. This is discussed further below.

What is the present view of the eschatological problem among scholars? The most remarkable fact to be noted is that in one way or another the concreteness or crassness of Schweitzer's presentation of the matter is being placed in question.

Goguel distinguishes between eschatology and apocalyptic. The latter always sees events as following a foreordained plan, whose successive phases can be recognized and predicted by signs. But Jesus abjured the calculation of the times and the speculative attitude of the true apocalyptist. In Jesus' assertion of ignorance as to the time of the Kingdom, "there is the germ, if not of denial, at least of the weakening of the eschatological conception. This leads us to think that this conception was merely the framework for the thought of Jesus provided by the surroundings in which he lived. He thought in eschatological terms just as he spoke Aramaic, but

[2] Cf. W. G. Kümmel, *Verheissung und Erfüllung* (Basel, 1945) pp. 35–37.

that which is most intimate and essential in his thought may not be connected any more closely with eschatological thought than with the Aramaic tongue."[3] This is surely going too far. The words "framework" and "scaffolding" recur constantly on the lips of those who are inclined to evade the dilemma of Jesus' outlook. But the general position insists on Jesus' independence of orthodox apocalypticism.

Windisch[4] and Sevenster[5] have canvassed the teaching of Jesus and shown clearly that large elements in it belong to the tradition of the wisdom teacher and the prophet, apart from those that belong to the tradition of the apocalyptist. The conclusion is clear that not all of it can be viewed as interim ethics. Repeated reference will be made below to these writers.

Perhaps the most significant correction of Schweitzer was that of Rudolf Otto in his work, *Reich Gottes und Menschensohn*.[6] There are two things we must note here. First is the theme of the essential irrationality of all eschatology as regards its expectation of the end. It expects the end and yet it does not! The eschatological type, he says, men like Zoroaster, Mohammed, Jesus, see the Kingdom or the end arriving, but they act as if history were still to go on. Such a combination of imminent eschatology with ethics for an enduring world is inconsistent, indeed. But from the point of view of religious experience they have a necessary relation to each other. Jesus reckons with the messianic woes and the coming of the catastrophic Kingdom in a brief time. Logically there is no time for an ethic, only for repentance. But Jesus nevertheless also can assume the duration of the world. Otto substantiates this by a striking presentation of the evidence for it on pages 47 and 48 (*The Kingdom of God and the Son of Man,* pp. 59–62). Many of Jesus' sayings as-

[3] M. Goguel, *The Life of Jesus* (New York, 1933), pp. 569–72.
[4] *Op. cit., (Bergpredigt)*. Abbreviated titles will be used after the first mention of a work. The reader is referred to the Bibliography for complete titles.
[5] *Ethiek en Eschatologie.*
[6] Munich, 1934; English translation: *The Kingdom of God and the Son of Man;* translated by Floyd V Filson and Bertram Lee Woolf; Grand Rapids, Michigan: Zondervan, n.d.

sume continuing historical conditions. The saying about forgiving
one's brother seventy and seven times does not reflect the mood
of the apocalyptist. Otto has an interesting treatment of the saying
of Jesus as to his rebuilding the temple. He takes it as genuine.
Jesus here, he says, as good as speaks of "a new service of God,"
"almost a new religion," *"in der Weltzeit selber."* In such discourses
of Jesus the thought of the inbreaking eschaton withdraws; we
have a continuance of history presupposed.[7]

The other point to note in Otto is his view of the Kingdom as in
one aspect already present. We have here the theme which C. H.
Dodd has emphasized and treated in his own way under the
phrase "realized eschatology." Otto deals with it without abandon-
ing in any such way as Dodd does the future aspect of the Kingdom.
He points us to the passage, "If I by the finger of God cast out
demons, then is the Kingdom of God come upon you," and to the
sayings about the strong man bound and the fall of Satan. Many
have insisted on the significance of these passages as evidencing
Jesus' thought of the reality of the present Kingdom or the pre-
monitory signs of the approaching Kingdom. Otto gives them a
more significant interpretation. He sets the theme of the overthrow
of Satan in its setting in the history of religions in both Israel and
Persia. He then concludes that the emphasis should fall on Jesus'
testimony that the Kingdom has come, that Satan has already been
overthrown in heaven. Jesus looks on his work of exorcism and
healing and witness as only part of a great redemption-transaction
in a concrete sense. The Kingdom has brought him, not vice versa.
Jesus is the witness to it. His work is to proclaim the Good News.
The Kingdom to him, says Otto, is *Gottessaat* not *Menschentaat.*[8]
The Kingdom comes of itself, unobserved, apart from men's effort.
In the individual it shows itself in the bringing forth of repentance
and the new righteousness. For Otto, Jesus expects the climax of
the Kingdom in full apocalyptic reality. The intense numinous
experience of this type, the "ekstatiker," the charismatic, inevitably posits the temporally future Kingdom in this way. So we have

[7] *Op. cit.,* p. 49; *The Kingdom of God . . . ,* p. 62.
[8] *Ibid.,* p. 93; *The Kingdom of God . . .* p. 113.

ourselves described it in the opening chapter. And yet he illogically acts and teaches as if the world were to continue.

H. Lietzmann in his summary of Jesus' work accepts the idea of the present aspect of the Kingdom. The following citation from the English translation of his work on the early church conveys his attitude to the apocalyptic question. "But the Kingdom was coming with no less reality even in the present, and the Messiah was passing unnoticed through the land, illumined only by the splendour of miraculous deeds . . . The new aeon had already begun, before the old had collapsed—the apparatus of time and space fails wherever a genuine prophetic message of divine reality is proclaimed."[9]

C. H. Dodd goes farther than Otto in the matter of realized eschatology. Dodd's views are to be found in his *Parables of the Kingdom*[10] and other writings and lectures about the eschatology of the Church.[11] The gist of it is that for Jesus the Kingdom had arrived as both salvation and judgment in his generation. The actual apocalyptic Judgment and world-renovation follow immediately. Yet here Dodd is difficult to follow for he sometimes leaves the impression that Jesus had spiritualized these away into symbol. From this point of view the Judgment and the new age were to Jesus implicit in his work and death.[12]

Dodd is led by this approach to ask whether Jesus did not after all anticipate a continuing order on earth. For one thing he believes that we must deny the interim character of Jesus' ethics. "We seem," he says, "to be confronted with two diverse strains in the teaching of Jesus, one of which appears to contemplate the indefinite continuance of human life under historical conditions, while the other appears to suggest a speedy end to these conditions. A drastic criticism might eliminate the one strain or the other, but both are deeply embedded in the earliest form of the tradition known to us.

[9] *The Beginnings of the Christian Church* (London, 1937), p. 63.

[10] New York, 1936.

[11] *The Apostolic Preaching and Its Developments* (Chicago, 1937), Appendix: Eschatology and History. Also, *The Kingdom of God and History,* (*Church, Community and State,* Vol. III) (London, 1938), chap. 2.

[12] See analysis of Dodd's view in John Knox, *Christ the Lord* (New York: Harper & Brothers, 1945), pp. 26–30.

It would be better to admit that we do not possess the key to this reconciliation than to do such violence to our documents."[13] Dodd himself suggests that a symbolic interpretation of the eschatological terms of Jesus might be admitted, in which case we would have the desired key. He shows how inherent the symbolic method is in apocalyptic. For in the Book of Daniel political events past, present and future are represented by apocalyptic symbols. But he finally waives any such solution and places the emphasis on the view that for Jesus the essential meaning of eschatology was fulfilled in the revelation of the reign of God there and then in himself and his ministry.

Other scholars while not accepting the exegesis of Jesus' sayings and parables which underlies Dodd's "realized eschatology" have interpreted the eschatology of Jesus in similar ways. That is, they have recognized that Jesus anticipated the coming of the Kingdom in the near future and in transcendental catastrophic form, but they have construed this language as indicative of the present crisis and opportunity of men under God's grace and judgment. Any genuine historical or futuristic significance of the proclamation is thus denied. To understand this development in relation to the work of the scholars we have already discussed we may turn to a notable volume by F. Holmström, *Das eschatologische Denken der Gegenwart*.[14] Holmström summarizes the movement of scholarship in this field from the first notable work of Johannes Weiss in 1892 on. But the particular value of this book lies in his account of the changing theological and philosophical context as it affected the conclusions of biblical scholarship and biblical theology in this area and in his account of the influence of the eschatological interpretation of the New Testament. The German edition was published in 1936 and brings the discussion down to that time.

Holmström's work is divided into three parts. The first part is devoted to the period still ruled by the orthodox historical approach of the nineteenth century ("Die zeitgeschichtliche Epoche"). This

[13] *The Parables of the Kingdom*, pp. 104–5.
[14] (Gütersloh: Bertelsmann, 1936), a translation and revision of *Det Eskatologiska Motivet I Nutida Teologi* (Stockholm: Berlingska Boktryckeriet, 1933).

is the period up through the work of Weiss and Schweitzer when the basic presuppositions were those of idealism and value philosophy. It was this setting that occasioned Harnack's interpretation of the Kingdom concept of Jesus in terms of inward experience of the individual and timeless values and his discarding of the eschatological element as merely a shell or husk. Even Schweitzer, whose work rested on similar rationalist and Hegelian assumptions, looked on this element which he made determinative in Jesus' teaching as a contemporary mythical vehicle whose significance ended with the cross and which had no continuing normative value.[15] From what appeared to him to be the bankruptcy of the quest for the historical Jesus, Schweitzer took refuge in an ethical mysticism which has its links with the timeless values of his predecessors and even with the timeless eschatology of the crisis theology.

The second period is marked, above all, by the influence of Karl Barth and is described as "unhistorical" ("Die ungeschichtliche Epoche"). The Kingdom is lifted above time, and the future disappears in favor of the eternal or recurrent Now. A sharp dualism between God and the world, between the absolute and the contingent, influences exegesis. This outlook stamped itself in different ways upon Bultmann's *Jesus* (in English, *Jesus the Word*), Dibelius' *Geschichtliche und übergeschichtliche Religion im Christentum,* and Lohmeyer's commentary on the Book of Revelation, all three of which came out in 1925 or 1926. The eschatological element in Jesus' teaching was fully acknowledged but was construed in terms of timelessness or the absolute, and the real future of the Kingdom and the Judgment were dissolved into a present or existential reality. The negative tendency of much form criticism contributed to this emphasis. Holmström also invokes the influence of cultural conditions and the impact of the first World War. The timeless categories of this movement are also significantly related to the timeless value philosophy of the preceding period to which they were at least unconsciously indebted, though the relation to phenomenological and existential philosophy was more immediate.

[15] Cf. Holmström, *op. cit., pp.* 92–99; C. C. McCown, *The Search for the Real Jesus* (New York: Scribner's, 1940), pp. 251–53.

On the title page of his third part Holmström cites the following passage from H.-D. Wendland's work on the eschatology of the gospels published in 1931:

Any theology which minimizes the element of the future and the end-time in the concept of eschatology departs from the outlook of faith of the New Testament. . . . The double meaning of the concept "eschatological," according to which eternity and the future end are maintained together, must therefore be insisted upon both in New Testament theology and in dogmatics.[16]

This third period is described as one in which there is a tendency toward a synthesis. In this period, history and the future are assigned concrete significance as in the first period, but the meaning of history is sought in the divine revelation recorded in the Bible rather than in immanent values. At the time at which he brought his work to a close, Holmström was obliged to recognize that no resolution of the theological problem had been reached. Various criticisms showed that the dialectical approach had been found unsatisfactory.

This author assigns the inconclusive character of the debate to the fact that systematic theology had not set its own house in order. Its presuppositions were still too much determined by secularized nineteenth century categories.[17]

The situation has not greatly changed since the middle of the last decade (1936) when Holmström's treatment ends. The suprahistorical viewpoint has continued to inspire both historical exegesis and general interpretation up to the present in many quarters, as, for example, in Bultmann's later work. Moreover, Schweitzer's analysis of Jesus' teaching has had a striking restatement in an important volume, Martin Werner's *Die Entstehung des christlichen Dogmas,*[18] published in 1941. Werner insists on the strictly futuristic

[16] H.-D. Wendland, *Die Eschatologie des Reiches Gottes bei Jesus* (Gütersloh: Bertelsmann, 1931), pp. 253, 255.

[17] McCown's *Search for the Real Jesus* provides a valuable parallel treatment to Holmström in many particulars and carries the story on down to 1940: *infra,* pp. 49–50; 61–64.

[18] Bern and Leipzig: Paul Haupt.

character of the coming of the Kingdom as proclaimed by Jesus, ruling out any present or realized aspects. He goes the whole way with Schweitzer in accepting the mission charge in the tenth chapter of Matthew as a discourse of Jesus genuine in all essentials. With this view of the original message which he supports by a review of the often debated sayings, he elaborates a new approach to the history of doctrine in the New Testament and the early church to set over against the organizing principle of Harnack's *History of Dogma*.

On the whole, however, the situation has somewhat clarified itself. The point of view toward the Kingdom of God in exegesis and theology which Holmström characterizes as the "nonhistorical" has been subjected to such effective criticism that its representatives, at least in the field of New Testament scholarship, have given ground. This shift is evident in the contrast between the earlier and later works of Lohmeyer and Dibelius as well as in the case of Paul Althaus, to the successive editions of whose *Die letzten Dinge* Holmström calls special attention. In the case of Bultmann it is worthy of note that he has been pushed to a radical and thoroughgoing attempt to justify the existential view of the eschatology of Jesus as it appeared in his *Jesus* (1929) and in his studies in *Glauben und Verstehen* (1933). In his volume *Offenbarung und Heilsgeschehen* (1941) he includes the eschatological elements in his characterization of almost everything in the primitive message as mythological, prescientific, and untenable today. He thus buttresses his older position that the teleological element in the message of the Kingdom is to be denied and finds the Gospel of John most faithful to the intention of Jesus. He thus also accommodates his interpretation of the gospel to an existentialist view of man and the world closely akin in many respects to that of Heidegger.[19]

On the other hand, we find little evidence that an interpretation which sets aside or minimizes Jesus' expectation of a transcendental and imminent Kingdom has much support today. The best recent

[19] See below, pp. 64–66, and discussion by R. Prenter, "Mythe et Evangile," *Revue de théologie et de philosophie*, XXXV (1947), 49–67; and O. Cullmann, *Christus und die Zeit* (Zürich: Evangelischer Verlag, 1946), pp. 25, 26.

canvass of the whole question from the point of view of historical-critical exegesis is probably that of W. G. Kümmel's *Verheissung und Erfüllung: Untersuchungen zur eschatologischen Verkündigung Jesu.*[20] Kümmel, indeed, agrees that Jesus showed no concern for apocalyptic speculation, lore, and cosmology. Jesus preached an eschatological message, not apocalyptic wisdom. But Kümmel is perfectly forthright in concluding that Jesus announced the coming of the Son of Man from heaven to judgment in his own generation. This scholar takes the now prevailing view that Jesus taught both the present and the future aspects of the kingdom. The present aspect is to the future as the grain of mustard seed is to the tree. Similar able presentations are found in Jean Héring's *Le Royaume de Dieu et sa venue* and in Oscar Cullmann's *Christus und die Zeit,* which, however, has wider interests. This volume insists on the naïve and concrete sense of time and history which Jesus and the first Christians shared with the men of the Old Testament. The Greek conception of eternity as timelessness or simultaneity is not found in the Bible even in the Fourth Gospel. Cullmann is only one of a number of writers like Ethelbert Stauffer[21] whose approach to the teaching of Jesus is in the framework of *Heilsgeschichte* and for whom therefore a reading of it in terms of a timeless decision is a forfeiting of the biblical point of view and open to the charge of Gnosticism.

Scholars in this country like F. C. Grant and C. C. McCown have been keenly aware of the dangers of nonhistorical and transcendental interpretations of the idea of the Kingdom, especially perhaps as it was thrown into prominence in English in the Oxford Conference volume, *The Kingdom of God and History* (1938). The earlier and continuing interest of both men in the social gospel and their full initiation in the social-historical study of religion (compare here the work of Shailer Mathews and S. J. Case) predisposed them to an important testimony and contribution. In different ways they have

[20] Basel: Verlag von Heinrich Majer, 1945. See also, by the same author, "Die Eschatologie der Evangelien," *Theologische Blätter,* XV (1936), 225–41.

[21] *Die Theologie des Neuen Testaments* (Geneva: Ecumenical Council of Churches, 1945).

insisted on the relevance of Jesus' outlook, along with that of the
Hebrew prophets, to man's social realities. In his *Gospel of the
Kingdom*[22] Dr. Grant delimits sharply the original apocalyptic element in Jesus' teaching, denies the dualistic character of his eschatology, and relates his outlook to the theocratic universalism of the
best of the Old Testament. There is here an abundance of relevant
observation and consideration, but the case for the this-worldly concern of Jesus fails of full demonstration.

Dr. McCown, on the other hand, accepts the full implication of
Jesus' Son of Man apocalyptic[23] and finds in it a special case of the
social revolutionary ideals of the Near East dating from ancient
times, one having surpassing significance for cultural history and
the social hope. The author's polemic is directed not at apocalyptic
versions of Jesus' utterance but at theologizing interpretations of it
which divest it of social relevance.[24] Like Holmström, Héring,
Kümmel, Cullmann, and others, Dr. McCown recognizes the teleological future import of the gospel of the Kingdom. But his view
is distinctive in proposing to relate that future aspect directly to
cultural evolution. He protests that the process of history need not be
accounted valueless even though man's aspirations or God's purpose
cannot be wholly realized there.

In any case he is convinced that a great deal of the exploration
of these questions is done in a dogmatic isolation from relevant
sciences. All the sciences of man have a contribution to make to
these large questions of human destiny and can also illuminate
the study of Christian origins and of the meaning of eschatology in
particular. We have here a most important corrective of the somewhat compartmentalized and rigid character of much biblical study
even at its best. The larger historical perspectives with which Rudolf
Otto and McCown himself have made their approach to our special
area have been abundantly fruitful, as has incidentally the corre-

[22] New York: Macmillan Co., 1940; see also his article, "Ethics and Eschatology
in the Teaching of Jesus," *Journal of Religion*, XXII (1942), 359–70.
[23] Cf. "Jesus, Son of Man: A Survey of Recent Discussion," *Journal of Religion*,
XXVIII, No. 1 (January, 1948), 1–12.
[24] "In History or beyond History," *Harvard Theological Review*, XXXVIII, No. 3
(July, 1945), 151–75; and see his *The Search for the Real Jesus*.

sponding approach to the Gospel of John. But historical method
at its best becomes scholastic and unreal unless new fertilizing insights, especially today from the psychology of religion and the
sociology of religion, are brought to bear upon the subject matter.[25]
Dr. McCown urges that the problem of the philosophy of history is
our underlying problem today and that it must be solved before
more agreement can be reached in the study of the career of Jesus.
This observation can be set over against Holmström's conclusion
that the disappointing character of such study is to be explained by
the indecisive situation in systematic theology. The difference here
is that the latter is calling for a theology (and a theology of history)
purified of nineteenth-century rationalism and determined consist-
ently by Christian presuppositions. Dr. McCown appeals to an
empirical philosophy of religion with a view of history in terms of
emergent evolution.

We may conclude this brief account of contemporary views of
the eschatological question. It will be seen that the simple thorough-
going eschatology of Schweitzer has been modified at some points.
There is a present aspect of the Kingdom as well as the future
aspect. Jesus did not teach an interim ethic in Schweitzer's sense,
but in this area often spoke as though the world were to continue.
Much of the apocalyptic assigned to Jesus by the Gospels is today
viewed as secondary.

Let us try to restate Jesus' teaching as to present and future.
We begin with Otto's formula that Jesus felt himself part of, and
witness to, a great redemption-transaction being effected by God
in his generation. This he proclaimed in both prophetic-messianic
and apocalyptic terms. That is, he could use terms drawn from the
older messianism, like the allusion to the thrones of David, or from
the newer apocalyptic, like the references to the Son of Man. The
main point is that he saw a world-process under way and moving

[25] "The problem of Jesus' place in history is therefore in part a problem for the
sociologist as historian. It is also in part a problem for the psychologist" (McCown,
The Search for the Real Jesus, p. 302). It may be mentioned here that a significant
and authoritative examination of the relations of psychology to the whole complex
of eschatological conceptions has been made by Dr. Anton Boisen in *The Exploration
of the Inner World* (Chicago: Willett, Clark, 1936).

toward its climax, and called on men to recognize it and to commit themselves to it. All this he saw and presented in terms of Israel first of all. His proclamation was both by word and by deeds of healing and exorcism. All these evidenced the arriving eschaton. Its outcome he saw as the Kingdom of God or the life of the age to come. On the other hand, he could speak of the future in less dualistic fashion. This is evident in the character of his ethical teaching as we have said; in the promise that his disciples would rule over the tribes of Israel, an allusion to the thrones of judgment of Psalm 122:5; and in the saying as to the Temple he would re-build after three days.[26] Jesus could envisage the future in non-dualistic, non-apocalyptic terms. Even where we find such terms it would appear from various considerations, better understood today than in Schweitzer's time, that we must not take the apocalyptic language of Jesus in the same opaque and concrete way that Schweitzer did. The future was beyond Jesus' knowledge. The decisive factor in it was the power of God. The apocalyptic char-

[26] This matter is so important that it seems best to dwell upon one of these sayings at this point, the saying about the Temple that Jesus will raise up. Study of Mk. 14:57–59, 15:29, (cf. 13:2, the D reading), Mt. 26:60, John 2:19, Acts 6:14, convinces most scholars that Jesus did utter a saying of the kind he was accused of at the Trial, most likely in the following form, "I will destroy this temple and in three days I will raise it up." We are to understand it as one of his sayings of deep rhetorical mood and profound import. Jesus speaks not so much in his own name as in that of the Spirit or Wisdom of God. The character of the Temple to be raised up is to be understood from the imaginative mood of the saying. The saying refers to the Temple as a figure for Israel itself or the Congregation. "I will destroy this Congregation," saith the Spirit of God, "and will raise up another after three days." In so far as it is a prophecy of the destruction of the nation it has its best parallel in the words concerning the fig-tree, "No fruit grow on thee henceforth for ever."

As far as the saying points beyond the destruction of the old Israel to a new Israel, the saying stands parallel to the eschatological forecasts of the coming Kingdom, but with a difference. Jesus' saying about the new Temple is not inspired by the sharp dualism of the apocalyptists. Like the sayings about the messianic feast and the thrones of judgment, it belongs in the sphere of the older messianism rather than in that of the later apocalyptic. It is true that we find passages in the apocalyptic literature describing the building of the new Temple by God or by the heavenly Messiah. (Enoch 90:28 ff.; 91:13; 53:6.) But there are also passages of this period that echo rather the older messianic conception, in the Psalms of Solomon 17:30 and in the Targum to Is. 53:5. See Otto's discussion of the saying as to the new Temple, *Kingdom of God* . . . pp. 61, 62.

acterization of it was the one most adequate to its full outcome. But he did not see it only in such terms. In fact, as Otto shows, the irrationality of the eschatological type was manifest in him: he could announce the imminent end of the world but live and teach as if it were to go on.

CHAPTER THREE

Historical and Transcendental
Elements in Jesus' View
of the Future

I T WOULD follow from the interpretation of Jewish eschatology
we have adopted that the use of apocalyptic terms whether by
Jewish writers or by Jesus in no way indicates an exclusively
otherworldly outlook. Allowance for the symbolic character of these
forecasts allows us to see that their concern is in part with the this-
worldly future of man. Those elements that appear to set a term
to the life of this world are in part transparent and disclose in
mythical form a future of men under divine judgment and grace,
indeed, but not translated to other conditions of existence. It is not
claimed that man's deepest intimation of a finally transcendent
destiny is absent from apocalyptic, but that this is joined in it with
equally compelling intimations of divine operation in the social-historical future. What form this latter would take could only be suggested by imaginative terms, and these merge imperceptibly into
the imaginative terms with which the final goal of existence is
described.

In some expressions of Jewish and Christian eschatology the
this-worldly historical element betrays its existence more clearly than
in others, being distinguishable from the transcendental elements
with which it is so intimately associated. This is true of the book of

Daniel for instance. Dodd discusses the symbolic character of apocalyptic sayings with illustration from Daniel as follows:

The symbolic method is inherent in apocalyptic. The course of history, past, present and future, with its climax in the Day of the Lord, is presented in a series of symbolic visions. So far as the apocalyptists use this method to describe history down to their own time, the interpretation is plain, because we have before us, as they had, the actual events corresponding to the images employed, and they sometimes themselves supply the key. But when they come to describe the supposed future course of history, there is no actuality within our experience, or theirs, corresponding to the imagery. How far did these writers suppose the images themselves to be actuality? The answer to the question would no doubt be different for different writers. For the author of the Book of Daniel, for example, the actuality corresponding to the victory of the "Son of Man" over the "beasts" is a victory of the Jews over the Seleucid monarchy, and the subsequent erection of a Jewish empire.[1] It had not happened when he wrote, but it had for him the actuality of an impending historical event.[2]

It is significant that our classic Old Testament apocalypse, Daniel, uses terms which became technical for eschatology in such a this-worldly sense and with such a this-worldly interest. It is true, as Dodd goes on to say, that other writers appear to be concerned with "that which lies beyond history altogether." But we would urge that even here under the symbolic terms the reader may justly find an historical preoccupation melting into the transcendental by imperceptible degrees.

What makes this probable is not only the example of Daniel, and not only the fact that the historical future can only be represented by symbolic language. More important is the following consideration. If Jewish eschatology in the late period had taken a sheerly

[1] Dodd here gives the footnote: "I do not mean that there is nothing 'supernatural' in the predictions of 'Daniel.' No doubt he may have conceived the victory as brought about miraculously, and the subsequent kingdom of the saints is certainly painted in supernatural colours. But there can be no doubt that the seer expected to experience, with his contemporaries, the events I have mentioned, on the plane of history."

[2] *The Parables of the Kingdom*, pp. 105–6.

transcendental direction, it would have been a complete reversal and denial of the main stream of Jewish religion. No religion has ever been so completely realistic in its concern for man's life in this world. The commanding, age-old and original concern of the prophets and psalmists of Israel was for a purified and holy Kingdom, an Israel disciplined and ministering to the world. Their interest was in the social-historical future of man. The later dualistic trends in eschatology should not be thought of as excluding this normative emphasis and tradition. They added to it. No doubt they at times so overlaid it as apparently to deny it. The new doctrines of the resurrection and the Judgment and of the cosmic scene of the conflict of God and evil, introduced elements that could not be harmonized easily with the age-old realism. But we should be prepared to scrutinize the ensuing representations, prepared to find the total picture still governed by the basic insights of the prophets, however sublimated. Especially in the teaching of Jesus, where on the face of it the ethical teaching often envisages a continuing order, and where the filiation with the prophets is so patent, shall we be surprised to find an otherworldly transcendentalism. We shall expect to find, indeed, a depth of perspective which includes the ultimate spiritual goal of mankind, but in the foreground we shall expect to see a characteristically prophetic concern with this world's future.

Examination of Jesus' total utterance, indeed, presents the student with a notable dilemma. We find some of his sayings that deal with the actual historical situation of his people and their historical prospects, but we also find much that is transcendental, bearing both on the present and the future. Dodd recognizes this twofold character of the teaching of Jesus as it concerns the *future*. "We seem to be confronted with two diverse strains in the teaching of Jesus, one of which appears to contemplate the indefinite continuance of human life under historical conditions, while the other appears to suggest a speedy end to these conditions."[3] But Jesus also interprets the *present* in a twofold way, sometimes realistic, sometimes transcendental. Is it not likely, then, that he saw the crisis of his day and its outcomes as a matter that could be viewed from either a

[3] Dodd, *op. cit.*, p. 104.

realistic or a transcendental point of view, that could be given either
a *geschichtlich* or *übergeschichtlich* interpretation? It would follow
that the transcendental characterization of the *future,* which is indeed the more common, need not be viewed as determinative by
itself.

We can briefly illustrate this twofold character of the teaching of
Jesus as follows. The Baptist now appears realistically as one who
came in the way of righteousness and whose baptism was from God,
and now eschatologically as Elijah. Jesus can present himself in
realistic terms as one of the prophets none of whom perish outside
Jerusalem, or in eschatological terms as one who is immediately
related to the Son of Man who is to come. The element of judgment
in the present crisis is seen historically in the rejection of the Israel
that now is, and especially in the destruction of the Temple. But it is
eschatologically seen in the advent of the Son of Man as Judge. The
ethical teaching of Jesus and his occasional non-dualistic characteri-
zations of the future contemplate a continuance of human society
and of a renewed Israel, and the eschatological conception of the
Kingdom of God does not exclude this but interprets it more
significantly.

Is not the right interpretation of this twofold character of Jesus'
view of the future as follows? The transcendental eschatological
element is the counterpart and overtone of the historical element.
Jesus' errand was one of this-worldly redemption. The apocalyptic
he uses lends a significance, motive and grounding to that redemption that could not otherwise be suggested. The interpretation of
Jewish eschatology that has been presented above fits with this view.
Creative eschatology, when ethically inspired and when springing
from a true insight into the ways of God with man, constitutes a
body of myth, a vehicle of profound and significant truth bearing
immediately upon historical-social realities. It follows that when the
purport of historical phenomena exhausts statement in immediate
and realistic terms, it can only be adequately conveyed by the imaginative terms of faith, in this case by eschatological terms.

With these points in mind we may outline the teaching of Jesus about present and future as follows, showing the relation of historical and transcendental more in particular.

Jesus, noting the forces and movements of his day, proclaims that the signs of the times indicate the great crisis or climax of Israel's vocation. It is a time when a greater matter than that of Jonah or Solomon is at issue. The generation is like a man on his way to a judge with his adversary. The period of the law and prophets is giving way to one representing their fulfilment. The promises of God are now to take effect upon and through his people. The meaning of this for Israel and for the nations was best suggested in the most moving passages of Scripture, but its full significance could only be conveyed by eschatological language. We therefore find the insight deepened and sublimated without being evacuated of its essential social-historical significance by the eschatological correlative: i.e., by the announcement that the Kingdom of God is at hand.

The prophet of the arriving crisis Jesus sees in John, the greatest born of woman, whose baptism was of God, and whom in eschatological terms he identifies with Elijah. Thus Jesus includes the period beginning with John as part of the eschatological time. Jesus himself, by contrast, is the prophet of the new order. We may fairly isolate in Jesus' self-consciousness those more realistic features and claims that can be distinguished from what Schweitzer and Wrede looked on in different ways as "dogma," i.e., eschatological self-interpretation. Jesus in his filial experience and sense of prophetic mission, felt a responsibility for the mediation of the new order which indicates a realistic historical errand. He may have invoked or permitted his disciples to use the category of Messiahship with regard to himself to convey more adequately the significance of his person and work, distinguishing between a present Messiahship of humiliation and a future Messiahship of glory. Or, more likely, he may have preferred the category of Son of Man with this same contrast. It appears more likely, however, that he was content to forego either such self-designation and simply to insist upon the direct relation between himself and the future Son of Man.

The new order already gives signs of its presence. It is there in the midst of men if they have eyes to see, evident in the working of God's spirit in the response to the Gospel, in the overthrow of Satan and the exorcisms and cures, and in the new kindred forming itself in despite of earlier ties. Not least is this new order evident in the divisions it creates. A wide range of Jesus' ethical teaching is concerned with the way of life of this new form of community. When Jesus speaks of the Kingdom of God as present he is using eschatological language, loaded with scriptural connotations, to more fully characterize this new situation. In particular it is shown in the later discussion how, when the present new order is checked and hindered by the hardness of men's hearts and the enmity of the authorities, Jesus can speak of the Kingdom of Heaven as stormed by and suffering violence from the world-rulers of this age, the evil angels and demons.

But the supersession of an old order by a new carries with it tragedy and cost. Its adherents in that temporary period are called on to fulfil the roles of persecuted witness and missioner. In particular the prophets of a new order are often its martyrs. Jesus comes to recognize this lot as his own. He has a baptism to be baptized with. In view of his sense of vocation we cannot doubt that he related his death to the fulfilment of Israel's calling, which had to do throughout all its great prophets with the effecting of a true community of men with men and of men with God. His death and his vindication and their significance for the new order Jesus magnificently asserted in transcendental terms. By a creative synthesis he bound together his passion with the session of the Son of Man at the right hand of God, and his role of judgment. The resurrection "after three days," i.e., after an indeterminate period, has the same meaning, being also related to the full manifestation of the Kingdom.

The actual advent of the new order Jesus anticipates in more realistic terms in rare allusions to the new Davidic reign or the new Temple. The lord of the vineyard will come and destroy the wicked husbandmen and will give the vineyard unto others. If Jesus does not speak more specifically of the actual historical future of his work in Israel, it is because the major aspect of God's operation in the future was so intimate and hidden (however mighty in its power and however significant ultimately for visible social-political institutions) that it could only be forecast in parables or in eschatological terms. Jesus anticipated a new and revolutionary this-worldly order, and the fact that here above all he necessarily had recourse to eschatological terms should not lead us to evacuate his outlook of social-historical significance. The eschatological perspectives include more but not less than this. Jesus felt himself the prophet and instrument of the coming of this new order and conducted himself with a fully realistic understanding of the circumstances involved. As Professor John MacMurray has pointed out in insisting on this conception of Jesus, there is an autobiographical light thrown on Jesus' own purpose by the parables of the builder of the tower and the general about to engage in battle. He set out to subserve a certain end *in* history, not outside it, and he chose the particular course and methods best calculated for success.

The richness of reference with which Jesus invokes the apocalyptic Kingdom and Judgment to lend significance and urgency to his message is well known. The judgment that is to fall on the present order in its manifold and intimate ramifications as the new order arises within it can only be conveyed in eschatological terms. For the travail and birth of a new age through the unsounded counsel of God does not lend itself to explicit prediction. Nor can the values and perspectives of his ultimate goals be stated otherwise than in the language of myth. Much of the difficulty that students have experienced in systematizing Jesus' view of the future is occasioned by their mistaken effort to fit sayings of different key or inspiration into a single program. It would be wiser to recognize that the sayings fall into two or more series rather than into one. They parallel each other in part. Significant historical events have their eschatological correlatives. But this correlative character of *geschichtlich* and *übergeschichtlich,* or historical and transcendental, does not exhaust the significance of the matter. The eschatological correlatives lend deeper meaning to present and future events, indeed. But a point comes where any possible inductive forecast of events must soon meet with ignorance, and at this point resort must be had by faith to the transcendental series and what it guarantees for this world's future.

Two objections to this view need to be considered. It will be pointed out that Jesus appears sometimes specifically to think of the life of the Kingdom as other than human. If his saying about the angelic condition of men in the resurrection applies to the conditions of life in the Kingdom, it would obviously forbid the social-historical significance of the eschatology that we have adopted. Jesus did of course believe in the resurrection of the individual and in the felicity of the righteous in the resurrection life. At some point the resurrection life and the life of the Kingdom meet. But it was not agreed in Jesus' time where this point of meeting was. We confront here two lines of eschatological conviction, that of the new age or Kingdom, and that of the eschatology of the individual. Jesus' sayings on the subject of the resurrection or the resurrection state belong to this latter vein or tradition of eschatology, that of the individual. This vein may sometimes overlap with, but is properly quite distinct from, the national eschatology centering in the idea of the Kingdom of God. Therefore there is no reason here why Jesus' typical eschatology with its main emphasis on the advent of the Kingdom and the judgment incident thereto may not be considered as symbolic of the historical crisis of his time and its outcome.

Again, it will be said that we have no right to suppose that Jesus' eschatological language was used symbolically, that we have no sayings of his that call his disciples' attention to such a use of it, and that we are ascribing a form of language to Jesus that was out of the question in his age. We call attention, however, to the double sense of the word symbol or symbolic. It is one thing for a person deliberately to employ figurative terms or symbols with the conscious knowledge that they *are* only symbols for the purpose of illuminating readily identifiable realities. It is another thing for a person in dealing with realities that are beyond express identification or characterization, i.e., ineffable, to use imaginative conceptions to suggest them. It is in this latter sense that we can speak of the eschatology of Jesus as symbolic.

In current interpretations of Jesus' message of the Kingdom there are three positions or emphases which are to be questioned. There is first the error against which the present chapter has up to this point been directed. This error consists in defining Jesus' expectation in solely otherworldly terms and in taking his transcendental language in literal fashion. Such a view recognizes the genuinely future reference of his message but assigns that future in a sheerly dualistic way to a fulfilment beyond the conditions of our present life.

A second error is the reverse of this. Either excising the transcendental eschatological elements from Jesus' utterance or treating them lightly, some scholars would throw the whole emphasis upon the this-worldly hope of Jesus. We recognize here the position especially of certain American liberal writers. In the preceding chapter we have drawn attention to the important contributions of men like C. C. McCown and F. C. Grant, contributions enriched by their formation in the social-historical school of Christian origins. The excesses of neo-orthodox interpretation of the message of the Kingdom have led to reaffirmations of the this-worldly character of the future hope. This appeared in the last writings of Shirley Jackson Case.[4]

The work of C. C. McCown is particularly significant in this connection. In the closing chapter of his book, *The Search for the Real Jesus* (1940), a chapter entitled "Jesus and the Problem of History," he warns against suprahistorical interpretations of Jesus and his teaching with special reference to the Oxford Conference volume, *The Kingdom of God and History* (1938). A subsequent article, "In History or Beyond History,"[5] carries on the thesis and presents an elaborate criticism of otherworldly and neo-orthodox views of the message of Jesus. McCown deals with what he sees as gross errors in the historical exegesis of the gospels but especially with archaistic conceptions of history in terms of which the meaning of the message is defined. There is a strange similarity between Mc-Cown and Bultmann in the sweeping way in which both dismiss the

[4] *The Christian Philosophy of History* (Chicago, 1943). See the discussions of Case's work by C. C. McCown in the Case memorial issue of the *Journal of Religion*, XXIV, I (January, 1949), 25–29, as well as that by Paul Schubert, *ibid.*, 30–46.

[5] *Harvard Theological Review*, XXXVIII, 3 (July, 1945), 151–75.

first century conceptions of history and man as untenable and useless today. In their conclusions, however, they part company. As we shall see below, the latter finds the essential significance of the obsolete "mythology" in the existential freedom and responsibility of the individual in confrontation with God. McCown affirms the this-worldly hope of Jesus which underlies the outworn conceptions in which it is expressed. He assigns the non-historical interpretations of Bultmann himself, as of H.-D. Wendland and C. H. Dodd, to a mood of pessimism induced by our period and to a refusal to take into account a realistic modern view of the social process and of social progress as measured by the whole story of man. He believes that archaic conceptions of man drawn from primitive Hebrew creationism and the dogma of the Fall determine the outlook of such New Testament theology rather than the observed data of the historical process and the actual empiricism of Jesus himself. McCown, indeed, recognizes that Jesus used apocalyptic eschatological imagery but construes its purport in terms of the emergent forces that work in history. Current tendencies to interpret this teaching in transcendental ways he assigns to a denial of the gains of modern historical study and of the new sciences of man and to a theological reaction characterized by supernaturalism, pessimism and determinism. Even though neo-orthodox biblical theology claims to accept the results of modern criticism, its exegesis is governed by subjective factors derived from present-day cultural moods and outlooks.

McCown is particularly insistent that the goal of history is not to be referred beyond this earth.

> The theory that the possibilities of life and history are to be fully realized in another world is only the recrudescence, in a slightly sublimated form, of the old demand that the righteous shall be paid for being good, that history has no satisfactory meaning unless the good receive their reward within history.[6]

In this protest against eudemonism certain forms of otherworldly Christian eschatology are effectively countered. But justice is hardly done to the varied grounds of the Christian hope of eternal life or

[6] *Ibid.,* p. 168.

to its view of the new age as a corporate matter. McCown's charge of irrelevancy, moreover, fails to see that the city of God of the consummation takes up into itself the historical life of man and its significant gains and is, therefore, by no means unrelated to our life in this age. This is the very point of the doctrine of the resurrection, both in the case of the individual and of the people of God as a whole. That the Kingdom of God in the age to come is a fulfilment of historical existence and not its abridgment is the chief thesis of Walter Künneth's work, *Theologie der Auferstehung.*[7]

Discussion of McCown's views in some detail has been called for here because the chief issues of our problem appear in his work, both as regards historical reconstruction and theological presuppositions. With his portrayal of Jesus' message the present work is in large agreement as with his rejection of a dialectical interpretation of it. But we would call attention to a basic theological issue raised by his approach which has representative significance in current discussion. An important methodological factor appears in his animus against views of the Kingdom which remove it "beyond history." Proper historical method—the thesis is—cannot employ categories of transcendence. The object of the historian is to identify events of the past and their relations in empirical terms and causal sequences. This is to be granted. Rather it is to be admitted that the historian's first task is to work within naturalistic presuppositions as the rules of the game and the necessary convention of scientific investigation. But McCown and others link with this methodological restriction a particular philosophical frame of reference which is best defined as an evolutionary naturalism. Here the transcendental interests of religion are in effect excluded in a much more significant way. Such presuppositions indispose the historian or the social scientist to appreciation of many of the chief concerns of religion. Strict historical method has its all-important rights, and an empirical philosophy oriented to the social process has offered necessary correctives to older views of man and history. But in these terms the historian cannot finally do justice to his subject matter. The ultimate mystery of existence and the

---

[7] Second edition (Munich, 1934). See also Holmström's discussion of its significance, *op. cit.*, pp. 382–88.

primal forces that underlie historical events and personal being cry
out for recognition, if necessarily in symbolic presentation. Even
where there is no disposition to limit critical analysis and empirical
investigation as far as these tools can go, our existence especially in
its religious aspects ultimately baffles scrutiny or exposition in these
terms. Here is the justification of categories of transcendence, indeed
of metaphysical transcendence excluded by McCown in his discussion.[8]

The third type of error in dealing with the eschatological symbol
of Jesus is that which not only reads it as purely transcendental but
refuses to recognize any real future or teleological element in it. Here
the eschatological language is viewed as the symbol for an absolute
value or a realized eschatology, a timeless or recurrent Now, which
points to no real sequel or fulfilment in the divine plan. These views,
included in Holmström's second or "unhistorical" period of interpretation, have their most notable continuing expression in the
writings of Rudolf Bultmann.[9]

This writer's treatment of the eschatology of the gospels is to be
understood in connection with his view first of their general world-
view and then of their view of salvation. Both are mythological. The
world-view presupposes a three-storey universe, a cosmological conflict between God and Satan, a future world-catastrophe and a new
age. The view of salvation construes the work of the redeemer in
both apocalyptic and gnostic terms through pre-existence, incarnation, redemptive death, exaltation and operation in the spirit. Both
aspects of New Testament mythology are obsolete and call for rejection. We must seek for the sense of human existence and divine
action which underlies them. Bultmann emerges from the analysis
with an existential, soteriological interpretation of the mythology.

---

[8] *Ibid.*, p. 174.

[9] "Neues Testament und Mythologie. Das Problem der Entmythologisierung der
Neutestamentlichen Verkündigung," in R. Bultmann, *Offenbarung und Heilsgeschehen* (Beiträge zur Evangelischen Theologie, Band 7), Munich, 1941; also reprinted in H. W. Bartsch, ed. *Kerygma und Mythos*, Hamburg, 1948. See discussion
of Bultmann's theses, in the last named volume, by Schniewind, Lohmeyer, Thielicke
and others; and the articles mentioned below by Kümmel and Prenter. Also Bultmann's review of Cullmann's *Christus und die Zeit* in *Theologische Literaturzeitung*
(1948), col. 659 ff.

In effect Jesus sees men as imprisoned in their own self-assertion and as clinging to the false security of their "world" of vanity and death, but offered the possibilities of freedom and true security in God's approach to them in the gospel. No real future of the world or of the self is intended in the promise of the Kingdom and the eschatological symbol, but rather the indeterminate possibilities of the creature under God. Thus the plan of salvation (*Heilsgeschichte*) so far as it means a concrete temporal future of the people of God and the world is dismissed as not only mythological but unavailable even as a symbolic expression of destiny and teleology. Bultmann sets his view over against orthodox views which accept the coming eschatological events literally, and over against liberal views which reinterpret them in humanistic or sociological terms. He also rejects a mystical interpretation of the promise of the Kingdom which would claim that it can be possessed and enjoyed psychologically, and distinguishes his position from that of Karl Barth especially as the latter deals with this problem in his book, *The Resurrection of the Dead*.[10]

Anyone who recognizes candidly the alien character of the world-view of the gospels and its pre-scientific elements must take seriously the problem with which this scholar has wrestled. His solution has greatness of conception and measures up to the depth and import of the New Testament faith, and his categories are well chosen to speak to many groups of our time. But it is the individualistic character of his interpretation which raises question. In defining the significance of the promise of the Kingdom in terms of the indeterminate possibilities of man under God, Bultmann touches on the center of Jesus' message, which was spoken out of a depth which does not distinguish between mundane and transcendental perspectives. But the "mythology" of the two testaments sees God's action always as having a social and corporate reference. The future in the gospel announcement is a future of the people of God, and the future of the individual is inseparable from it. It is at this point that the "plan of salvation" is to be maintained. It is here that Bultmann's reinterpretation verges toward gnosticism and psychologism. His critics.

[10] Translated by H. J. Stenning (New York, 1933).

have pointed out in this connection that "mythology" is indispensable to the gospel, in one form or another. Only by such rich symbolic expression can the fulness and wholeness of the message be conveyed and safeguarded. If in the interests of a modern scientific apologetic we are tempted to reject the pictorial vehicles we end in either rationalism or psychologism.[11]

⸰ The danger involved in any reinterpretation of the eschatological language or of the terms of the Bible generally has been well stated by Paul E. Minear. The chief emphasis in his volume, *Eyes of Faith*,[12] and in various papers has been on the distinctive character of the outlook of the men of the Bible. This carries with it a distinctiveness of language which cannot be translated without falsification. Their terms, symbols and conceptions all belong together, and no part can be separated from the whole or placed in a different context without loss. Their key words "are the structural girders that support an entire edifice of thought. They bear not only their own weight, but a mammoth construction of assumptions, implications and affiliations." Thus, he continues, with regard to the interpretation of biblical eschatology:

It is a problem not of modernization but of communication; communication, not across the barriers of language but across the barriers between one structure of experience and another. Or, to use pedantic jargon, the terminological problem arises out of an epistemological problem, and the latter out of an ontological problem.[13]

This observation does not relieve us of the task of reinterpretation but it cautions us against any too facile simplification or against any too hasty depreciation of an ancient outlook.[14] It follows, moreover,

[11] R. Prenter, "Mythe et evangile," *Revue de theologie et de philosophie*, XXXV (1947), 49–67; Kümmel, "Mythische Rede und Heilsgeschehen im Neuen Testament," *Coniectanea Neotestamentica*, Lund, 1947, pp. 109–131.

[12] Philadelphia, 1946.

[13] "Some Eschatological Quandaries—and How They Grew"; unpublished paper, 1947.

[14] McCown in the article discussed above writes as follows: "Eschatology, it must be remembered, had to do originally with the 'last things' (*ta eschata*) which were to happen just before the 'end,' the conclusion, of 'this age' and the beginning of the 'next'. . . . The more quickly the word 'eschatology' drops out of theological terminology and comes to be confined to factual description of ancient views which

that when scholars assign an exposition of the eschatological teaching
of the New Testament to the closing pages of a work on the religion
of the canon, they do not do justice to its original significance and
context. The idea of the Kingdom presupposes all of existence: cosmology, philosophy of history, conception of man, and other areas.
All such provinces may in fact "take their significance from this
over-all perspective."

Dr. Minear also draws attention to another issue of which we shall
hear a great deal more in discussion of these matters. The distinctions between "history" and "suprahistory" or between "history" and
"myth" which have become so common today are untrue to biblical
thinking. It is just because the conception of the "historical" has
been so confidently assumed that the category of "myth" has been
invoked. This dichotomy is hazardous, as are such current terms
as "suprahistorical," *Urgeschichte,* "prehistory," "posthistory," and
Heilsgeschichte. "They all presuppose a prior and more adequate
knowledge of history than of the category that is related to it. In
all of them the 'suprahistorical' tends to fade off into wisps of fog."
But, as Dr. Minear says in the same paper, "the early Christians did
not so distinguish between history and myth. If we may use Dodd's
terms, all history was for them permeated by mythological struggle
and all events were significant only in terms of this struggle."

If this line of thought is cogent, it would mean that such phrases
as "God's invasion of history" are untrue to New Testament thinking. God's relation to the world is that of creator and redeemer,
indeed; but this is a different context of ideas. At this point a basis
of understanding is possible between the new biblical theology and
those who on other grounds protest against dualistic and suprahistorical categories. Dr. McCown and Dr. Minear are both repu-

---

are no longer tenable and which make no contribution to our understanding of the
universe and of God, the sooner progress will be made." ("In History or beyond
History," p. 166.) But the gospels have a doctrine concerning not only the last days
but also the new age to follow. General usage at least justifies extension of the term
eschatology to cover both. Moreover, if these "ancient beliefs" have as McCown
admits "a moral core which must not be discounted or forgotten," they have also a
religious core of faith and hope of which the same is true. Here lies the validity of
the use of the term eschatology as a theological as well as a historical concept.

diating rationalistic categories and a dualistic metaphysics, the former in favor of an evolutionary naturalism, the latter in favor of a scriptural world view.

In dealing with the teleological significance of the idea of the Kingdom, Dr. Minear is content to confine himself to the New Testament teaching. The age of salvation will succeed the age of sin; that which is hidden in our present order will be revealed; the whole creation will be redeemed. "Perhaps all that we can affirm about the kingdom of God is that it is the resurrection and the life which God shares with men who share the faith and love of Jesus the Lord."[15]

We believe that the tendency of New Testament scholarship and of New Testament theology since the "suprahistorical" emphasis described by Holmström is in the direction of a more positive interpretation of the future of men's life on the earth. The matter is well stated by Dr. Jean Héring in his *Le Royaume de Dieu et sa venue.*[16] He points out what is *not* refuted by the failure of the parousia to materialize. This is, above all, our hope in the advent of the Kingdom at a given moment in the story of humanity. According to Héring, this hope is composed of two factors:

1. The aspiration toward an ideal "kingdom" which is neither purely celestial nor purely terrestrial, because it must safeguard and take up into itself the values which manifest themselves in the creation or even those elaborated by history, while uniting together both the living and the dead (which excludes the coexistence of this future kingdom with the laws of our existing human life). This aspiration is by no means universally human. Buddhism does not know it, nor a spiritualistic gnosticism. But it has proved itself ineradicable from the soil sown by the preaching of Mazdean, Jewish, and Christian prophets.
2. Belief in the effective realization of that aspiration by divine forces. This belief, founded on the words of Jesus or on particular spiritual experiences, cannot be either confirmed or refuted by history. It is often accompanied by a pessimistic judgment on history. . . . *But it is equally compatible with an optimistic conception which places its hope in a progressive purification of humanity up to a relative state of*

[15] "Some Eschatological Quandaries—and How They Grew," p. 18.
[16] (Paris: Félix Alcan, 1937), pp. 49, 50.

health realizable in this age and leaves to God the responsibility for the great final transfiguration.[17]

It is more important and timely today than ever to urge that the teaching of Jesus concerning the Kingdom means in part a genuine hope for the future of men in this world. The restriction of the meaning of the Kingdom to a present "decision" or "possibility" or to an exclusively "realized" category excludes that element of hope for human destiny which is of the essence of Jewish and Christian faith. The hope of Jesus is, indeed, transcendental in many sayings and "mythological" in expression, but this does not warrant our setting aside its teleological concern or its bearing on what we distinguish as "history." This hope relates to man's destiny both in this world and in the world beyond—certainly in the world beyond, since it concerns ultimates and assumes the ripe hopes and insights of late Judaism. But the eschatological anticipations and language of faith are too fluid and varied for us to confine their meaning to this otherworldly reference alone. We do not have here a categorically dualistic outlook. These terms and symbols speak of the human future, human possibilities, human destiny generally, without any consistent or sophisticated distinction between this world and the next. They were spoken out of a level of experience where the world and man are made and unmade and out of an intensity of vision that is concerned with the creative work of God in its most general aspects. The mythical conceptions of the "future," therefore, are not unrelated to ongoing "historical" existence. There is no more important task for apologetics than to clarify the gross libel on Christianity of its chief rivals today—the charge, namely, of false asceticism and social irresponsibility at the heart of the gospel. This is not to deny that Jesus proclaimed the imminent end of the age often in apocalyptic terms. But it is to ask what that announcement meant in his context.

[17] *Ibid.*, pp. 49–50. (My italics.) Héring here adds in a footnote: "But curiously enough such is the force of these aspirations among the people who have received the seal of one of these three messianist religions that even the absence of a faith in a divine intervention, even the extinction of belief in the existence of God, cannot abolish it. It manifests itself then, as everyone knows, in a 'godless' messianic expectation."

If there is one confusion more than any other which is responsible for the apostasy from Christianity of extensive groups and strata today, it has to do with this charge of false otherworldliness. Actually a whole group of confusions are involved: Jewish apocalyptic eschatology was a form of escapism; its messianism was a compensatory vision of a frustrated people; Jesus was a naïve dreamer conditioned by a simple society or was a deluded fanatic; his ethic was an impracticable perfectionism and the early church's version of it a slave morality which offered a sentimental and ascetic code in lieu of that *arete* or virtue from which they were disqualified by their social position. Even Christian moralists have difficulty in coming to terms with these issues. There is no area which demands more attention today in Christian apologetics, and biblical scholarship and interpretation are crucial at this point.

Jesus' proclamation of the kingdom was not a fantasy projection or the portrayal of an escapist's paradise. It was a prophetic forecast of human destiny resting on the whole of Israel's best experience and her witness to the agelong purpose and work of God the creator. This forecast had to do with ultimates; and it rested on ultimates. It had to do with last things, and it rested on first things. But it was directed to the present moment and to the actual scene and was lived out in the concrete process of history, and it bore on that concrete process in its future aspects. It conveyed an intimation of the ineffable fruition of life, and from some real fulfilment of that hope our present existence is by no means excluded.

PART I

Eschatology and the Sanction
of the Ethics

CHAPTER FOUR

Eschatology as Sanction of the Call to Repentance

OUR consideration of the teaching of Jesus concerning the future together with our discussion of Jewish eschatology has prepared us for our central task, a consideration of the relation of eschatology to ethics in his teaching. We have found that the Kingdom had two aspects to him, a present and a future. But both aspects are eschatological. Thus "the relation of eschatology to ethics in the teaching of Jesus" includes both the usual issue of the relation of the Judgment to ethics, *and* the bearing on ethics of the fact of the present "messianic times." These two problems we will handle in that order. Part I will deal with the sanction for repentance and ethics found by Jesus in the coming of the Kingdom in its future aspect, with the Judgment, rewards and punishments. We shall note, however, that this sanction is a "formal" one, not the essential one; and this observation will agree significantly with what we have said in the Introduction as to the symbolic character of Jesus' eschatology and of Jewish eschatology at its best. Turning then to the relation of the present Kingdom or present messianic times to the ethical teaching in Part II, we shall see how Jesus found in this fact warrant for recognizing the advent of new conditions of the moral life and a deepened ethical demand.

The Last Repentance

The relation between eschatology and ethics in the teaching of Jesus is nowhere illustrated in more striking fashion or in more condensed form than in the immediate connection established between the coming event and the ethical reform involved in repentance. The Gospels represent the preaching of Jesus as beginning with the words, "Repent ye; for the kingdom of heaven is at hand" (Mt. 4:17; Mk. 1:15). Understanding of this saying in the light of others and in the light of contemporary anticipations shows us that Jesus made the coming eschatological event at least the formal motive and sanction for his whole ethical summons, here summed up in the idea of repentance.

It is first to be noted that John the Baptist was the preacher of an eschatological repentance. It is no doubt true that Mt. has assimilated the teaching of John to that of Jesus in respect of the actual formula above quoted, assigned to John in Mt. 3:2. However, in the Baptist's preaching both the catastrophic features and the theme of repentance are indubitable (Mt. 3:8, 11). The primary place of repentance in the message of John is expressly set over against the imminent Judgment, represented by a variety of graphic images which we need only allude to here: the wrath to come, the axe at the root of the tree, the mightier than himself coming to baptize with fire of judgment. For John, it was the Day of Judgment typified by these that enforced the call to a change of heart and to the bearing of fruits of conduct approved by God.

The true significance of Jesus' words in Mt. 4:17 is further illuminated by other passages where repentance is brought into relation with judgment. We read in Mt. 11:20 ff., cf. Lk. 10:13-15:

Then began he to upbraid the cities wherein most of his mighty works were done, because they repented not. Woe unto thee, Chorazin! woe unto thee, Bethsaida! for if the mighty works had been done in Tyre and Sidon which were done in you, they would have repented long ago in sackcloth and ashes. But I say unto you, it shall be more tolerable for Tyre and Sidon in the day of judgment, than for you.

Similarly, he goes on to make more explicit the "woe" in the case of Capernaum with the words, "And thou, Capernaum, . . . shalt go down unto Hades." Here, then, Jesus' preaching and announcement of the Day of Judgment, authenticated by mighty works, is represented as properly motivating repentance, though in the case of these cities it had failed. Likewise in Mt. 12:41 the repentance of Nineveh at the preaching of Jonah and its escape from destruction is adduced as a contrast to the impenitence of the then generation and Jesus presents himself as a preacher of repentance in an occasion greater than that in which Jonah was concerned.

From the Sermon on the Mount we extract this parable of warning:

> Agree with thine adversary quickly, while thou art with him in the way; lest haply the adversary deliver thee to the judge, and the judge deliver thee to the officer, and thou be cast into prison. Verily I say unto thee, Thou shalt by no means come out thence, till thou have paid the last farthing. 5:25–26.

This graphic picture of the generation going to judgment and called upon to make its peace at the eleventh hour represents in its original intention and in its Lukan use a perfect dramatization of the words, "Repent ye, for the kingdom of heaven is at hand." In Mt. the original force is obscured, and it becomes a warning to the individual who is tempted to neglect his duty of reconciliation for the lesser duty of sacrifice. However, the original meaning shines through.

A further passage that deserves notice is the parable of the two sons. Jesus here draws attention to the repentance of the publicans and sinners and the refusal of the authorities to do likewise despite their religious diligence, and relates it to the Baptist's preaching of repentance and to his own. The eschatological sanction is present in the word, "the publicans and harlots go into the kingdom of God before you," and in the penalties evident in the two associated parables that follow. Such passages prove that if Mt. 4:17 is not genuine, it at least summarizes the preaching of Jesus in one of its main aspects.[1]

We may add to these examples the following, wherein we find that the message assigned to the Twelve on their journey was identical with that of Jesus himself.

---

[1] See also Lk. 13:1–5, "except ye repent, ye shall all likewise perish," and the following parable of the fig-tree given a last chance to bear fruit, 6–9.

And as ye go, preach, saying, The kingdom of heaven is at hand . . .
And whosoever shall not receive you, nor hear your words, as ye go
forth out of that house or that city, shake off the dust of your feet. Verily
I say unto you, It shall be more tolerable for the land of Sodom and
Gomorrah in the day of judgment than for that city. Mt. 10:7, 14, 15.

This enforcing of the motive of fear of judgment is in relation to
repentance here also. For wherever we have the expression preach
the gospel, or preach the gospel of the Kingdom, we may conclude
from the form of Jesus' preaching as given in Mt. 4:17 that repentance was linked with the proclamation of the coming of the
Kingdom.

The significance of Jesus' initial summons is illuminated, finally,
by the associations of the words "repent" and "repentance," and this
will emerge from our analysis of these to which we now turn. For
repentance had come to be especially assigned to the days of the
end, and the very fact of a general call to repentance on the part of
John and Jesus could be interpreted as an indication of the approach
of the end of the age.

In the word "repent" Jesus sums up his whole ethical summons.
The word μετανοεῖν connotes a complete moral and religious change
of heart, canonized in this sense by the use of its equivalent throughout the prophecy of the Old Testament. We can illustrate both the
force of the word in the Old Testament and in addition the usual
association with it of drastic sanction or eschatological sanction by
the following representative citations.

If that nation, concerning which I have spoken, turn from their evil,
I will repent of the evil that I thought to do unto them. Jer. 18:8.
Cast away from you all your transgressions, wherein ye have transgressed; and make you a new heart and a new spirit: for why will ye
die, O house of Israel? For I have no pleasure in the death of him that
dieth, said the Lord Jehovah: wherefore turn yourselves, and live. Ezek.
18:31–32.
And Jonah began to enter into the city a day's journey, and he cried,
and said, Yet forty days, and Nineveh shall be overthrown. And the
people of Nineveh believed God; and they proclaimed a fast, and put on

sackcloth, from the greatest of them even to the least of them. And the tidings reached the king of Nineveh . . . And he made proclamation . . . yea, let them turn every one from his evil way . . . And God saw their works, that they turned from their evil way; and God repented of the evil which he said he would do unto them; and he did it not. Jonah 3:4–10.

And He is righteous also in His judgment, And in the presence of His glory unrighteousness also shall not maintain itself: At His judgment the unrepentant shall perish before Him. Enoch (Parables) 50:4.

We see especially two elements present in the older references to repentance; one, the completeness of the change looked for; and, secondly, the presence of sanctions that are eschatological: life, or death and destruction. Thus we find that John's preaching of repentance is strictly in line with the past and that of Jesus with his, except in so far as the eschatological sanction is now more definitely formulated as universal and imminent.

But the prophetic calls to repentance never succeeded in any full sense. This failure of the prophets gave birth to the idea of a repentance eventually worked by God himself in the last time. It is notable that the later reflective period of Israel's thought is so pessimistic as to the moral capacity of human nature that only a resort to divine initiative is left. "Who can bring a clean thing out of an unclean?"[2] This general resignation to the weakness of human nature found its present solution in institutions like the Day of Atonement to pacify the conscience, and its solution as regards the future in the dogma of the eschatological cleansing. The apocalyptic literature especially took up the latter topic. Windisch argues[3] convincingly from the numerous aspects of this expectation to be found that there was finally in Jewish thought a rather fixed and generally accepted dogma of the final repentance and conversion of Israel at the end, with established features like the return of Elijah, the great preacher of repentance. His work was to be one aspect of that re-

[2] Job 14:4.
[3] *Taufe und Sünde im ältesten Christentum bis auf Origines. Ein Beitrag zur altchristlichen Dogmengeschichte* (Tübingen, 1908), pp. 43–45; *Bergpredigt*, p. 73.

storing of Israel, the *apokatástasis*. Such a dogma if accepted as the background of the announcement of the Kingdom by John and Jesus abundantly illuminates it. "Repent ye, for the kingdom of heaven is at hand." That is, now is the time of the promised, divinely aided restoration of Israel to its proper disposition and obedience as preliminary to the great things of salvation and renewal that had been promised. Now was "the acceptable time."

B. W. Bacon distinguishes the role of the Baptist from that of the prophets in the following terms. "If Jesus went beyond this general verdict to proclaim John's mission a 'greater' than those of the former time could claim, it was because this mission seemed to fulfil the promise of Mal. 4:4–6 of a last Great Repentance, turning the heart of the children to the Father and the Father to the children, as when Elijah at Carmel 'turned the heart of Israel back again' from following the *baalim*. Without this Great Repentance the coming great and terrible Day of Jehovah, would prove a curse instead of a blessing. Because his message of warning is ultimate, because he voices Jehovah's last summons to erring Israel before the great Day, John is to Jesus 'greater' even than Elijah, something 'more than a prophet.' "[4]

We subjoin now a considerable number of citations from the older literature each of which illuminates from some angle, whether repentance, restoration, cleansing, washing, the gift of the Spirit or forgiveness—the eschatological repentance preached by John and Jesus. It is to be noted that the conceptions of the great renewal vary from writer to writer. The ideas concerning the restored Israel are so fluid that there was no clear distinction between the closing phenomena of this age and the phenomena of the new age itself. The sinless men of the time of salvation were to become sinless by God's cleansing. This process was variously represented. Such a repentance movement as that of John and Jesus could well be interpreted as a fulfilment of the prophecies.

Wash you, make you clean; put away the evil of your doings from before mine eyes; cease to do evil; learn to do well. Is. 1:16.

---

[4] *Studies in Matthew* (New York, 1930), p. 390.

Note the word "wash" here in connection with the demand for repentance; surely one of many such expressions in the prophets borne in mind by John in establishing his rite of baptism.

In that day shall the branch of Jehovah be beautiful and glorious . . . when the Lord shall have washed away the filth of the daughters of Zion, and shall have purged the blood of Jerusalem from the midst thereof, by the spirit of justice, and by the spirit of burning. Is. 4:2–4.

Here we get the action of washing and purging in an explicitly messianic passage.

For I will pour water upon the thirsty (land), and streams upon the dry ground; and I will pour my Spirit upon thy seed, and my blessing upon thine offspring . . . One shall say, I am Jehovah's . . . Is. 44:3–5.

This passage gives us the significant connection of the time of salvation with the pouring out of the Spirit of Jahweh.

And I will build them . . . and I will plant them . . . And I will give them a heart to know me, that I am Jehovah: and they shall be my people, and I will be their God; for they shall return unto me with their whole heart. Jer. 24:6–7.
But this is the covenant that I will make with the house of Israel after those days, saith Jehovah: I will put my law in their inward parts, and in their heart will I write it; and I will be their God, and they shall be my people . . . for they shall all know me . . . for I will forgive their iniquity, and their sin will I remember no more. Jer. 31:33–34.
And they shall be my people, and I will be their God; and I will give them one heart and one way, that they may fear me for ever, for the good of them, and of their children after them: and I will make an everlasting covenant with them . . . Jer. 32:38–40.
And I will cleanse them from all their iniquity, whereby they have sinned against me; and I will pardon all their iniquities. Jer. 33:8.
In those days, and in that time, saith Jehovah, the iniquity of Israel shall be sought for, and there shall be none; and the sins of Judah, and they shall not be found: for I will pardon them whom I leave as a remnant. Jer. 50:20.

As we read these passages from Jeremiah and the prophets we are struck anew with their immediate relevance and importance for understanding the time and work of Jesus. These prophecies of Jeremiah of the time of deliverance with the promise of forgiveness, a new heart, a new covenant, and the knowledge of Jehovah, were of the kind that were cherished, though continually set ahead and deferred into the future, and assigned to the growing many-featured dogma of the times of the end, after the arrest of prophecy.

And I will give them one heart, and I will put a new spirit within you; and I will take the stony heart out of their flesh, and will give them a heart of flesh; that they may walk in my statutes, and keep mine ordinances, and do them: and they shall be my people, and I will be their God. Ezek. 11:19-20.

Such passages throw light not only on the relation of cleansing and conversion to the times of the end, but also upon the ethics and ethical capacity of the new condition.

The doctrine of the heart of flesh prepares us to understand the new ethical standard and requirement Jesus took up. His extreme demands and his emphasis on motive and his doctrine of making the tree good, show that he judged men now to be capable of a higher righteousness. He assumes, as it were, that they have the heart of flesh. He comes close to saying so in his words, "Moses suffered men . . . on account of the hardness of their hearts, but . . ."

In that day there shall be a fountain opened to the house of David and to the inhabitants of Jerusalem, for sin and for uncleanness . . . and also I will cause the prophets and the unclean spirit to pass out of the land. Zech. 13:1-2.

For the prophet Zechariah's expectation of the removal of wickedness from Israel, cf. 5:5-11.

In that day shalt thou not be put to shame for all thy doings, wherein thou hast transgressed against me; for then I will take away out of the midst of thee thy proudly exulting ones, and thou shalt no more be haughty in my holy mountain. But I will leave in the midst of thee an afflicted and poor people, and they shall take refuge in the name of Jehovah. The remnant of Israel shall not do iniquity, nor speak lies;

neither shall a deceitful tongue be found in their mouth; for they shall feed and lie down, and none shall make them afraid. Zeph. 3:11–13.

As it is written in the law of Moses, all this evil is come upon us: yet have we not entreated the favor of Jehovah our God, that we should turn from our iniquities, and have discernment in thy truth . . . Seventy weeks are decreed upon thy people and upon thy holy city, to finish transgression, and to make an end of sins, and to make reconciliation for iniquity, and to bring in everlasting righteousness, and to seal up vision and prophecy, and to anoint the most holy. Dan. 9:13, 24.

And the righteous shall be victorious in the name of the Lord of Spirits: And He will cause the others to witness (this), that they may repent And forego the works of their hands. Enoch 50:2.

This repentance of the "others" (perhaps Gentiles) is assigned to the time of the victory of the righteous here in the Parables of Enoch.

With these examples in mind we can agree with Klostermann that John's baptism of repentance "would thus depend upon the prophetic idea of a great 'lustration' in the messianic time."[5] But Jesus' call to repentance is but a continuation and a development of John's call. He too is proclaiming the last repentance over against the imminent, nay the arriving, judgment and the arriving salvation. And this leads us to other considerations. We have now to note two remaining aspects of this general topic of the relation of the Kingdom to repentance: the Kingdom as promise as well as warning, and repentance as hastening the Kingdom.

The Kingdom as Promise as Well as Warning

The Kingdom of God in the eyes of the prophets and apocalyptists, had always had a double aspect of promise and warning. It was a supreme good whose coming meant reward and vindication for the righteous, and it was therefore a threat to all unrighteousness. Since the occasion of so much prophecy was the sinfulness of the times, the feature usually emphasized in the older writings and in the preaching of the Baptist was the menace in the imminent visitation. This circumstance explains the presence of the same theme in the preaching of the Baptist and of Jesus, and in its recording in the

[5] E. Klostermann, *Das Markusevangelium,* Zweite Auflage (Tübingen, 1926), p. 7.

gospels, where the danger of the Last Judgment is the most prominent consideration urged in respect of the coming Kingdom. Jesus is seen as addressing his summons to an unrepentant nation and in such preaching the menace needs to be uppermost. The evangelists all no doubt tended to emphasize unduly this aspect of the preaching because of the final issue of Jesus' career and because of the rejection of the gospel by Israel and the later history of the church. Mt. in particular[6] has sharpened the indictment of Israel's leaders and the formulation of the warning in Jesus' sayings.

We may be confident that Jesus himself spoke a message of a more positive mood. The evangelical announcement, before the situation was complicated by opposition and the shadow of the cross, was in the mood of Deutero-Isaiah[7] as we can see in Luke's account of the preaching in Nazareth or his saying, "Fear not little flock, it is your Father's good pleasure to give you the kingdom." In contrast with the comparatively forbidding form of the Baptist's preaching, that of Jesus was in the first instance, in its central mood and inspiration, gracious. It was a gesture of invitation, not of exclusion. And this attitude was his to all, both to the older son as well as to the prodigal. We may infer this spirit of his teaching from the spirit of his person and action, though enough of his utterance in this vein remains to confirm us. Like Deutero-Isaiah, Jesus announced the year of the Lord's favor. The favor or bounty of God was thus urged as a reason for repentance. The coming of the Kingdom in its aspects of promise is a sanction for ethics, as well as its aspect of peril. The use of the Aramaic equivalent of "gospel," the mood of the Beatitudes, the connection made between man's forgiveness of man with man's forgiveness by God and man's mercy to man with God's mercy to man, the references to God's bounty, are examples that testify to this conception in the gospel. Parables that deprecate the merit conception should be recalled as well as the general bearing of Jesus himself as the spokesman of the Father to the needy and undeserving. It is not too much to say that

[6] See Emmet in B. H. Streeter, *Immortality* (New York, 1917), pp. 187–90; 194–98.
[7] For promise as a motive to repentance and righteousness note Is. 55:6–7; 61.

the positive sanction is the more fundamental, though the negative sanction is the more prominent. This topic will concern us later in our analysis of the various sanctions.

Repentance as Hastening the Kingdom

The connection of repentance with the time of salvation has another aspect. If repentance was in order because of the immediacy of the Kingdom, could repentance on the other hand hasten the Kingdom? Could men themselves have any hand in "shortening the days"? Was this in Jesus' mind? An ambiguous passage understood in one way would seem to indicate this. But first we recall the evidence in Jewish literature that would encourage the supposition. Strack-Billerbeck give a considerable number of examples from the rabbinic writings relative to the hastening or postponing of the end. Another group deals with the hastening of the time of the Messiah by repentance, by fulfilment of the commandments, by the study of the Torah, by good works.[8] These include the oft-quoted:

> If all Israel together would only repent for a single day, the redemption would be vouchsafed almost immediately and the Son of David would come. Pesiq. 163b, R. Levi (c. 300).

But there are earlier sayings. R. Jose the Galilean about A.D. 110 is quoted as saying, "Great is repentance; for it causes the redemption to draw near."[9] Similarly, R. Eliezer ben Hirkanos of about A.D. 90 said, "When Israel repents it will be delivered."[10] This thought has its obverse in the possibility of delaying the time of salvation by wrong conduct.

Along with these rabbinic passages we recall the passage from the Apocalypse of Baruch 20: "the calamities of Israel were designed by God in order that he might the more speedily visit the world." That is, through the calamities Israel would be led to repentance, and repentance would permit God to bring in his Kingdom.

[8] H. L. Strack und P. Billerbeck, *Kommentar zum Neuen Testament aus Talmud und Midrasch* (Munich, 1922), I, 598; cf. Moore, *op. cit.*, II, 350–51.

[9] Joma 86b.

[10] Sanh. 97b.

With these in mind we turn to the saying Mt. 11:12:

And from the days of John the Baptist until now the kingdom of heaven suffereth violence, and men of violence take it by force.

We shall see that, as Mt. gives this saying, those that storm the Kingdom are not the righteous but the evil spiritual powers. At least the meaning is so uncertain that even if the former view were favored it would not have great weight. We are left then with only dubious evidence in the gospel that supports the view that repentance can hasten the Kingdom. The prayer for the coming of the Kingdom in the Lord's Prayer and the unique insistence of Jesus upon importunity and importunate faith, however, encourage us to hold open the possibility. We are confronted here with the old dilemma of predestination and free will. Jesus and the Church held surely that the consummation of God's plan for his people was fixed in his secret counsel both as to its time and manner.[11] But the universal feature of all predestinarianism that the free will and agency of men are inconsistently called upon, none the less, leads us to anticipate a similar inconsistency here. The prayer and sayings and activity of Jesus are such as to convince us that he felt that the Kingdom could be hastened by repentance, when taken in connection with the Jewish passages we have given. Jesus laid great weight on earnestness and importunity and action in securing personal benefits. He called attention to such examples as illustrations of the attitude he most desired in his disciples to the Kingdom itself. The parables of the importunate widow and of the traveler at midnight,[12] both Lukan, originally applied to the Kingdom:

And the Lord said, Hear what the unrighteous judge saith. And shall not God avenge his elect, that cry to him day and night, and yet he is longsuffering over them? I say unto you, that he will avenge them speedily. Lk. 18:6–8.

[11] "But of that day or that hour knoweth no one, not even the angels in heaven, neither the Son, but the Father." Mk. 13:32. "It is not for you to know times or seasons, which the Father hath set within his own authority." Acts 1:7.

[12] Coming immediately after the Lord's Prayer whose central petition is for the Kingdom.

In Jesus' mind, certainly, trust in the Father's dispositions and obedience to his omniscient will take first place, and his main message is that the Kingdom is near and that men should repent in view of it. But in another mood which we may or may not find inconsistent we note Jesus giving expression to the thought of the immense power of importunate faith in affecting the advent of the Kingdom.

Bultmann denies that the Kingdom can be hastened. This is a corollary of his position that the Kingdom of God is not "the supreme good" humanly considered, but "in keeping with its eschatological character a sheerly supernatural affair." It is therefore nothing toward which human will or conduct can direct themselves nor is it anything which can be realized by human behavior. It grows of itself according to the parable. One sees how this view fits in with Bultmann's radical treatment of Jesus' teaching. We must defer to the conclusion of the study criticism of what seems a dogmatic and ultra-simple presentation.

We conclude this chapter, then, with the summary that the nearness of the Kingdom, conceived both in its threatening and promising aspects, was stressed by Jesus as a motive and sanction for repentance; and that, vice versa, repentance was thought of as in some way a factor in the hastening of the Kingdom, here thought of in its aspect of blessing. We defer until the close of the next section a discussion of the formal nature of this sanction.

CHAPTER FIVE

Sanctions of Reward and Penalty

W E HAVE seen that repentance was a term that summarized the ethical reform that first John and then Jesus in their respective ways preached. It included both penitence and good works, both sentiment and act. The Scriptures gave it significance as a term involving a radical change of life and as having eschatological associations. But while *metanoia* involved for Jesus the whole range of practice that full obedience implied, it was inevitable that various of the requirements involved should be specified. Thus we find in the records ethical teaching. This, however, is by no means a fully worked-out code. What we have of such instruction appears to have been spoken on the spur of particular occasions and to vary widely in nature. Indeed, it varies all the way from the most general principles to the most precise commands. Now as the summary of these in repentance was brought into close relation with the Judgment and the Kingdom of Heaven, which served as formal sanctions to enforce it, so the ethical requirements are enforced, often by emphatic eschatological rewards and penalties. Every particular demand does not necessarily have its accompanying sanction drawn from penalty or blessing at the Judgment, but many have. The fact of the presence or absence of such is not specially significant. These enforcing motives may in some cases have been adventitiously attached to or detached from the precepts by the evangelist or others. The fact remains that these imperatives are very generally uttered in inseparable connection with eschatological warning or promise. And when such are lacking it will be found that the thought is not far to seek in the context or the sense. Moreover, it is to be remembered that even where another motive may be the ruling one, the eschatological motive is not excluded. This is evident especially in the way in which series of ethical requirements are concluded with general invocation of the eschatological sanction.

As the best way of examining this problem, we have gone over the ethical teaching of the gospels, identifying the eschatological sanction where present, and in addition noting what other motivation is present. Thus we are in a better position to judge the real part played by the former.

In distinguishing between a considerable number of types of ground on which ethical summons is rested in the gospels we have elected to use the word sanction in its wider sense as the most convenient. By sanction we shall mean any objective consideration, tacit or expressed, that enforces a moral imperative. Such a consideration might be one of possible reward or penalty (and in its more limited sense sanction usually refers to penalties). But such a consideration might equally well be one of elements of fact or truth to which the assent of the hearer is invited, or of one or other type of authority that would weigh in prompting obedience. The advantage of this wide conception of sanction is that it permits us to study in its very deepest aspects the grounding of Jesus' ethics.

The drawback of the word "motive" for our purposes is that, on the one hand, it applies to any kind of action and not only ethical action and is thus in one sense too general. On the other hand, it is too limited in its bearing in that it does not properly cover grounds for action that are non-affective; i.e., its most characteristic associations are with such appeals as those made to fear, love, gratitude, but not to reason, discernment or consent. Thus G. F. Moore groups[1] the "motives" of Jewish ethics under the following heads: desire of reward, fear of punishment, love of good for its own sake, the fear of God, the love of God, the hallowing of the Name, the imitation of God, etc. "Motive" here emphasizes the subjective and affective reasons for obedience. "Sanction" would stress the ob-

[1] *Judaism*, II, 89 ff.

jective and impersonal aspects of such reasons, and would include other considerations. The two words overlap, however, to a large extent, and in many cases either word is proper.

As a result of our canvass of the precepts of the gospels and the sanctions assigned or implicit we can venture the following analysis of such sanctions. Such an analysis must needs partake of the arbitrary in that we are dealing with a body of prophetic and creative utterance which is made up of elements spoken under diverse impulses and in diverse situations. But rough classification of the sanctions is possible and cannot but further our understanding of the profounder assumptions.

We can draw first, then, a distinction between the sanctions that depend upon rewards and penalties of whatever kind, and those from which this feature is absent. The distinction is clear, even though the two types be not mutually exclusive. Of the former type, eschatological rewards are the typical kind, though there are other types of consequences envisaged. Of the latter type, an example is found in the summons to mercy or generosity, where grounded in the nature of God or in some other religious-prophetic affirmation. Consequences of good or ill may be implicit here, just as the religious-prophetic insight may be implicit in the appeal to rewards and punishments. But the distinction is helpful. There then follows the discrimination of types within these two main classes of sanctions.

We turn first to the sanctions of reward and penalty. The appeal in this group is essentially an appeal to self-interest. In the other it is an appeal to the moral discernment, to the conscience and reason of the hearer, sometimes fortified by the authority of the Scriptures, of the speaker, or by the example of God, or that of Christ himself. Both appeals recur throughout the ethical teaching of Jesus. That the notion of reward and a frank appeal to it is present in Jesus' teaching and is even fundamental to it appears from many instances. The passage Mt. 6:1–6, 16 is pertinent. "Thy Father who seeth in secret shall recompense thee." Even the reward of those who parade their religion is acknowledged.[2] And it is recognized that there will

[2] Cf. Windisch, *Bergpredigt*, p. 16.

be a distinction in rewards and penalties: few stripes and many stripes.[3]

The appeal to self-interest involved in the proposal of rewards and punishments is not hastily to be condemned. Morality motivated by reward is inferior only as the reward is arbitrary and external. Where the reward is of the nature of necessary consequence flowing from the conduct and the conditions, it escapes this indictment. The punishments and rewards assigned in the teaching of Jesus are sometimes, usually for reasons of concreteness, presented in a way that makes them appear external, but closer study shows that this aspect is not primary.

We should not be hasty to conclude that the ruling mood of the gospels is one of warning before punishments to come. Such a mistake is easily possible for one who neglects the other motives urged or who fails to see the often merely formal aspect of the former. It is interesting to note the impulse of Bacon to turn to the Hellenistic gospel of John as doing "better justice than the Synoptic (i.e., Mt.) to the true 'heart of Christ.'" . . . "there has come with this growing loss of cogency in the cry 'Flee from the wrath to come' a dawning apprehension that perhaps Jesus' gospel of peace, his message of reconciliation to the compassionate Father, did not chiefly consist of a new and higher legalism, appealing with redoubled vehemence to men's hope of reward and fear of punishment."[4] But though the early community appears to have colored this aspect more highly, even so the intrinsic and selfless sanctions remain in the Synoptic accounts.

Recognizing the large place, however, that the sanction drawn from rewards and punishments has in Jesus' teaching, the following considerations are pertinent.

In dealing with simple people good pedagogy demanded that Jesus and the disciples lend concreteness to their teaching. The urgency of the moral demands could best be dramatized for unphilosophical minds by the picturesque conceptions drawn from human compensations.

[3] Lk. 12:4–8.
[4] *Studies in Matthew*, p. 428.

The Jewish rabbis, as G. F. Moore points out,[5] explained the importance assigned to rewards in their Scriptures by holding that only thus are men educated to a loftier motivation for right conduct. "There is sound insight into human nature in the saying ascribed to Rab: Let a man always occupy himself diligently with the study of the Law and the doing of the commandments, even if not for their own sake; for out of doing it not for its own sake comes doing it for its own sake."[6]

The Jews were not philosophical and did not think abstractly about ethics as Plato and Kant did.[7] Moreover, their theism was unique. Jahweh was for them a highly personalized individual whose rule over the world was immediate and discretionary, rather than mediated through a reign of law or second causes. Therefore the individual had to do, in a unique way, immediately with God, and the feature of God's personal blessing or discipline was thrown into high relief. Further, "God has put himself under obligation by his promise of reward, and in this sense man, in doing what God requires of him, deserves the recompense."[8] Especially is reward merited by suffering for the Name.[9]

We must distinguish between reward and punishment sanction (a) in a form truly vicious, where the future retribution is held out as an arbitrary and external lure or inducement, and (b) in such unobjectionable form as is found in Jesus' essential teaching, where the compensation is announced as an inevitable consequence flowing out of the nature of the moral and spiritual world. One can illustrate the two kinds of inducement by the way an unwise and a wise parent will put pressure on a child. In the latter case, "The result

[5] *Op. cit.*, II, 90.

[6] Pesahim 50b, cit. Moore, *op. cit.*, II, 98.

[7] "Thus the concept of moral personality is lacking, as well as any moral philosophy proper such as inevitably develops wherever the Greek conception of man prevails. It follows further that there can be no 'value-ethic' since nothing is regarded as possessing value in and of itself. Obedience alone gives meaning to conduct." Bultmann, *Jesus*, p. 65; cf. pp. 75–76.

[8] Moore, *op. cit.*, II, 90.

[9] A. Schlatter, *Der Evangelist Matthäus, seine Sprache, sein Ziel, seine Selbständigkeit* (Stuttgart, 1929), pp. 143–44.

is contained in the premise, as surely as the result of health-giving medicines or death-dealing drugs is already contained within them ... Thus the sting of the supposed eudaemonism is removed."[10]

It is all very well to say that virtue is its own reward, but the reward motive is still present for him who thus reflects. We see how natural and almost inevitable for human thinking is the concept of reward. Plato's thinking on ethics is not free of such motivation. He conceives of the just man: just not because of any external incentive but because it is the proper nature of man to be just, and he dwells upon the harmony in which the just man will live among just men. But the appeal to self-interest is there in the thought of the common harmony making for the individual's well-being, and even more clearly in the prospect of immortality open to the just man, a truly eschatological sanction.

The concept of reward has this in its favor, moreover; it goes with a view of life that affirms the worth of the self and the validity of the best personal satisfactions. "And herein is Jesus' attitude set over against a strictly ascetic view, against the view namely that annihilation of the self is the claim that God makes of men."[11]

Montefiore justly points out that "to seek salvation and felicity after death is not selfish, unless it is taught that A's salvation means B's damnation or neglect. Moreover, the teaching of Jesus is that it is *service* which secures salvation; it is by serving others and seeking to redeem the 'lost,' that we save our souls."[12]

But Jesus invokes other and more fundamental sanctions than that of reward, appealing to reason and conscience and the nature of God. The same Jewish scholar we have quoted above thus explains the reward sanction in Jewish ethics: "It does not follow, because one believes strongly that righteousness and felicity must, and will, in the long run, be joined together, that therefore the desire for felicity is the only, or even the strongest, motive for moral

---

[10] C. G. Montefiore, *The Synoptic Gospels* (Second Edition; London, 1927), II, 42.

[11] Bultmann, *op. cit.*, p. 76; *Jesus and the Word*, p. 80.

[12] *Op. cit.*, II, 43.

well-doing. Judaism, and Rabbinism more especially, know and lay the utmost stress upon other motives, such as the Sanctification of the Name, Lishmah (virtue for virtue's sake), the love of God, and so on."[13]

Finally, we note that Jesus goes out of his way often to minimize the reward motive and the merit concept by pointing to the hidden will, secret dispositions, and unreckoning grace of God as having the final word in the rewards of men. The last shall be first. Grace shall submerge reckonings. The Kingdom is a gift. "When we shall have done all, say, We are unprofitable servants; we have done that which it was our duty to do."

Bultmann deals interestingly with what he calls the paradox that Jesus promises reward to those who are to be obedient regardless of reward. He notes that certainly Jesus demanded obedience irrespective of ulterior motives. "Yet, to be sure, for Jesus it is quite certain that men *do* receive reward or punishment from God. And the sayings in which Jesus points to these possibilities are to warn men of the consequences of their conduct. In the strict sense such cannot be accounted motives where the concept of obedience is carried out to its limit."[14] Bultmann agrees with our interpretation of rewards as essentially an indication of consequences. But he abandons the main problem by calling it a paradox, where we would rather point out the inner connection of the two kinds of motive.

It will be shown that the sanction involved in the appeal to the moral and religious discernment is the more fundamental. The prophetic-religious intuitions and experiences, and the objective concept of God that they yielded, these are the ground of Jesus' ethical teaching and living. The thought of consequences derives from these apprehensions. But the primary announcement of Jesus is positive. It is not negative as was that of the Baptist. It is a positive announcement of the reign of God as a gift, this aspect being evident in the very word "gospel." The Beatitudes in so far as they are declarations rather than hortatory, and in so far as they then correspond to the thought of Jesus' first sermon in Nazareth ac-

[13] *Ibid.*, p. 43.
[14] *Op. cit.*, p. 75; *Jesus and the Word*, p. 79.

cording to Lk., reflect this same fact. But the ethical sanction that fits with this conception is not one of rewards and punishments. The appeal is to gratitude, homage, imitation. God is bringing in his reign and his great deliverance. Do good, avoid evil, that you may be the sons of such a Father, that men may see your good works and glorify him, that you may sanctify his name. The particular conduct urged is urged as the only conduct compatible with such a God.[15] Any blessings envisaged are thought of not as reward but as free gift. The blessings precede the obedience or at least the announcement of these precede it. God's work of blessing is fixed and sure, in any case. His mercy is the motive for conduct. Men do not live well to secure the mercy but in gratitude for it.

This positive character of the preaching of Jesus must be held in mind as the background of the teachings of rewards and punishments. In this way we secure ourselves against overemphasizing the rewards feature. Good conduct is acceptance and acknowledgment of a great blessing, and its reward is simply the appropriation of it. Evil conduct is unwillingness and rejection of a positive blessing, and its punishment is the missing of that good. "If I had not come and spoken unto them, they had not had sin: but now they have no cloak for their sin." The prophet, therefore, is rightly understood as "making the heart of this people fat, and their ears heavy, and shutting their eyes," and as rejecting all but a remnant. The prophet is always the touchstone that serves to discriminate the many called and the few chosen, and is the stumbling-block to designate those unfitted for the new thing. His new truth is the reagent that reveals the elect and the rejected. The prophet makes manifest the blindness of those that see not, and in so far he causes it. His appearance, indeed, provokes to further blindness. He precipitates the moral forces in individuals and in society and crystallizes error.

The negative emphasis, that on vivid eschatological punishments, and the invocation of these as sanctions for conduct, seems to arise in Jesus' career at that stage where his rejection by Israel becomes more and more clear. The note in his teaching passes from that of

[15] Cf. Bacon, *Studies in Matthew*, pp. 345–46.

God's positive deliverance to that of God's discrimination between good and bad. This latter aspect remains the most prominent in the time of the evangelists.

So much being said we can take up our enumeration of the sanctions attached to the ethical teaching under this first head of rewards and penalties.

1. *The Last Judgment and Its Retributions*

This is the dominant sanction and is, in fact, an almost universal one. "His preaching, above all his exposition of the will of God for us, is therefore eschatologically framed in a double sense; the nearness of the salvation and the danger of missing it are the leading motives in this proclamation."[16] As with the general call to repentance, so with the specific precepts, and with the summons to vigilance, the motive assigned is the nearness of the Kingdom of Heaven, thought of especially in terms of its leading feature, the Judgment. The extreme urgency with which the people is summoned to obedience is enforced above all by the graphic and drastic punishment promised to those who neglect it. This eschatological sanction is, indeed, normal for Jewish ethics of the later period. But the assured immediacy of the Day is a particularity of the Baptist's warning and that of Jesus.

We shall study this sanction under the following heads: A., the use of the sanction, B., the evangelists' special emphasis on and application of it and their occasion therefor, and C., the non-explicit use of the sanction.

A. *The use of this sanction.* We would call attention to outstanding and representative examples of the use of this eschatological sanction in what immediately follows. It is well to bear in mind that occasional references to the Judgment and the end of the world may entirely lack the feature of immediacy, and therefore belong by their derivation or mood to quite a different type of sanction. Similarly, we recognize a category of penalty which like much Jewish sanction falls in the class of the eschatology of the individual. Yet both these groups, especially the former, when found in the

[16] Windisch, *Bergpredigt,* p. 6.

total atmosphere and setting of Jesus' preaching really link themselves with the characteristic eschatology, namely, the imminent
universal Judgment with its retribution.

To make clear the omnipresence and forcibleness of the transcendental eschatological sanction in the teaching, and to give opportunity for attention to the form in which it appears, we shall review
it briefly under the following characteristic heads: (i) judgment by
the Son of Man, (ii) the finding or losing of life, (iii) entrance into
the Kingdom of Heaven, (iv) treasure in heaven, (v) the penalties
of Gehenna, (vi) the suddenness of the coming.

i. Judgment by the Son of Man. Warning of eschatological
penalties is most clearly conveyed by Jesus in his prediction of the
coming of the Son of Man in judgment. The Markan saying, 8:38
with its parallels and the Q saying, Mt. 10:33 = Lk. 12:9, point to a
genuine utterance, though their variations need to be scrutinized.
The gist of the sayings is that the Son of Man at his coming will
confess or deny before the angels of God him who now confesses
or denies Jesus. In connection with the latter passage the saying, Mt.
10:26b, "for there is nothing covered, that shall not be revealed; and
hid, that shall not be known," is a warning or encouraging allusion
(as the case may be) to the Judgment.[17] The sayings in either context
that stress the imminence of the coming of the Son of Man (Mt.
10:23; 16:28) may or may not be genuine, but this imminence is in
any case understood from the basic announcement by Jesus of the
nearness of the Kingdom.

Judgment at the last day is less explicitly taught in those passages
where forgiveness by God is connected with forgiveness of one's
neighbor. Thus in the Lord's Prayer the sanction for the summons
to forgive is the granting or withholding of God's forgiveness,
presumably at the Judgment. Similarly with the passage, "Judge
not that ye be not judged." In the parable of the unforgiving servant, the sanction is only indicated parabolically: "the tormentors,"
however, point to the penalties of the Judgment.[18]

The most graphic representation of this sanction in our gospels,

---

[17] So Lk. 12:2, also Mk. 4:22 = Lk. 8:17.
[18] Mt. 18:32–35. See Mk. 11:25.

one probably not genuine, is found in the description of the Great Assize in Mt. 25:31–46. Here we have the formidable tableau of the Last Judgment with the following indication of final rewards and penalties:

And these shall go away into eternal punishment: but the righteous into eternal life. 25:46.

It is worth mention here as illustrating what is implicit in the more genuine sayings. And it is possible that Jesus himself chose this familiar tableau of the Judgment, nationalistic in its original bearing, in order to play a new variation on it.

ii. In Mt. 10:38–39 and its parallel the finding and losing of one's life are stressed as considerations for conduct, and as we recall how closely "life" is linked up with life in the world to come, we see the eschatological sanction. In the similar passage Mk. 8:35 and its context we see how inseparable the gaining or losing of life is from the thought of the day of the Son of Man.

iii. This leads to another class of sayings in which the eschatological event plays the part of sanction, namely, those in which entrance into the Kingdom is envisaged. The positive sanction of acquittal at the Judgment is usually assigned in this form which pictures entrance into the Kingdom as the reward of righteousness. How typical it is for Mt.'s arrangement in particular is evident in the words of Windisch, "The entire ethical and religious instruction of the Sermon on the Mount has this intention, then, to stretch every power to win access to the Kingdom of God; through and through it is eschatological. It is a proclamation through the mouth of Jesus of the conditions of admission as God himself has disposed them."[19] The relation of this formulation of the sanction to similar conceptions in the Old Testament and among the rabbis is instanced by the same writer.[20]

[19] *Bergpredigt*, p. 10.
[20] Compare conditions of entrance to the Temple (Pss. 15; 24; 118: 19 ff.), to the Promised Land (Deut. 4:1 ff.; 16:20), to God's Rest (Heb. 4:1 ff.) "Thus the Sermon on the Mount appears at still another point as the companion piece to the Mosaic legislation." *Ibid.*

A slightly different form of the idea is presented to us in the saying,

> Enter ye in by the narrow gate: for wide is the gate, and broad is the way, that leadeth to destruction, and many are they that enter in thereby. For narrow is the gate, and straitened the way, that leadeth unto life, and few are they that find it. Mt. 7:13–14.

The entrance to the World to Come is a Needle's Eye and is hard to get through (Lk.), hard to find (Mt.), and passed by few (Lk. and Mt.).[21] The passage tacitly equates "life" with the Kingdom. Compare the rabbinic passage,

> Lord of the world, would'st thou tell me which πυλῶν stands open to the life of the World to Come! (the answer is given: the fear of God, and suffering).[22]

It is such passages that most clearly bring out the topic that we are now studying, and show that it is the nearness of the Kingdom that is the dominant motive, at least on the surface, for the urgency of all this ethical teaching. The passage, indeed, lacks the express note of immediacy of the Judgment, save in its Lukan form, which implies that those not saved were too late. For in Lk.'s sequel to this passage Jesus illustrates the "narrow door" theme by his parable of the master who has "shut to the door" and who repudiates the appeals from outside with the words, "Depart from me, all ye workers of iniquity."

iv. A fourth class of cases in which the eschatological sanction is invoked is that in which reference is made to treasure in heaven, reward in heaven, or to being rich toward God. Jesus refers to it usually in contrast with the treasure of this world which is insecure, which is to be prized lightly, and in one case is to be given away entirely, in the form of alms. That treasure in heaven was thought of as first of all related to the Judgment we note from the following passage in Enoch,

[21] E. Klostermann, *Lukasevangelium*, Zweite Auflage (Tübingen, 1929), *ad loc.*
[22] Pesiqtha 179b, cit. in Klostermann, *Matthäusevangelium*, Zweite Auflage (Tübingen, 1927), p. 68.

> When the congregation of the righteous shall appear . . . and when the Righteous One shall appear before the eyes of the righteous, *Whose elect works hang upon the Lord of spirits . . . When the secrets of the righteous shall be revealed.* 38:1–3.

That is to say, at the Day of Judgment the "works" of the righteous that "hang upon" God shall be there for a witness to their innocence and a guarantee of their acquittal. Gressmann cites the following clear passages:

> Thou hast a treasure of good works that remains guarded for thee before the Highest. 4 Ezra 7:77.
> Since they have a treasure of good works before Thee which will be guarded in the treasure chamber. Apc. Bar. Syr. 14:12.

The Testament of Levi has an interesting parallel which is not explicitly eschatological:

> Work righteousness, therefore, my children, upon the earth,
> That ye may have it as a treasure in heaven,
> And sow good things in your souls,
> That ye may find them in your life,
> But if ye sow evil things,
> Ye shall reap every trouble and affliction. 13:5–6.

Reward in heaven or the simple promise of reward by God is a conception very closely related to that of treasure in heaven, and similarly means reward before God, accumulated against the Day of Judgment. Compare here Rev. 22:12.

v. In the teaching of Jesus about the future severe penalties are announced for the wicked. One instance will illustrate this group.

> But I say unto you, that every one who shows anger to his brother shall be in danger of the judgment; and whosoever shall say to his brother, Raca, shall be in danger of the Gehenna of fire. Mt. 5:22.[23]

Here we have an example of explicit eschatological sanction of penalty to give urgency to the teaching. It is significant for our

[23] Among various reconstructions this seems preferable, given in Montefiore, *Synoptic Gospels*, II, 59, citing K. Köhler.

understanding of it as formal throughout to note that it is here based upon the Jewish retributive scheme. Thus, the antecedent in the Law is the occasion for the form in which the teaching is cast and grounded. We note that Windisch minimizes the eschatological sanction here, speaking of Jesus' saying as follows: "In every way it follows a regular type of the Pharisaic method of exposition. 'Gehenna' is a constant dogmatic concept in the Pharisaic eschatology. In our present passage, thus, it is only a final case, and the intention of the saying is not to proclaim an eschatological teaching but to impose the will of God in all its sharpness."[24] The penalty belongs in the class of the eschatology of the individual, like so many other allusions to Gehenna in the teaching. But such uses of the traditional penalty of Gehenna really are taken over in Jesus' teaching into its prevailing Judgment-eschatology, so dominant is this outlook.[25]

vi. Mt. presents his eschatological sanction with peculiar force in warnings in chapters 24–25 that impress the duty of vigilance on the disciples. The "watching" urged represents a general attitude and conduct fulfilling all the various particular demands of the ethical teaching. But the force of the word emphasizes the probability of sudden danger. The suddenness of the coming of the Son of Man and of his election of the saved is conveyed by the parallel of the coming of the flood in the time of Noah, and the warning is enforced thus:

Watch therefore: for ye know not on what day your Lord cometh. Mt. 24:42.

The same warning of sudden danger is conveyed by the figure of the thief coming at night when none is on guard:

Therefore be ye also ready: for in an hour that ye think not the Son of man cometh. Mt. 24:44.

[24] *Op. cit.,* p. 16.
[25] The denunciation of the scribes and Pharisees carries the traditional penalty, "How can ye escape the judgment of hell?" Mt. 23:33, but the imminence of this judgment is assumed as we can see from v. 56, "this generation."

Again, the suddenness of the coming is represented in the return of
the lord of the household, and the rewarded servant and the one
punished are set before us in language that calls up to mind the
Judgment of the Last Day.[26] The parable of the ten virgins enforces
the same vigilance and closes with the typical warning:

Watch therefore, for ye know not the day nor the hour. Mt. 25:13.

The parable of the talents throws its main emphasis upon the nature
of the rewards for various services and not on the suddenness of the
return. But the parable is assimilated to the foregoing by the feature
of the lord's return:

Now after a long time the lord of those servants cometh, and maketh
a reckoning with them. Mt. 25:19.
And the rewards and punishments indicated are eschatological:

And cast ye out the unprofitable servant into the outer darkness: there
shall be the weeping and the gnashing of teeth. Mt. 25:30.

With such a review of the use of the eschatological sanction of the
immediate and transcendental type before us, we are in a better
position to compare it with our other sanctions. We have, of course,
left unmentioned many significant passages like the Beatitudes, the
Lord's Prayer, the important verse Mt. 6:33, etc., where the thought
of retributions at the Judgment is of importance. As to these and
other passages a sentence of Windisch will again summarize the
matter: "The Sermon on the Mount, taken as a whole, is a proclamation which takes the expectation of eschatological judgment and
salvation as its foundation, as the guide-post for living and for conduct, for the attitude towards men in this life as for that towards
God."[27]

    B. *The evangelists' special emphasis on and application of this
sanction and their occasion therefor.* We have said that this sanction

[26] Mt. 24:45–51. Note here Lk.'s unique addition, "Take heed . . . watch . . .
that ye may prevail to escape all these things that shall come to pass, and to stand
before the Son of man." Lk. 21:34–36.
[27] *Bergpredigt,* p. 20.

is universal in the teaching. It is impossible to distinguish strands in it from which it is absent. It is impossible to presume an absence of it in the teaching of Jesus himself and a subsequent overlaying of Jesus' supposed non-eschatological teaching with this sanction. It is impossible to assign it exclusively to Mk. or to pretend its absence from the Source. It is omnipresent in whatever elements or strata we would seek to isolate. It is present in the parables as in the non-parabolic teaching.[28] It is present in the elements that are typically narrative such as the scene of the Trial, as it is present in the discourse material.[29] It is present in the unique Matthean matter as in the sections dependent upon Mark and the Source,[30] and in the peculiar Lukan material.[31] We have seen that Mt. tends to loosen the sense of the phrase, the Kingdom of Heaven, and to give it a contemporary application, but if we presume on this to try to evaporate the concrete eschatological expectation we soon have to give up the attempt. We find that there are other sanctions present but these do not supplant the eschatological sanction.

It is of especial interest, however, to note how the evangelist, Mt., reflecting the outlook of his times, has extended this sanction and sharpened its lines. The intense moral crisis of the church in its struggle against the false brother and "acute Hellenization" led to a diverting and intensifying of the sanction. Bacon brings out the special circumstances that drove the writer in this direction. "Mt. hopes to stem the tide of moral relaxation and the inroads of the false prophets who teach 'lawlessness,' by sanctions of everlasting reward and punishment. As we have seen, this is characteristic of Jewish-Christian effort at the time. In the struggle against 'acute Hellenization' and the perils it involved in the post-apostolic age the remedy of eschatological sanctions was eagerly applied by leaders of the Church."[32] Bacon notes how systematically this evangelist has incorporated this theme. "Every one of its five great Discourses

[28] Mk. 13:33–37; Mt. 24:43–44 = Lk. 12:39, 40; Mt. 13:24–30, 47–50, etc.
[29] Mk. 14:62 (Trial); Mt. 8:11, 12 = Lk. 13:28–29; Mt. 23:39 = Lk. 13:35 (Discourse).
[30] Mt. 10:22, 23; Mk. 16:28; Mt. 10:32, 33 (Q).
[31] Lk. 21:34; 12:35–38; 17:28–30. Cf. 13:1–5, 6–9.
[32] *Studies in Matthew*, p. 428.

concludes with a more or less extended reference to the rewards and penalties of the Day of Judgment. In addition every opportunity afforded by the material is availed of for heightening the colors of the apocalyptic judgment scenes or emphasizing their nearness."[33] Both in view of the moral issues of the time and of exciting contemporary events and of persecution, we are not surprised to find the eschatological sanction invoked in ways that go far beyond its use in Jesus' own words and outlook.

Windisch in his study of the Sermon on the Mount points out that the evangelist's point of view has been stamped on the composition as a whole and therefore on the various parts, but that inspection of the parts permits us to see the wholly different light in which many of the units were originally conceived. This is particularly true in regard to the eschatological element. "It follows for the eschatological question, (1) that the Sermon on the Mount as a whole, like all other long discourses of Matthew, is conditioned by the eschatological expectation, but that (2) the evangelist has conformed a great deal of material to this setting which originally had no relation to eschatology."[34] As he indicates, this applies to all the Matthean discourses of Jesus more or less.

Mt. goes beyond Jesus in his adducing of positive sanctions of compensation as well. Bacon notes of these sayings, "The Father that seeth in secret will reward thee," and "Your Heavenly Father will give good things to them that ask him": "It is habitual with Mt. to introduce, whether from his written sources or from any other, such sanctions of the commandment."[35]

To observe now how the eschatological sanction is employed by Mt. to safeguard the church we have only to look at chapter 18. This chapter reads like the charter of the early Christian community, rather than a group of sayings to the disciples in Jesus' lifetime. The ethical emphases are on avoidance of jealousy, fair treatment of the humbler classes of Christians, self-improvement, church discipline and the conserving of the fellowship. Note the

[33] *Op. cit.*, p. 412.
[34] *Op. cit.*, p. 9.
[35] *Op. cit.*, p. 347.

sanctions. For him who sets a stumbling-block in the way of a weaker brother,

it is profitable for him that a great millstone should be hanged about his neck, and that he should be sunk in the depth of the sea. Mt. 18:6.

Rather than be an occasion of stumbling to a fellow-Christian one should cut off hand or foot, or pluck out the eye, for the other alternative is the Gehenna of fire.[36] The certainty of judgment is increased by the assurance of the presence before God of the angels of those injured. Finally, the forgiving spirit is urged upon the brethren by the parable of the unmerciful servant who was delivered "to the tormentors." Windisch takes the passage, vv. 7–9, as one of the examples where the form of the imperative is most immediately and most crassly determined by the fearful conception of the lake of fire. This is exceptional, for usually the human or religious reasonableness of a particular precept is present as motive in addition to the eschatological motive.[37]

We have here, then, an interesting case of how drastic sanctions, invoked by Jesus in his original preaching for the imperatives he found crucial, are taken over and used to enforce the ethical demands that are central for the early church. What the evangelist began to do was to give a picture of Jesus transposed from his real setting and become an oracle for the situation of the time. In effect the synoptic evangelists did what the author of the Fourth Gospel did.

Apart from the occasion for use of drastic sanction by the evangelists found in the moral crisis of the church, they found further occasion in contemporary events, especially in the fall of Jerusalem. In the parable of the king who made a marriage for his son, the impenitence and violence of the invited guests is denounced, and the sanction appears in the passage:

But the king was wroth; and he sent his armies, and destroyed those murderers, and burned their city. Mt. 22:7.

[36] Mt. is following Mk., indeed, in these verses and their context, but the whole is brought to bear on the situation of the church by being related in this chapter to a group of other sayings evidently concerned with the church.
[37] *Op. cit.,* p. 19.

This is peculiar to Mt. and probably reflects the destruction of Jerusalem. The Lukan form merely proclaims that "none of those men that were bidden shall taste of my dinner." Mt. has wholly converted this simple supper parable into an elaborate allegory of the rejection of the Messiah, like that of the Wicked Husbandmen, and has included a clear threat of penalty. We should ask ourselves how far the marked eschatological note of Mt. throughout is a reflection of the same tendency. Assignment of verse 7 above to the fact of the fall of Jerusalem may give us a clue to much of the drastic sanction peculiar to this gospel. An evangelist writing after the destruction of the city would be inclined to develop to the full the indefinite prophetic penalty present in the reports of the words of Jesus. This would apply certainly to non-apocalyptic penalties. Experience of the events of A.D. 66–70 would, however, also intensify the significance of properly eschatological sayings of Jesus, and we would expect to find this element in the teaching of Jesus given its full value and even emphasized beyond its proper proportions. For to Christians of that decade historical events appeared as fulfilment and confirmation of Jesus' own eschatological announcements, and as immediately introducing the whole program. Such a reading of events we have before us certainly in the use of the apocalyptic chapter, its relating to the saying concerning the destruction of the Temple, and the way it is edited to reflect the events and circumstances of the time.

The detail of the guest without the wedding garment standing in forced relation with the parable we have just discussed, and peculiar to Mt., offers us an example of the use of graphic eschatological sanction in relation to the "false brother" of the early community. The false brother or false prophet comes before us repeatedly in the writings and must have been a major issue in the problems of the ecclesia. We see the evangelist here laying upon him the full force and weight of Jesus' most devastating eschatological menace. This suggests to us again the probability that in a gospel so immediately reflecting the life of the ecclesia we shall find the retributions of the Judgment invoked by the evangelist in relation to ethical issues of his own situation, a sanction indeed having its antecedents in Jesus' own words and outlook, but here often extended in its application.

C. *The non-explicit use of the sanction.* The recurrent eschatological sanction is not always invoked in explicit form. For one thing, as we have seen, the immediacy of the Judgment is often left unmentioned, but it is implicit everywhere in view of the basic announcement of Mt. 4:17 and of similar passages. There are also many references to the punishments of Gehenna which are invoked in connection with the teaching in such a way as is usual in Old Testament and rabbinic writings, without being related to the coming of the Son of Man and the Judgment.[38]

Again, it is interesting to find that blessing and penalty are often indicated in metaphorical ways which only remotely, if at all, imply the eschatological dogma. An excellent example, because it bears on so large a body of ethical precept, is the double parable of the builders found at the conclusion of the Sermon on the Mount. This expected storm and flood does not represent an eschatological sanction in itself any more than in the parallels in Jewish literature.[39] For the evangelist it could not but be associated with the time of persecutions the early church witnessed; cf. Mt. 13:21, "when tribulation or persecution ariseth . . ." But, all in all, in view of the eschatological character of Jesus' teaching (compare for instance the phrase two verses before, "in that day," referring to the Judgment), we must understand this parable of the builders as constituting an eschatological sanction.[40]

One recalls likewise the figure of the tree cut down because it bears no fruit, or the parable of the tares (apart from its explanation), or the even simpler parable of the net full of fish, or the figure of the salt cast out and trodden under foot of men. Here again, one would be tempted to say that the original sanction of the ethical teaching of Jesus was in such simple metaphorical form, and that

[38] See Sevenster, *Ethiek en Eschatologie,* pp. 79–81, dealing with the penalties of the rich fool and of Dives.

[39] Ps. 37:6; Job 1; Wis. 4:4; Is. 28:16 ff.; Pirqe Aboth III:17.

[40] So Windisch, *Bergpredigt,* p. 10.

the eschatological sanction was a later rendering explicit and dog-matic of this merely prophetic or wisdom type of sanction. Thus, "blessed are the merciful for they shall obtain mercy," simple here as in Ps. 18:25, would be transformed into the dramatized es-chatological picture of the parable of the unforgiving servant or, indeed, into that of the picture of the Great Assize. Such, indeed, we consider to be the *logical* genesis of the eschatological retribu-tions. But the explicitly eschatological is too closely interwoven into all elements of the teaching to permit any such analysis. The con-clusion must be that of all the sanction of reward and penalty which does not refer to the present age, some was implicitly eschatological and some explicitly. For later Jewish thinking was so steeped in the conception of the ultimate Judgment that a metaphor like that of the tree cut down, or "the harvest," or "the prison," or abandonment to the tormentors, or such conceptions as those of "treasure in heaven," or "reward in heaven," "your names . . . written in heaven," or hire, or the promise of comfort or mercy or satisfaction, were inevi-tably eschatological in their first connotation.

Windisch, indeed, points to a body of teaching in the Sermon on the Mount from which, when isolated from the evangelist's context, eschatological preoccupation and sanction are absent.[41] His conclu-sion, however, is not that this is typical of Jesus' own proclamation or of any particular strand in the gospel, but that it is one of two main streams of utterance of Jesus, the wisdom-type and the escha-tological, and that these spring from a common source. The escha-tological sanction is never far away, and it is our contention that the appeal to the discernment and to the facts of the nature of God, etc., inevitably ushers in the thought of consequences, hence of the Judg-ment.

There are rare instances among the sayings of Jesus where prom-ises or warnings are not in any sense eschatological, but of the strictly sapiential type. "All they that take the sword shall perish with the sword." "If the blind guide the blind, both shall fall into a pit." In the former case, for instance, the saying does not invoke supernatural

41 *Op. cit.,* pp. 20–21.

retributions, but, in a profound aphorism, the return of violence upon the head of him who employs it.[42] So Shakespeare,

> we but teach
> Bloody instructions, which being taught, return
> To plague the inventor.[43]

Again, Jesus now and again gives counsels of a "common sense" variety with a utilitarian, this-worldly motivation, in a vein we recognize as characteristic of the wisdom literature. Note the advice to take the lowest place at a feast, to reconcile yourself with your adversary on the way to the trial, to be wise as serpents, and note the commendation of the unrighteous steward. But such precepts are usually, as in the cases above, not straightforward counsel for this world's life, but illustrations from this world's wisdom of considerations having to do with the Kingdom. Here we believe that Sevenster errs in seeing in some of the above sayings a common-sense, this-worldly instruction.[44] And in general that teaching of Jesus that resembles the utilitarian teaching of the wisdom literature will be found to have a larger bearing.

There are numerous other sanctions or motives invoked in the ethical teaching besides the eschatological. We note first what further sanction there is that can come under the general head of reward and punishment.

2. *Rewards and Penalties in the Present Age*

We find here a second sanction for ethics, namely, the promise of reward or of satisfactions here in this present age, or reassurance as to the conditions of life here. This prospect is sometimes placed in deliberate relation to that of reward in the future world.[45]

---

[42] Cf. Gen. 9:6, "Whoso sheddeth man's blood, by man shall his blood be shed." Also Rev. 13:10, "If any man shall kill with the sword, with the sword must he be killed."

[43] *Macbeth*, Act I, Sc. 7.

[44] For example, *op. cit.*, p. 82.

[45] Compare on the negative side, "It shall not be forgiven him, neither in this world, nor in that which is to come." Mt. 12:32.

Verily I say unto you, that ye who have followed me, in the regeneration when the Son of man shall sit on the throne of his glory, ye also shall sit upon twelve thrones, judging the twelve tribes of Israel. And every one that hath left houses, or brethren, or sisters, or father, or mother, or children, or lands, for my name's sake, shall receive a hundredfold, and shall inherit eternal life. But many shall be last that are first; and first that are last. Mt. 19:28–30. Cf. Mk. 10:29–31; Lk. 18:29–30; 22:30.

Here the Twelve themselves are promised a place with the Son of Man in his reign over the renewed Israel. In this life, in the pre-parousia era, moreover, there shall be an hundredfold return of all those things sacrificed. The double sanction here of present indemnification and eschatological promise is further illustrated in another Q passage, Mt. 6:33: "But seek ye first his kingdom, and his righteousness; and all these things shall be added unto you." "All these things" refers to the bare necessities of life, and while it lacks the definite reward aspect of the saying above, it yet bears on the satisfactions of the faithful in this age. The present saying approximates closely to that of the Agraphon, therefore:

Seek the great things, and the little shall be added to you, and seek the heavenly and the earthly shall be added to you.

The promise of abundant return is made in somewhat proverbial form (and therefore with application to the present life) in the passage,

Give, and it shall be given unto you; good measure, pressed down, shaken together, running over, shall they give into your bosom. Lk. 6:38. Cf. Mt. 7:11.

It is difficult to say whether the rewards or rather assurances of the Beatitudes should be thought of as referring in part to the present age. No doubt on the face of it the promise of the Kingdom which is the characteristic "blessing," should indicate that they are eschatological in character. The Lukan form of the Beatitudes would confirm this.[46] But we should be on guard against too systematic an

[46] Also our conclusions above as to the eschatological character of inheriting the earth and seeing God.

interpretation, and what we have discovered with regard to the connotation of the Kingdom will make us hesitate. The assurances of Jesus to the hearers of his word seem to carry a double aspect corresponding to the twofold aspect of the Kingdom. Thus, to use Mt.'s form which is not more than a legitimate interpretation of the Q beatitudes, those that mourn are *already* comforted and that comfort shall receive its complete fulfilment at the parousia. Those that hunger and thirst after righteousness or salvation *already* are blessedly fed, yet remain in expectation of the definitive victory of Christ.

The early church out of its rich experience naturally read a very great deal into these assurances of Jesus concerning the present age, and probably extended the sayings of Jesus that bore on this point, or even applied to itself promises of Jesus of an eschatological character. It is worth while to pause and note how in the gospel of Mt. such is the case.

Thus words of Jesus bearing on promise for the present age are found in the offer of "rest" to those that accept his invitation, and in his assurance that he would be "in the midst of" those that should gather in his name. The passage promising rest lacks all eschatological reference,[47] and this fact is perhaps to be assigned to the origin of the passage in some pre-Christian wisdom writing. Jesus' promise to be in the midst of his followers gives us the most extreme expression of pre-parousia promise, and while it probably belongs to the latest element in the gospel, it only expresses clearly the tendency of the community to assign much of the eschatological promise to the church itself. In Mt. 18:15–20 the binding and loosing actions of the church are assigned divine sanction and this confirmation in heaven is thought of near the end of the first century as God's present vindicating action in the church and in the world. One evident example of such action to the church was the destruction of Jerusalem. Mt. includes in the parable of the wicked husbandmen the prophecy (a present fact to the church): "Therefore say I unto you, The kingdom of God shall be taken away from you, and shall be given to a

---

[47] It is not justifiable to find it in the words, "All things have been delivered unto me of my Father," as though they were a parallel of 28:18 ("All power is given unto me in heaven and earth."). In the former it is all wisdom that has been committed to Jesus; the associations of the passage are with Jer. 6:16 and Ben Sira 51:27.

nation bringing forth the fruits thereof" (21:43). Here Jesus was
thought of as forecasting the power of the pre-parousia ecclesia.

The emphasis by the evangelist on sayings of Jesus urging lowli-
ness of mind may well have arisen from the need of such teaching
on the part of the faithful, especially of their leaders, in his time. We
refer to that tendency to assertiveness and rivalry which the Epistle
of James combats with the admonition, "Be not many masters
(teachers)"[48] and Paul with various appeals. Where the sayings of
Jesus attach promises of true precedence in the Kingdom to instruction on meekness, we can readily believe that the church understood
it of the pre-parousia time:

Whosoever would become great among you shall be your minister; and
whosoever would be first among you shall be your servant: even as the
Son of man came not to be ministered unto, but to minister, and to give
his life a ransom for many. Mt. 20:26–28.

The precedence here referred to as won by self-abasement is not,
first of all, for the evangelist, that in the coming Kingdom, but in
the present community.[49] Similar assurances of places of true honor,[50]
or of authority to bind and loose, or of greatness or exaltation, may
be included among the satisfactions promised to those who shall take
on them the yoke of the Kingdom. A further case, this time not set
against the virtue of humility but that of faithfulness to the law, is
found as follows:

Whosoever therefore shall break one of these least commandments,
and shall teach men so, shall be called least in the kingdom of heaven:
but whosoever shall do and teach them, he shall be called great in the
kingdom of heaven. Mt. 5:19.

[48] James 3:1, cf. Mt. 23:8; Rom. 2:20.
[49] So Klostermann on Mk. 10:41–45, *Markusev.* p. 21: "There are places of honor
among the disciples too, but they are to be won by humble service: Jesus is thought
of as talking about the question of rank in the Christian community, not of present
service in expectation of future splendor." But no doubt Jesus himself in such passages
spoke with reference both to the present and the future age.
[50] Cf. Mt. 23:10–12 and parallels.

The evangelist may well here be assimilating the Kingdom to the church, and disapproving those of his time who were for relaxing the law too far in certain respects.

Whatever the church did with such sayings we may be sure that this sanction of reward and penalty in the present age had a part in the actual teaching of Jesus himself. Dealing with the typical promise of reward in the sayings concerning alms, prayer and fasting: "Your Father who seeth in secret, will reward you," Windisch says, "But it is not stated that the compensation is thought of as exclusively eschatological. . . . It may also, as in the Jewish Wisdom thought, show itself in the life of this age."[51] We should recall here that these rewards of the present age are really eschatological, if not in the same sense as those rewards that were to follow the parousia of which we have spoken in the preceding section. For we have concluded that the eschatological era had really begun at least with the work of Jesus, and that the prophesied messianic age with its blessings was already present in a measure, awaiting its fulfilment indeed with the Second Coming. Therefore these blessings or rewards of the pre-parousia age properly belong among our eschatological sanctions in the wider sense.

As we have seen, the gospel of Mt. is rich in intimation of the fulfilment in the life of the community of the promises made by Jesus to his followers. A church fellowship is reflected in which, though family ties have been severed, a new set of even more close relationships has been set up. The present reward of this new family bond in the ecclesia is certainly reflected in the passage 12:46–50. "And he stretched forth his hand towards his disciples, and said, My mother and my brethren! For whosoever shall do the will of my Father who is in heaven, he is my brother, and sister, and mother." The same holds for the promise of the hundredfold return of "houses, or brethren, or sister, or father, or mother, or children." Any reward promised by Jesus that is not explicitly eschatological in the strict sense, takes on for the Christians of the evangelist's time a present application. It is in the Beatitudes that one can most easily

[51] *Bergpredigt*, pp. 16–17.

observe this. The Kingdom of Heaven becomes a phrase loosely used and often denoting a condition of things in the ecclesia. The evangelist is not far removed from the point of view of one who could say that "the kingdom of God is not eating and drinking, but righteousness and peace and joy in the Holy Spirit."[52]

But we observe that with whatever sanction drawn from present satisfactions, the strictly eschatological sanctions do not fade into unreality in the least. The twofold considerations of blessing are retained: God's Kingdom and his righteousness, beyond; and all these things added, here. In the world to come, life everlasting; and in the present world, one hundredfold return for all renunciation. Here, mercy, comfort and satisfaction; in the new age, the eschatological salvation and vision of God.

Before we turn from this review of the first kind of sanctions, namely those involving rewards or punishments, we pause to note that Jesus on various occasions went out of his way to deprecate attention to reward. We have alluded to this in the considerations urged above that explain the use of such sanctions. Here we wish to show just what treatment Jesus is represented as giving to this point. The effect of several sayings of his is to set aside or transcend the reward-conceptions and to show that the appeal to compensations is at best only secondary. This is of importance, and it prepares us to understand that the second class of sanctions which we are next to take up are more fundamental.

We turn first to the Beatitudes. These sayings are not merely statements of fact, but are hortatory.[53] Yet the declarative form in which the Beatitudes are cast has significance. We are here in a different atmosphere from that of much Jewish and Christian ethics, where ethics are brought into conjunction with reward and punishment. The matter is of great importance because it is typical of the

[52] Rom. 14:17.

[53] "The promises are words of comfort. . . . But they also sound like imperatives: be poor in spirit, hunger after righteousness . . . for only so can you be sure of the Kingdom." Windisch, *Bergpredigt,* p. 10, speaking of Mt.'s form of the Beatitudes. So Bacon, "Mt. has expanded the Beatitudes to double their original number, giving all but the last the form of commandments, by obedience to which admission may be won to the joys of the kingdom. He makes them anti-Pharisaic admonitions." *Studies in Matthew,* p. 346.

whole of Jesus' ethical teaching, both in its original spirit and its presentation. The ethics called for in the Beatitudes are not so much ethics of obedience as ethics of grace. This innocence of heart and disposition, this earnestness of heart striving for the reign of God through reconciliation and mercy, are the ethics of a new moment in Israel, springing out of a new apprehension of God. The rabbis were feeling their way to such a position, but the evangelical utterance goes far beyond them. The Jew held, indeed, that "all have sinned. Hence for him too divine grace and forgiveness are determinative of future blessedness."[54] But Jesus goes very far in intensifying this stress upon divine grace. The Beatitudes seem to indicate the fulfilment of the time of the new covenant anticipated by Jeremiah and Ezekiel when a new order of moral capacity was to be present.

The blessings assigned in the Beatitudes are not so much held out under conditions as they are immediately declared. The conduct that is praised and the blessing assigned to it are, indeed, presented indirectly in the form of condition and reward, the reward being eschatological. But here all desert aspect is precluded,[55] and the reward is rather the gift of God. Luke's account of the first preaching at Nazareth corroborates this. The year of the Lord's favor is announced as a matter of great rejoicing to the poor, the brokenhearted, the captive, the blind, the bruised. These groups correspond to the Beatitudes groups of Mt. and Lk.; actual poverty, mourning, captivity, etc., are identified with the receptive spirit toward the freely given Kingdom. If the Beatitudes are typical, we are led then to see that sanctions of reward and penalty are formal and stylistic rather than ultimate. The eschatological or other blessings are a matter of grace rather than being conditioned on obedience, or rather the obedience is itself part of the positive gift of the Kingdom.

We now turn to the parable of the laborers in the vineyard.[56] Jesus has been promising dazzling rewards to his disciples, for they shall sit on twelve thrones judging the twelve tribes of Israel. He has been promising great things to all who make great renunciations

---

[54] C. H. Kraeling, ms. note.
[55] Schlatter, *Der Evangelist Matthäus*, p. 141; Klostermann, *Matthäusev.* on 5:11.
[56] Mt. 19:30–20:16.

for his sake, for they shall receive an hundredfold and shall inherit eternal life. "But," he says, "many shall be last that are first; and first that are last." Thus he warns against too literal an understanding of his reward language. He is quick to repel any tendency on the part of his hearers to exploit the reward prospect by measuring their merit or presuming to anticipate God's criteria of judgment. And the evangelist continues with the parable of the laborers in the vineyard as an illustration of verse 30 cited above: "For the kingdom of heaven is like unto a man that was a householder, who went out early in the morning to hire laborers into his vineyard. . . ." The parable is best understood as portraying the respective entrances of the "righteous" and of the publicans and sinners into the Kingdom. It justifies God's invitation to the latter classes, and their admission at the eleventh hour. A parallel cited by Klostermann illustrates it:

Many a man wins his World (to come) in one hour, and many only in many years. Aboda zara 10b.

Important for our notice is the fact that while the reward of a shilling at the end of the day stands for the eschatological reward, yet the element of merit is forcibly excluded by the emphasis on the bounty of the householder.[57]

The rabbis reproved service with an eye to reward, a good example of their thought being the following:

Be not like servants that minister to their Lord on condition of receiving a reward; but rather be ye like servants that do not serve their Lord on condition of receiving a reward. Abot 1:3.

So also:

If thou hast learnt much Torah, ascribe not any merit to thyself, for thereunto thou wast created. R. Jochanan ben Zakkai.[58]

Not because of our righteous acts do we lay our supplications before Thee, but because of thine abundant mercies. Jewish Liturgy.[59]

[57] Cf. the parable of the prodigal son, Lk. 15:11–32.
[58] Cit. Montefiore, *Synoptic Gospels*, II, 544.
[59] *Ibid.*, p. 543.

The thought is forcibly expressed in Lk. 17:7–10, the parable ending with the words, "Even so ye also, when ye shall have done all the things that are commanded you, say, We are unprofitable servants; we have done that which it was our duty to do."

We note finally that in the episode that follows so closely on the parable of the workers in the vineyard, that of the request of the mother of the sons of Zebedee, Jesus again deprecates the concept of desert or reward. His answer, "are ye able . . ." presumes, indeed, a relation between fidelity and the coveted honor, but he goes on to divert attention from this aspect by pointing to the secret dispositions of the Father as ultimately determinative.

CHAPTER SIX

The Fundamental Sanctions

PASSING from the first group of sanctions which we saw included all that involved rewards and punishments, we come to the remaining sanctions, those from which the appeal to self-interest is absent, and which speak rather to the reason and conscience of men, reflecting upon the facts of the nature of God, man, etc. We do not fail to recognize that Jesus in invoking retributions often appealed to the discernment of his hearers in approving his proclamation of the consequences of conduct. Thus he called on them to recognize themselves the signs of the times. But in such cases, none the less, the real motive for conduct was the consequences recognized. In our present sanctions Jesus is appealing not to the consequences, feared or desired, but to realities, and he is striving to make men discern these realities. And it is not solely to men's intelligence or reason, if such can be isolated, that he appeals, but to the whole man as the Jewish heritage had made him. He was appealing to the God-conscious moral nature of his hearers, and he was stimulating that God-consciousness by every means possible, by his own authority, by appeal to the Scriptures, and by whatever illuminated the true nature of God.[1]

It is important at this point to emphasize and illustrate how much Jesus relied upon the sheer validity of his truth and on the native discernment of his hearers. It becomes more evident, then, that his

[1] "What God's will is is not stated as though it came from an external authority such that its content is a matter of indifference, but men are trusted and expected to see for themselves what is required of them. The requirements of God are therefore self-accrediting." Bultmann, *Jesus*, p. 73; *Jesus and the Word*, pp. 76–77.

appeal was finally not to fear, or avidness for safety, but to the assent of the heart. This confidence of Jesus in the persuasive power of the truth and in the ultimate moral discernment of common men seems to have taken precedence with him over other enforcing features. His final plea, all eschatological menace apart, is,

And why even of yourselves judge ye not what is right? Lk. 12:57.[2]

Even the appeal to the Scriptures as we have noted above is subservient to this appeal to the reason. The unanswerable rhetorical questions that Jesus puts when an issue is raised involving the authority of the law are appeals to common sense.

How much then is a man of more value than a sheep! Mt. 12:12.

And the assignment of first place of authority to one feature of the law over another is determined by reason. Thus the appeal to the passage,

I desire mercy, and not sacrifice (Mt. 9:13; 12:7).

We need to make a distinction here. On the one hand Jesus is found frequently appealing to the reason of his hearers in respect to illustrations and analogies that he proposes. These often do not touch the fundamental moral issue except by analogy. In fact this appeal to reason is "brought into play especially where situations are met which are least apt to be acted upon on reasonable grounds."[3] Thus Jesus calls on his hearers not to be anxious for the morrow, for (and here is the telling appeal to the abundant mother-wit of the Galileans) they cannot add a cubit to their stature, any more than they can (in another reference, with regard to oaths as presumptuous) make a hair of their hair white or black. In such sayings there is an appeal to the reason: we find Jesus counting upon the shrewd consent of men; we are grateful to note that his method as tested even here is not one of coercion but of appeal. The force of the indictment of hypocrisy against the scribes and Pharisees lies in the immediate

[2] Cf. "Are ye so without understanding also?" Mk. 7:18; "And he called to him the multitude, and said unto them, Hear, and understand." Mt. 15:10.
[3] C. H. Kraeling, ms. note.

appeal to the hearer's sense of discrepancy. The rhetorical questions, "Which is greater, the gold, or the temple that hath sanctified the gold?" etc., constitute a plain appeal to common sense. Again, so graphic a figure as that of the gnat and the camel have their force in the same appeal.

But such incidental appeals to reason are not what we have first of all in mind. In some cases they serve only negatively, and in others they serve merely to intimate by vivid analogy. "If the salt have lost its savor, wherewith shall it be salted?" The observations drawn from nature are expected to convince by their own truth, and then serve as a ground from which to rise to a higher order of truth, not this time by "reason" but by a moral discernment. Jesus deals with certain issues by the unanswerable figures of the new patch of cloth and the new wine. But once the justice of the homely figures is recognized, it still is necessary for the hearer to perceive the propriety of the analogy.

Over and above the first type of appeal to reason in respect of analogies and illustrations, then, we find Jesus appealing to the discernment and consent of his hearers in more fundamental ways. Even when he is calling upon his disciples for conduct that is on the face of it unreasonable from a lower ground, he yet appeals to a deeper discernment or a deeper reason for this very conduct. It is one of the glories of Jesus' teaching that it is thus fundamentally confident of man's native insight and free moral responsiveness. This optimism shows itself on the one hand in the cases we have referred to above, and similarly in more significant appeals. For instance, the Golden Rule, while it involves the sanctions of Scriptures which it summarizes in Mt.'s form, is counted on really to carry its own conviction. The same is true of the double great commandment as a summary of the law. "Take heed, and keep yourselves from all covetousness," says Jesus. "Why?" we answer. And he calls our attention to a fact that we cannot but assent to: "for a man's life consisteth not in the abundance of the things which he possesseth."[4] The recognition of what defileth a man is left to the hearer's discernment, assisted by the analogy drawn from the body. The issue

[4] Lk. 12:15.

of divorce turns upon the proposal that in view of the nature of the sexes, "in the beginning," Moses' concession was not valid (at least so Mt. understands it). For a true discernment recognizes in the old account of creation the essential relation of man and woman and the enduring nature of marriage, and its conclusion will therefore override custom and "Moses." Jesus puts Sadducees and Pharisees to silence with his unanswerable conclusions, "Render unto Caesar the things that are Caesar's," and "God is not the God of the dead, but of the living." That he lays immense weight on the responsibility of men to perceive and to understand comes out well in the denunciation of the hypocrisy of the Pharisees, the burden of which is summed up in the words, "fools and blind."[5]

We turn now to the first of the sanctions of this second group, the third in order of the significant sanctions as we are listing them.

3. *The Nature of God*

This fundamental sanction, that of the very nature of God, presumes on the one hand a powerfully vivid experience of the divine, of the *mysterium tremendum,* or the numinous experience itself; and in addition a special conception or group of conceptions of the object thus known. The objective aspects of God's character significant for ethics[6] such as his holiness (here, separateness in its moral aspect), his justice and his mercy in their various forms, these are attributes derived from the religious experience itself yet distinguishable from it. Yet we would err to make too much of such a distinction. In knowing God the Jew felt that he knew One who was holy, just, good, purposeful. The content of the vision of Jahweh included all such aspects as of his very nature.[7] An experience of God was in itself an experience of his holiness and his goodness. The "Abba" apostrophe of Jesus made no discrimination of God's majesty and his righteousness. And while one might say that, objectively considered, only God's moral attributes could be motives for human holiness or goodness, yet it would also be true to say that the experience of God

---

[5] Cf. the author's "Equivalents of Natural Law in the Teaching of Jesus," *Journal of Religion,* XXVI (1946), 125–35.

[6] Cf. G. F. Moore, *Judaism,* I, 336–400.

[7] See Ex. 34:5–7; 19:16–20:1; Is. 6; Ps. 36:5–10.

itself was both the ultimate sanction of ethics, and their inspiring source.[8]

We shall therefore distinguish two aspects of the sanction drawn from the nature of God, (a) his character as the objective sanction for imitation and gratitude, and (b) his godhead (i.e., his glory, sanctity, holiness,[9] power, etc.) as the ultimate sanction of obedience and of the sanctification of the Name.

a. God's character as the objective sanction for imitation and gratitude. The imitation of God is a motive invoked for ethics. "That ye may be the sons of your Father which is in heaven" is the end Jesus proposes for generosity, impartiality and "perfection."[10] This section of the Sermon on the Mount is instructive at this point. "The address . . . lays down the principle of imitation of the Father's goodness as the true basis of moral conduct. . . ."[11] In Mt. 5:38–41 Jesus teaches, "Resist not him that is evil," and gives three illustrations. The next verse on giving to him that asks and on acceding to the borrower exalts generosity and likewise has no explicit motive attached. Mt. 5:43–48 that follows teaches the love of enemies,

> that ye may be sons of your Father who is in heaven: for he maketh his sun to rise on the evil and the good, and sendeth rain on the just and the unjust . . . Ye therefore shall be perfect, as your heavenly Father is perfect.

This motive, then, applies to at least the foregoing counsels if not to the whole Sermon as Bacon holds.[12] The sanction of the nature of God matches the important sanction of the Old Testament found

[8] We recall that very often to enforce such duties as were left to the conscience of the Jew (masūr-la-lēb), the divinity rather than the attributes of God are recalled in the phrase, "And thou shalt revere the Lord thy God." Moore, *op. cit.*, II, 82.

[9] The essential meaning of the sanctity or holiness of God is his divinity. "God hallows his own name (himself) by demonstrating his supreme godhead . . ." *op. cit.*, II, 102.

[10] In the sense of drawing no lines in one's benevolence. Cf. James 1:4, "perfect and entire, lacking in nothing." To be conceived in a positive or activist sense.

[11] Bacon, *Studies in Matthew*, p. 347.

[12] If we turn to the corresponding material in Lk. we find much the same instruction closing with the words, "And your reward shall be great, and ye shall be sons of the Most High: for he is kind toward the unthankful and evil. Be ye merciful, even as your Father is merciful." Lk. 6:35b, 36.

in its classical form in the verse, "Be ye holy for I am holy."[13] It is interesting to note that there is no eschatological sanction immediately attached to this section. "In the case of the saying as to the love of enemies, the absence of eschatological ground is clear. The motives that are named here that should lead to the love of enemies in both disposition and action, are the example of God, the perfection of God, which are to be imitated, and also the expectation that the faithful who belong to God and to Jesus and who anticipate a reward from God must do more than the publicans and the heathen, that is, than those men who had withdrawn from God."[14] It is significant to find that so important an ethical section as this is grounded alone on the nature of God.

Windisch in his discussion of the Sermon on the Mount treats the passage, "Resist not evil . . . ," with special attention because of its selection by J. Weiss as one of the classical examples of interim ethics in Jesus' teaching. Weiss, that is, thinks that only the imminent Judgment can have led Jesus to offer such an inhuman teaching. To put it in the language of Montefiore,

> Jesus is giving counsels of perfection for those who are entering or want to enter the "Kingdom." He is not providing rules for ordinary society. He is telling what men must do in or amid the greatest crisis in the world's history, how they must behave to endure the crisis, and then to become members of a kingdom in which the need and the occasion for such conduct will no longer exist.[15]

Windisch denies that this eschatological mood and sanction is uppermost in the passage. He shows that its immediate connection with the sayings on the forgiveness of enemies indicates that its true grounding is, as there, the generosity and example of God, even more clearly recognized in Lk.'s arrangement. But, Windisch says, Mt. does have a theory of his own which leads him to radicalize Jesus' demands throughout this whole section (and so to lend plausibility to the interim ethics interpretation). He has, in this general

[13] Lev. 11:44. Sevenster discusses this sanction with illustrations from the Wisdom Literature, the Testaments and the Letter of Aristeas, *op. cit.*, pp. 100–2.

[14] Windisch, *op. cit.*, pp. 12–13.

[15] *Synoptic Gospels*, II, 73–74.

section of the Sermon, so edited the sayings as to draw a primary motive from sheer contrast with the ethics of the old dispensation.[16] Therefore, the radical nature of the summons is due largely, in Mt.'s form, to the wish to make the contrast thorough-going, and to eradicate every impulse of retaliatory spirit from the heart. In reading Mt.'s version of these sayings of Jesus we need therefore to make some allowance for this emphasis of the evangelist (not absent from the original: cf. Lk. 6:32–34). We then find that in Jesus' original utterance the main motive for the section was the imitation of God. This understanding of the matter led Windisch to reject the view he had formerly shared with J. Weiss, in accordance with which the whole passage represented interim ethics.

Sevenster chooses this passage as one in connection with which to urge his often-repeated theme that the radicalized ethical teaching of Jesus has its ground in a correspondingly radicalized conception of God. He points out that for the Wisdom Literature, God loves the good and hates the wicked. Hence man is allowed to hate those whom he thinks God considers evil. But for Jesus God loves all, and this change in the premise concerning God requires a change in the ethical obligation.[17] The significance of this for understanding the differentia of the ethics will be considered in the second part. Here we note that in any case the theme of the imitation of God is basic.

The total contradictoriness of the conception of God in Mt. 5:45 and Lk. 6:35–36 and that in the catastrophic eschatological passages is one of the most significant points made by Windisch. This is a God "who in his rule over the world according to fixed laws, has renounced the right of favoring the just and punishing the godless, and who since the covenant with Noah has certainly renounced every form of catastrophe. . . . All thought or anxiety connected with catastrophe are therefore absent from this beautiful saying." And he contrasts the avenging God of Luke 18:7 and of Romans 1:19 ff.[18] The conception of God here as impartial in his active beneficence brings this passage among those where the positive aspect

16 Mt. 5:38, 43.
17 *Op. cit.*, p. 101; cf. pp. 106 f., 109 f., 118.
18 *Bergpredigt*, p. 13.

of God's action, his grace and generosity, are stressed. This note is not, however, essentially incompatible with the thought of the God of judgment, however it may be with the realistic pictures of catastrophe. The incompatibility of the two pictures of God, the scandal of the God of apocalyptic judgment, arises only for logic and the literal mind. The antinomy runs through the whole of Hebrew prophecy. Jesus' radicalized teaching of the goodness of God sharpens the problem, indeed. If we interpret his eschatology in a crass way we are indeed face to face with an insoluble contradiction. But we need to recall that Jesus spoke as a preacher, concerned to move the wills of men by terms they would understand, and that righteous indignation and insight into disastrous consequences naturally resort to forensic language and to parables drawn from human behavior and human compensation. Thus the radical distinction made by Windisch, Sevenster and others between eschatological and non-eschatological moods is not justified.

Ethical summons, next, grounded on gratitude to God is found in the saying in Mt. 10:8b, "Freely ye have received, freely give." It is not easy to distinguish the motive of gratitude and that of imitation. We have brought out the fact that the bounty of God in giving the Kingdom was the positive motive for repentance and acceptance of the lighter yoke of conduct. This sanction of gratitude is notable in the later New Testament ("we love, because he first loved us"), but is present also in Jesus' teaching.

b. His godhead as ultimate sanction of obedience and of the sanctification of the Name. We turn now to a more difficult aspect of this sanction of the nature of God, that namely drawn not from his character but from his godhead itself. Here, rather than the righteousness or the bounty of God, it is the majesty of God that is invoked. Here, rather than imitation or gratitude, it is reverence that is called for. Here it is the nature of God not in respect of some attribute that has affinity with human virtues, but in its essential and divine quality that is urged: in its majesty, sanctity, hallowedness, glory, power. The old thought of the "jealousy" of God is inseparable from these conceptions. This aspect of the nature of God does not so much determine the kind of ethical conduct as lay immense weight on obedience and on reverence and on single-minded devotion to the things of God.[19] Thus this aspect of the nature of God (the discernment of which by men Jesus again counts upon) is more fundamental than the others. It really can be reduced to the recognition by men of the reality of God, but of God as understood by Jesus; yet that reality carries with it inseparably not only divine power and glory but all manner of ethical connotations.

The simplest expression of this ethical motivation is as follows: Do the will of God because he is supremely great. His power and glory are such that they are to be reverenced by whole-hearted obedience. In its most elementary form, therefore, it is just the Old Testament plea for obedience to One who is ruler and king over all men, to One who is the Almighty, the Lord of Hosts, the King of Kings. Not only the Scriptures but the rabbis could reduce the motives for conduct to the simple one of obedience. "That it is the will of his Father in heaven is the all-sufficient reason and motive for abstaining from what he forbids. On Lev. 20:26, R. Eleazar ben Azariah says:

> A man should not say, I have no desire to wear a garment of mixed stuff, I have no desire to . . . etc. He should say, I have the desire, but what shall I do, since my Father in heaven has laid a prohibition on me . . ."[20]

In the teaching of Jesus the duty of obedience to God is implicit throughout. The prestige of the Scriptures as representing the will of God, the precepts of God and not of men, is sustained. Pervasive in the proclamation of the Kingdom, moreover, is the view that Christ speaks as the spokesman of God who is to be obeyed, even as the Ninevites obeyed him when he spoke through Jonah. Thus the gospel is the Word from God. Here, then, the nature of God in its aspect of authority and dominion serves as a sanction for ethics. It is notable, however, that Jesus does not seem to rest the urgency of his ethical teaching on such extrinsic authority alone. While he calls

[19] "We have to do with a God who is holy and jealous, who has authority over men and will have complete sway over them, who demands their entire dedication and calls for their service $\dot{\epsilon}\nu$ $\dot{\alpha}\pi\lambda\dot{\delta}\tau\eta\tau\iota$." So Sevenster, *op. cit.*, p. 191, with references to Mt. 6:24; 5:22, 28; 6:1 ff.; 23:5–7, 9; 6:22–23 and their parallels.

[20] Moore, *Judaism*, II, 205.

for obedience, it is always to a commandment whose authority lies equally in the cogency with which it appeals to the discernment of the hearer. This has been sufficiently evident from our discussion of Jesus' appeal to the reason and the discernment of the individual.

Some contrast with Jewish ethics is evident here, at least with Jewish ethics in its orthodox statement, as for instance in the following: "what are called Jewish ethics are in substance and form more exactly described as preceptive morals; they are the morals of a religion, and their obligation lies not in the reason and conscience of men but in the authority of the sovereign Lawgiver."[21] Yet a considerable sphere of duty in Judaism, as we have seen, has no detailed prescription, and is "left to the conscience and right feeling of the individual. These are . . . masūr-la-lēb, 'committed to the heart.' "[22] Yet in commending such undefined obligations to the Jew with the phrase, "And thou shalt revere the Lord thy God," the Scriptures enforce them by a reminder of the reality and authority of God.

But the sanction drawn from the godhead itself has other expressions. Indeed, in the form in which we have stated it, it is not found except tacitly. The typical expression of it is somewhat indirect: Do righteousness so as to glorify the Father in heaven or to sanctify his name.[23] Jesus bids his disciples let their light shine before men, "that they may see your good works, and glorify your Father who is in heaven." This motive echoes an old theme in Jewish exhortation. Do righteousness that the God of Israel may be sanctified in Israel and before the nations. George Foot Moore calls this "the supreme principle and motive of moral conduct in Judaism."[24] If so, we may confidently reckon the present passage which reflects the same thought as one of the utmost significance. But we must believe that the form of this motive, both in the Old and New Testaments, is a transposition or special application of what is very much more central

[21] *Ibid.*, II, 81–82.
[22] *Ibid.*, II, 82.
[23] "To glorify God is the equivalent in this passage, 5:16, of the sanctifying or hallowing of God." Montefiore, *Rabbinic Literature and Gospel Teaching* (London, 1930), p. 35.
[24] *Op. cit.*, II, 103.

and fundamental, that is, the sanctity or glory itself of the heavenly Father. God is to *be* sanctified; but this means that his sanctity *is*. It exists already; it exists as a tremendous fact and as determinative of conduct. Men "glorify" God by praise or by righteousness, especially by martyrdom, but basic in the summons to glorify him is the Isaiah-like vision of his existing holiness and power, i.e., his deity.[25]

With this introduction we turn to the passages in which Jesus directly and indirectly invokes the glory of the Father. They lead us into realization of the immediate religious experience of Jesus, that which was the central and essential source of all his teaching, and the ultimate ground of his ethical demands. And we note by anticipation that this emphasis on the glory and power of God is closely related to the eschatological sanction. They both spring from an overpowering sense of the august reign of God. The eschatological anticipation just goes a step farther and sees this same power in imminent action of judgment. The call to hallow the Name springs from the sense that all power and rule is lodged with God and all obedience is due him. This sense of the majesty and reality of the divine rule is really primary, and in studying this sanction we are at the root of the derived and more formal sanction found in its dramatization in act of judgment. We therefore consider it crucial in its significance for our study and shall examine it closely.

The clearest use of this sanction is found in Mt. 5:16:

Even so let your light shine before men; that they may see your good works, and glorify your Father who is in heaven.

In the writings of the Old Testament the glorification of God or of the name of God is a frequent theme, finding its roots in the Decalogue. It stands for the recognition in praise or obedience of the

[25] Montefiore illustrates by citations the dilemma of the rabbis as to whether God needs men's sanctification; whether it is possible for men to add to the sanctity of God. "We may observe with them a curious see-saw. God, as it were, needs man for the full sanctification of his kingship and divinity; he even needs man, as it were, for himself; and yet he does *not* need man; he is holy, he is divine in himself. Moore cites Sifra 86c (on Lev. 19:2) to show how man can make God holy: he really cannot do so, but God imputes it to man if man is holy."

power and rule of God, and is often found in a context bearing on God's deliverance of his people. So Ps. 22:23 ff.:

> Ye that fear Jehovah, praise him;
> All ye the seed of Jacob, glorify him;
> And stand in awe of him, all ye the seed of Israel . . .
> For the kingdom is Jehovah's.

Compare here Ps. 86:9–10:

All nations whom thou hast made shall come and worship before thee, O Lord;
And they shall glorify thy name.
For thou art great, and doest wondrous things:
Thou art God alone.[26]

Our passage 5:16 is peculiar to Mt. Peculiar to Mt. also is the understanding of the candle and the light here as conduct rather than as true doctrine.

Another use of this sanction appears in the Lord's Prayer. We find in both the Matthean and the Lukan form of the prayer the clause,

Hallowed[27] be thy name.

The Lord's Prayer presupposes a readiness and therefore involves a summons to do the will of God. It constitutes therefore an ethical imperative, whose sanction is the ascription of the reign and the glory to God. This ascription is to be found in verses 9 and 10 in the optative clauses rather than in the secondary 13b. Here the hallowing of the Name is closely tied to the advent of the Kingdom.[28]

But the most developed emphasis on the glory of God as sanction

---

[26] See also Mal. 1:6; cf. I Peter 2:12 (which interestingly connects the glorifying of God with the Day of Judgment), and Jn. 12:28.

[27] "It is noteworthy that ἁγιάζω, the more direct equivalent of 'sanctify' (as contrasted with δοξάζω), is only found once in Synoptic Gospels, namely, in the Lord's Prayer, Mt. 6:9; Lu. 11:2." Montefiore, *Synoptic Gospels*, II, 35.

[28] "The Lord's Prayer is the prayer-formula of an eschatological community. It is sheer religious eschatology like the first half of the Beatitudes." Windisch, *op. cit.*, p. 20.

comes in two sections dealing with oaths or vows. We recall the passages:

> But I say unto you, Swear not at all; neither by the heaven, for it is the throne of God; nor by the earth, for it is the footstool of his feet; nor by Jerusalem, for it is the city of the great King. Mt. 5:34–35.
>
> He therefore that sweareth by the altar, sweareth by it, and by all things thereon. And he that sweareth by the temple, sweareth by it, and by him that dwelleth therein. And he that sweareth by the heaven, sweareth by the throne of God, and by him that sitteth thereon. Mt. 23: 20–22.

The effect of these two passages is to exalt into startling reality and majesty the sovereignty of God, symbolized especially by his "throne." But the reign of God is assigned not only to the heavens, but also to the city, Jerusalem, and to the Temple. These great assertions of the reality of the godhead, especially in reference to the scribes and Pharisees, recalls a pertinent passage in Malachi:

> A son honoreth his father, and a servant his master: if then I am a father, where is mine honor? and if I am a master, where is my fear? saith the Lord of hosts unto you, O priests, that despise my name. 1:6.
>
> And now, O ye priests, this commandment is for you. If ye will not hear, and if ye will not lay it to heart, to give glory unto my name, saith the Lord of Hosts, then will I send the curse upon you. 2:1–2.

These several passages, then, show that discernment and consideration of the transcendent greatness, glory, sanctity ("jealousy" and separateness, rather than moral holiness) of the Father are urged as a fundamental motive for reverence, obedience, doing the will, making the light of worthy conduct shine before men. Again we note that this persuasion of God's reality and majesty cannot practically be divided into a religious and a moral aspect. It is all one. We are here face to face with the fact that the grounding of ethics in the gospel is religious, and we do well to lay hold of the fact anew that our deliberate discrimination of ethical aspects is artificial. The ground and source of Jesus' life and teaching, the objective sanctions of his moral imperatives, and that which in the life of his hearers rendered them practicable, all these are reducible finally to the vision of God that Jesus mediated, a vision whose import we find most simply stated in the emphasis on the glory of God and the sanctity of his Name. Thus, other aspects of sanction drawn from the nature of God, imitation of his goodness, gratitude for his generosity, etc., are subordinate, finding their real force in the further truth of his greatness and reality. For apart from that his beneficence would be a matter of comparatively little consequence or convincing power.

It is the prophetic vision of God's sanctity and glory that animates everything in the evangelical proclamation. And we wish again to set these passages exalting the name and power of God over against the eschatological sanctions. They are closely related to them. It is the same unclouded religious apprehension of God that is expressed in the one and in the other. The same sensitive moral and spiritual discernment that beholds like Isaiah the glory of God also recognizes the inevitability of judgment and the inevitability of salvation. To know the Father is to know that he acts and will act. To know something of his inconceivable ways and power is to be assured that the human will and the human order are like clay in his hands or like silver ore to his fire.

We pass to the other sanctions of this second group, noting that while they differ from the first their real function is not to annul the appeal to the individual's free discernment and response, but rather to assist this.

4. *The Scriptures*

A fourth sanction that appears for the ethical instruction is the authority of the Scriptures. We understand authority here in the sense of immense prestige, rather than in that of binding law. Jesus and his hearers meet on a common ground of assumption that the Scriptures are authoritative in this sense, though Jesus himself may wish to weigh their various elements.[29] The twofold Great Com-

---

[29] Bultmann holds that Jesus' departure from the scribes in the matter of the authority of the Scriptures is in his readiness to play them off against each other and to decide what is essential and what is unessential. But here, he notes, the

mandment and the Golden Rule assume the authority of the law of
Moses: "on these two commandments hang all the law and the
prophets"; and, "for this is the law and the prophets." We note also
Jesus' resort to the law in the account of the Temptation.

The evangelist Mt. is distinctive for the manner in which he
presents Jesus' attitude to the Mosaic law. In general it may be said
that Jesus here recognizes a very high and continuing authority in it.
He has not come to destroy the law but to effect its fulfilment: that
is, to lead Israel to carry out its demands in their full meaning and
spirit (though the outcome of "fulfilment" of the law is transcendence of the law, already glimpsed in Jesus' action and teaching in
Mt.). The concern of such sayings as that referring to the "jot and
tittle," and that on the greatest in the Kingdom who do and teach
these commandments, is with the "greater matters" of justice, mercy
and truth. These things, which the scribes teach and do not, Jesus
demands of his hearers.[30] Sayings that emphasize mercy rather than
sacrifice, and the summary of the law with its emphasis on the love
of one's neighbor show the same truth.

But even in matters of piety, ceremonial and ritual, Jesus in this
gospel recognizes a high authority in the law. These also are precepts of God, and it is only certain rulings of the scribes, certain
aspects of the oral law, those in which the real and deeper intention
of the written law is obviated, that he attacks as precepts of men.
The jealousy of the evangelist in conserving the authority of the
Jewish law is explained by the "lawlessness" of certain Christians in

formal authority of the Scriptures is really abandoned. *Jesus,* pp. 71–72; *Jesus and
the Word,* pp. 74–76. In this Jesus only went farther along a road entered on by
the scribes themselves, however.

[30] Convincingly analyzed in Schlatter, *Der Evangelist Matthäus,* pp. 666–67. There
is a flat contradiction between the "all things" of 23:2, 3a, and the "every jot and
tittle" of chapter 5, *and* the representation of the attitude of Jesus that we get
throughout the gospel. Jesus could not have meant here to require the whole body
of scribal precept and interpretation of the common man, nor could the evangelist
so have represented him. Mt. gives too many cases of Jesus' neglecting the requirements for us to be able thus to understand the passage. The authority or sanction
invoked for the law and for those that sit in Moses' seat, therefore, has in mind the
divine oracles on the side of their "weightier matters"; these were the points at
which "they say, and do not." They *performed,* of course, the minutiae of the
interpretation. Jesus is, therefore, not speaking of these.

the church of his time. In order to point their error he emphasizes attitudes of Jesus that exalted the moral and pietistic law of the old dispensation. The most significant expression of this in Mt. is found in the gospel's special treatment of two incidents: that of the plucking of the ears of corn on the Sabbath, 12:1–8, and that of the healing of the man with the withered hand on the Sabbath, 12:9–13. Mt., in contrast with the other evangelists, adduces extra precedents from the Old Testament, the effect of which is to show that Jesus was not really infringing the law. They tend to show that "Jesus' action was fully justified by precedent as an entirely proper application of the law." [31]

Mt.'s representation of Jesus' attitude to the law in his own conduct and sayings is probably at this point truer than that of Mk. or Lk. It comes out most clearly of all perhaps in the controversy over ceremonial washings and the duty to parents, 15:3–20. Here Mt. does not, like Mk., "make all meats clean," but confines Jesus' teaching to the topic of ablutions. The "precepts of men" here, therefore, are not the food discriminations of the written law as in Mark's account, but merely the oral decisions, that "plant which my heavenly Father planted not," in this case comparatively recent. Mt. does, indeed, account the food requirements provisional, and anticipates their loosening by Peter. Bacon finds Mt.'s gospel thus more truly historical throughout in not anticipating in Jesus' own words and actions what really first appeared later, whether in the matter of "meats" or of approach to the Gentiles.[32] The error thus avoided is illustrated by the view of Bultmann who says that the whole code of clean and unclean is discarded with the saying concerning what defileth a man.[33] It is truer to say that this discarding is latent and prepared in Jesus' words, but only took effect in the time of the early church.[34]

We conclude then that for Jesus the Torah and its guardians

[31] Bacon, *Studies in Matthew*, p. 350.
[32] *Ibid.*, pp. 351–53.
[33] *Jesus*, pp. 72, 73; *Jesus and the Word*, p. 76.
[34] For further discussion of Jesus' attitude to the Mosaic law see Part II, chap. IX, where it is shown that Jesus as the prophet of the arriving new order asserts the authority to rule freely upon ethical issues, the fulfilment of the law passing over logically into transcendence of it.

(those that "sit in Moses' seat") had their real authority, and that this constituted a motive for conduct along with the sanctions of reward and punishment, etc.[35] Yet the relative importance of this motive is another matter. Jesus' use of the Scriptures is represented less as a decisive court of appeals than as an arsenal from which to fortify his own and his hearers' personal discernment in things spiritual and ethical. The conclusion of Sevenster after a study of the ethical teaching of Jesus and that of the rabbis is that Jesus differs from them in determining his ethical teaching directly from the concept of God, rather than from that of the law.[36]

5. *The Authority and Example of Jesus*

The example of Jesus is invoked in the call to minister, "even as the Son of man came not to be ministered unto, but to minister." We find it also in Mt.'s phrase, "is not worthy of me" in 10:37–38, where, however, Lk. has, "cannot be my disciple." Moreover, the verses Mt. 10:24–25 (Q) point to the example of Jesus himself in being blasphemed and to the naturalness of the rejection of disciple with master. In all cases the sanction from the example of Jesus is complicated by the thought of reward present in the context.

Similarly, the authority of Jesus is set forth as a sanction to compel obedience. This sanction is usually related to the eschatological sanction in that Jesus speaks as one related to the coming Judge, if not as identical with him. In the secondary saying, Mt. 28:18, the charge of Jesus to his disciples at the ascension, we have the assertion by Jesus of his messianic authority in its most unqualified form, and we can infer from it the tendency of the church increasingly to look to Jesus' personal authority as sanction for the new law of the community, and to read and modify the records in this direction. The authority of Jesus as justifying his *own* freedom with the law is another aspect which we have alluded to just above, and concerning which we have referred the reader to a later chapter (Chapter IX).

[35] "Their authority (i.e. that of the O. T. writings) stands fast for him as for the rabbis," says Bultmann, *Jesus*, p. 71; *Jesus and the Word*, p. 74, and he illustrates from Jesus' answers to the questions concerning the way to life and the first commandment.

[36] *Ethiek en Eschatologie*, pp. 144–45. See also B. H. Branscomb, *Jesus and the Law of Moses* (New York, 1930), pp. 128–31.

CHAPTER SEVEN

The Significance of the Eschatological Sanction

W E ARE now in a position to draw our conclusions as to the nature of the sanctions invoked by Jesus for his ethical summons, whether in his call to repentance generally or in his particular precepts.

The nearness of the Kingdom of Heaven, viewed both as promise and as menace, is the dominant sanction for righteousness.

This dominant eschatological sanction is, however, a formal sanction only, secondary to, if closely related to, the essential sanction.[1]

The essential sanction for righteousness is the nature of God.

The essential sanction represents an appeal simply to the reason and discernment, to the God-conscious moral nature of men, assisted by the witness of Scripture and the example and authority of Jesus.

The formal sanction represents an appeal to self-interest in view

[1] "The eschatological outlook is the decisive motive for the special form of presentation of the ethical teaching as well as for men's decision, performance and attitude. In the main the commended conduct and attitude carry their own religious validation; but this is never unrelated to the salvation that they involve and the God that promises such salvation." Windisch, *Bergpredigt*, p. 19. Compare Bultmann, "One could say quite simply: the performance of the will of God, obedience, is the *condition* of a share in the Reign of God, for entrance into the Kingdom of God. That is in a certain sense true, but this answer is not wholly satisfactory. For one could interpret this relationship superficially to mean that sharing in the Kingdom is the reward sought for obedience, and thus the radical character of obedience would be missed. Herein the unique way in which Jesus speaks of obedience would be misunderstood." *Jesus*, p. 112. Thus both writers decline to place the emphasis upon the retributions.

of the rewards and punishments that are to follow on the Judgment; and, incidentally, that are to be present in a degree in the present interim, which is a phase of the messianic times, in which the Kingdom of God is already present in a sense.

We have in several connections above anticipated the discussion of these conclusions. What has been said in the Introduction as to the nature of Jewish eschatology bears especially upon it. It was there emphasized that in the eschatological tableau the Jewish mind was—in a way most suitable to its Weltanschauung—dramatizing its conviction of the holiness of God in its dealing with men. This tableau therefore partakes of the nature of myth or symbol, and while the anticipations were real to them and represented indubitable actualities of the divine action, they should never be taken in a crass sense. The apocalyptic ideas are "fictions." They are fictions naïvely held; that is, they are not conscious symbol and deliberate metaphor. As fictions, it follows that, however vividly they might compel the imagination of the eschatologist, they could never serve as a final and determinative sanction. A fiction however vivid and compelling has not the substance to serve this purpose. The only exception here is when it has grown so impoverished and conventionalized that men begin to take it with a crass literalism. We are not surprised, therefore, to find that the eschatological sanction, in the vital and creative stage in which it appears in our gospels, is always in the form of a fictional or formal sanction.[2] But what real force there is in this sanction, properly enough, springs out of its immediate relation to that from which the fiction springs, that is, the experience of the holiness and power of God. For our gospels, indeed, it must be recognized that the eschatology falls sometimes below this level of creative power. The original creative symbol or "fiction," the true heart of all apocalyptic, here as elsewhere has advanced some steps on the way of literary crystallization. It is by way of becoming dogmatic and crass. The lengths to which this can go we can see in contemporary millenarianism or in some of the Jewish writings or later

[2] Prof. W. E. Hocking of Harvard, in a conversation, stated that many of the world's ethical teachers have, either consciously or unconsciously, been obliged, as though by the very conditions of thought and speech, to employ an *als ob* or fictional sanction.

Christian writings. In the gospels both the original and the conventionalized or impoverished stages of conception are found, and these in varying degrees. The former are pervasive enough to save the whole from misrepresenting the teaching of Jesus. Behind Mt.'s elaborations of the judgment motif and his constant invocation of penalty, for instance, we feel the fresh religious experience of the early church animating and validating these.

Discussion of our conclusions has also been anticipated above during our analysis of the sanctions when we have had occasion to show how intimately related are the two kinds of sanctions which we have called formal and essential. For vivid evocation of the glory and power of the Father has been seen to lead insensibly and inevitably into reflection upon that power asserting itself in redemption and judgment, and into the impulse to anticipate or forestall such action. Again, we have shown in another connection how inevitable and how pardonable is the tendency to deal in the sphere of consequences when questions of ethics are being handled. The evocation of a tableau of consequences is a most natural and human impulse in such exhortation; and, similarly, the dramatization and stylization of such a tableau is an inevitable result given the human mind and imagination as they are.

The double aspect of sanction is recognized by Windisch from another point of view in speaking of the reward aspect of the sayings concerning almsgiving, etc.: "Meanwhile it must be recognized that alongside the thought of reward a purely religious principle determines the content of the teaching: the content, namely, of the right and fitting performance of the various religious practices. Jesus would extricate the worshipper from all human concerns in which he may be entangled, and throw him entirely upon God. That God holds ready a reward for such a right attitude to him *also,* is unquestioned, but this consideration is secondary."[3]

Examination of Jesus' teaching permits us to catch in the moment of transition this tendency we have indicated to pass from one type of sanction to the other. Jesus says: do so and so because such and such is the evident nature of man, the world and God. But such a

[3] *Op. cit.,* p. 17.

grounding of ethical choice and conduct, if in the least developed, seems immediately to involve a reflection upon consequences of conduct in a world where the realities are such as Jesus describes. But *consequences are most naturally conceived in the light of rewards and punishments among those for whom the personal rule of God is so much an axiom. By these stages we thus pass from the sphere of essential sanction to that of retributive sanction, and from disinterested or impulsive virtue to calculative virtue.* Jesus himself and the people to whom he talked were not dialectical enough to raise the issue discussed in the *Republic* as to disinterested virtue. The rabbis indeed warned against obedience for the sake of reward. But the Jewish mind as we have seen conceived of right conduct as obedience to the will of a gracious Jahweh, and intrinsic and extrinsic sanctions were confused and mingled.

Jesus' essential appeal to the nature of God and man and their relation as the ground of his ethical demands led, then, immediately to the envisagement of consequences as a further sanction. We find an illustration of how inevitable this transition was in the following parable:

> The lamp of the body is the eye: if therefore thine eye be single, thy whole body shall be full of light. But if thine eye be evil, thy whole body shall be full of darkness. If therefore the light that is in thee be darkness, how great is the darkness! Mt. 6:22–25.

By means of the illustration of the eye Jesus appeals to the hearer to assent to the all-importance for one's life of the condition of the will (which is the lamp of the life as the eye is the lamp of the body). If the will and disposition are corrupted, then the life is in utter confusion ("how great is that darkness"). But with this realization the consequences immediately loom, and therewith the sanction for single-mindedness drawn from the fear of consequences.

In fact, any appeal to reason and conscience like that of Jesus necessarily evokes a moral order in which consequences are patent and inescapable. It was a reminder that the nature of man, the world and God and their relation were such and such, and that this nature demanded such and such attitudes and actions, and penalized

the actions of folly and blindness. Such insight into moral consequences is found in the Old Testament in various forms. Sometimes
we find it, here in the least developed stage, in the form of a wise
aphorism, like the many found in the Wisdom Literature, where
merely the natural this-worldly consequences of conduct are pointed
out. Jesus' saying concerning those that take the sword falls in this
class. Not far from it are such sayings as, "Blessed are the merciful
for they shall obtain mercy," and "With what measure ye mete, it
shall be measured to you again." Similarly with the parable of the
two builders. In such ethical teaching, the appeal to the moral sense
and moral insight has compelled recognition of the moral order
conditioning conduct. Then, at a deeper stage of insight, this merely
sapiential sanction, a discernment of natural and social consequences,
begins to pass over into a truly religious sanction, a discernment of
divine retributions. The important reality conditioning conduct is
now the majestic God of righteousness. The further step is when
this sanction becomes dramatized and perhaps eventually dogma-
tized in a scheme of eschatological rewards and punishments.

We see therefore the natural connection between the essential
sanctions of Jesus, his appeal to moral and spiritual realities, and his
eschatological sanctions. The former is not merely an appeal to the
reason. It is an appeal to the whole man, to his God-conscious moral
nature. As such it has in it implicitly all possible divine sanctions.
Once one recognizes and vividly apprehends the will of the Father
determining all destinies and the destiny of the world, wide vistas
of his favor or disfavor are immediately opened up. As someone has
said, "When I pass in review the appalling injustices that continue
in the world, I tremble to recall that God is just." The portrayal of
divine reward and punishment is, therefore, inevitable for the religious consciousness when it is in any degree ethicized. And it
follows that the eschatological sanctions in the gospel may not be
impeached as a type of motivation. While they are formal and while
they partake of the nature of dramatization, they are not adventitious. The appeal to realities demands them or their equivalent.
They are not merely arbitrary lures and menaces, arbitrary incen-
tives. They stand for inevitable consequences.

The prominence of the reward feature in the gospel can then be understood. Jesus, with the instinct of the consummate teacher, speaking as he is to simple people, casts his vision of moral consequences into concrete pictures of compensation, "hire," reward and punishment. The eschatological conception itself—the Judgment and its retributions—rises from the same dramatizing necessity. The mind of Jesus senses the terrible and glorious issues of human choice, and the eschatological drama is the only adequate representation that could then be given of such a range of spiritual fact. But this resort to the concrete and dramatic is not a consciously artistic or deliberate move; it is the natural action of the imagination. The "fictions" involved in the eschatological picture and sanction is of the very stuff of the mind here; it is an *als ob* inherent in the conditions of thinking.

Windisch has isolated a considerable body of units in the Sermon on the Mount which he thinks can easily be detached from the eschatological sphere because the teaching grew for a great part in a non-dualistic sphere, or because the eschatological motive present in it is not original. He thus analyzes the Sermon into two main streams: radicalized wisdom teaching, and eschatological announcement of judgment. He traces both back to Jesus' conception of God and his consequent radical deepening of both heritages.[4] Where we have tried to go a step farther is in showing the logical relation of these two elements. When this relation is realized, whereby wisdom teaching and prophetic teaching pass over insensibly into envisagement of consequences, and these take on conventional forms, we are prepared to see that the two types and moods of preaching are not to be so sharply distinguished as Windisch does without danger. Part and parcel of the solution, however, is recognition of the imaginative quality of the eschatological conceptions.

Bultmann holds well that the authority of the demands lies in their sheer convincing power; he writes of the *"Einsichtigkeit der Forderung."* He recognizes two aspects of Jesus' teaching, moreover: first, Jesus as scribe (where the teaching is sapiential, a radicalized obedience-ethics), and second, Jesus as prophet (where the teaching

[4] *Op. cit.,* p. 20.

is radicalized eschatology). But his main point with regard to the intuitional nature of the ethics is that they are not based on any accepted conception or ideal of human nature and its virtues or values. Jesus' precepts win the assent of the hearer through their own validity, but he denies that this validity grows out of any observation of or congruity with the human situation. Rather, they are valid to the native discernment as the only proper response and as the necessary total obedience of the will over against the recognized presence of God calling for immediate choice. "Nun, sie erwachsen sehr einfach aus der Situation der Entscheidung vor Gott, in die der Mensch gestellt ist."[5] He goes on to say that this answer is meaningless except to him who sees men and himself placed in this situation. But the conception is too simple or too abstract. "He who sees man placed continually in the act of choice, and he who regards this as the true angle from which to understand human existence, he recognizes that man is capable of knowing *now* what is good and what is evil; knowing, that is, not on the basis of any experiences or rational considerations whatever, but out of the very situation of the moment."[6] This is unreal. Bultmann is right in his point that the source of Jesus' ethics is not to be sought in the field of human precedents, relativities and theories of ethics. And he is right in assigning to the assisted human discernment power to recognize and choose the good. But that good must be given some content and reality.

Suppose as Bultmann has it that in Jesus' summons all antecedents and circumstances and thought of consequences are banished for the moment, and that the hearer is raised to a moment of moral freedom and choice over against the summons of God outside of time, as it were. His reaction then will be one of obedience, indeed. And the justice of this author's position appears when we limit our consideration of Jesus' sayings to those drastic sayings which present the duty of his hearers in the form of a choice or a call to complete obedience. But that obedience must then be conceived in terms of a

[5] "They arise simply enough out of that situation of choice over against God in which man is placed." For this and previous paraphrase, *Jesus*, pp. 82–83; *Jesus and the Word*, pp. 85–87.
[6] *Jesus*, p. 83; *Jesus and the Word*, p. 88.

human situation and human relations. And our recognition of the validity of the ethical teaching will be based on our understanding of such human circumstances. Bultmann is anxious to deny any fixedness of human nature and ethics so as to magnify the creative factor in God's action and in Christ's work, but even the creative freedom of God with our wills requires some human and social "character." Bultmann is going all lengths to simplify Jesus' ethics by reading it as absolute, and treating it in a metaphysical way. But Jesus' various instruction cannot be all assimilated to the one ultra-drastic mood here selected. And the second and even greater draw-back in this analysis is the forbidding nature of the Deity over against whom he sees men placed in the moment of choice. The fact is that what Bultmann means by the *Einsichtigkeit* of the ethics is not so much the consent of the individual to a range of moral duties as the capitulation of the individual to the divine authority. This emphasis on obedience as the key-note of Christian ethics is disturbing.[7]

We accept therefore only with reserves Bultmann's view of the self-convincing nature of the teaching of Jesus. The distinction that he like Windisch draws between Jesus as wisdom teacher and as eschatological prophet is again too unnatural, and the unity of these two aspects of teaching and sanction we have tried to make clear.

We conclude this first part, then, with the statement that as regards the sanction of the ethics Jesus' teaching concerning the future is by no means of first importance. The announcements of rewards and punishments may be ubiquitous and highly colored; certainly Mt. has lent this motive to righteousness more weight than the other gospels. Yet this should not blind us to the fact that even in this gospel the fundamental motives are religious-prophetic. What Sevenster says of the synoptic gospels generally is true here: "We

---

[7] See criticism of Bultmann's treatment in Windisch, *op. cit.*, pp. 34–35. Also, Otto, *Reich Gottes und Menschensohn*, p. 38; Otto speaks of "borrowings from a fashionable 'existence' philosophy; in this way points of view . . . are imported into the preaching of Jesus . . . which falsify it. For it is not my existence which Christ's call to repentance places in question but my righteousness before God . . ." *The Kingdom of God and the Son of Man*, translated by F. V. Filson and B. L. Woolf (Grand Rapids, Mich.: Zondervan, n.d.), p. 51.

can conclude then that by far the larger portion of the synoptic ethics brings no interim ethics, not even eschatologically conditioned ethics, but common religious ethics."[8] What we have pointed out as to the stylistic and imaginative quality of the eschatological imagery, as to Jesus' depreciation of merit-considerations and calculations of reward, as to the more essential sanctions of gratitude, obedience, discernment of the truth, etc., as to the Kingdom as freely given— these justify us in seeing the eschatological sanction as derivative and formal. We do not wish to rule out entirely the place of such sanction in the teaching. He would be foolish who would try to do so in the face of the Judgment parables and pointed summons to vigilance. Even read as dramatizations such passages definitely bring into play, and legitimately, the self-regarding motives as over against the future. But these formal sanctions should be looked upon as supplementary rather than as compromising the fundamental sanctions. And for him who wants to lay hold on the essential appeal made by Jesus for repentance and obedience and righteousness, it will remain unquestionable that these vistas of reward and penalty are definitely subordinate to the call upon men to act worthily of those who are the sons of the Father in heaven, and in ways consonant with his glory.

[8] *Op. cit.*, p. 195.

PART II

Eschatology and the Differentia of the Ethics

CHAPTER EIGHT

Ethics in the Time of Salvation

OUR first part has dealt with the sanction aspect of the relation of eschatology to ethics. We have to turn now to an even more significant aspect. How did the eschatological conception affect the content and nature of the ethics, if at all? Does Jesus call for a different righteousness, and if so, how is it related to the conception of the end?

In the first section we have assumed that eschatology meant an event still in the future. As long as we thus confine ourselves to the thought of the coming Judgment with its rewards and penalties, our problem is comparatively simple. The coming event is, then, motive for repentance and for urgency in doing righteousness, and the particular demands are looked on as conditions of entrance to the future Kingdom. If this were all, the problem would be much simplified. Then the Baptist and Jesus would be prophetic exponents of the law in its inner meaning, calling the nation to prepare itself by righteousness for the coming day of Jehovah.

But in our analysis of the eschatology taught by Jesus we have seen that it includes elements anterior to the parousia and Judgment. The eschatological period begins with the proclamation of the Baptist and the work of Jesus, and goes on through the death and resurrection of the latter to the coming of the Son of Man. This interpretation by Jesus of the events of his own lifetime and of the days immediately to follow it is evidenced throughout, as we have seen, especially by such words as those designating the Baptist as Elias who should come and by the significance assigned to his own work.

This whole reading of events is based upon the Scriptures. Logically, we would suppose that a clear distinction would be made between the present age and the age to come, with all evidences of God's work of salvation strictly confined to the latter. It was not so in fact. Lake and Jackson point out that there was no fixed doctrine of the future, and that the "Good Time Coming" at times included both the Days of the Messiah as well as the Age to Come proper.[1] That is, the Scriptures warranted the expectation of various aspects of the time of salvation before the decisive catastrophe itself. We can understand this when we recall the history of Jewish eschatology. The earlier Davidic messianism envisaged a redeemed people living in the world in conditions not greatly changed. When the apocalyptic ideas came in with their picture of a regeneration and a transcendental Kingdom, it was not easy to submit the older earthly ideals to the new, and the older were not therefore abandoned or subsumed under the new entirely. Thus many details in the Scriptures there loosely assigned to the coming time of salvation, could be legitimately interpreted as fulfilled in the days of John the Baptist and Jesus. The return of Elijah and the preaching of a Last Repentance were of course most naturally assigned to the last days before the new age. But there was hardly less difficulty in seeing a present fulfilment of the prophecies of the washing away of the sins of the people, the purifying of the priests and the Temple, the outpouring of the Spirit, the giving of a new heart of flesh to Israel, the overthrow of Satan and the demons, the forgiveness of sins and other features of the messianic days. Thus Jesus found abundant warrant for his interpretation of the phenomena of his day as evidence of the expected time of salvation, as part of the eschatological program in the larger sense. Many prophets and wise men had desired to see these days. "Today hath this scripture been fulfilled in your ears."

This fact presents us with a new aspect of the relation of eschatology to ethics and opens up an essentially different problem. The eschatological period is already present. It is now not the sanction of the ethical teaching that is in question, but its very content. How is

[1] *The Beginnings of Christianity*, I, Part I, chap. VI.

the ethic affected by the fact of the present eschatological situation? This new situation is constituted by the presence of the Kingdom in its first and humbler manifestation, with its accompanying benefits and powers, and by the activity of Jesus, whose humble role was none the less closely related to the coming of the Son of Man in power. In these circumstances it is not surprising to find that a correspondently modified ethic is taught.

1. *A new situation has arisen with the presence of the Baptist and Jesus which has a significant relation to ethics.*

Some students would have us believe that Jesus taught no other righteousness than that of the law. But Jesus speaks as though the *present* Kingdom of God presupposes a different relation between man and man, and man and God, and therefore a different ethic. We have noted that on occasion Jesus speaks of the Kingdom as present. The overthrow of Satan is another aspect of the present Kingdom. And in so far as the Kingdom is already come a new order of relationships and responsibilities is offered.

Jesus' reference to a new covenant (Mk. 14:24 and parallels; cf. I Cor. 11:25 and Lk. 22:29, 30) is questioned by many scholars advisedly. Yet it is clear that he thought of his generation as living in a time like that foreshadowed in such passages as Jer. 31:31 ff., Ezek. 24:8, Zech. 9:11. "Jesus nowhere refers to these promises," says Windisch of the Jeremiah and Ezekiel passages, "yet he assumes that the inner condition of his hearers is such that they can 'live according to God's statutes' or that he himself it is who by his word has put the command of God 'in their inward parts' and written it 'in their hearts.' "[2] It is notable that a feature of Jeremiah's picture of the new covenant has to do with God's "law."

But this is the covenant that I will make with the house of Israel after those days, saith Jehovah: I will put my law in their inward parts, and in their heart will I write it. 31:33.

Similar promises, in terms of future sonship, are found in Hos. 1:10, Is. 43:6, Ps. Sol. 17:27, Jub. 1:23–25. Jesus looks on his followers as

[2] Windisch, *Bergpredigt*, p. 73.

heirs of these promises. The new situation is there for those who respond.

The new condition of things is evidenced also by Jesus' power in exorcism. By the spirit of God he casts out devils and the presence of the Kingdom is manifest. The strong man, Satan, is bound, as is evidenced by the overthrow of his agents. The passage (Mt. 12:28–29)[3] and context connect all this closely with Jesus himself. The reduction of Satan to impotence has significance for ethics.

Again, of the parables of the Kingdom, at least those of the mustard seed, the seed growing of itself and the leaven, show us Jesus' thought that the Kingdom is present in anticipatory form already before the parousia. In these three the relation of the outcome to the initial action is so essential as to call attention to the intervening phase.

In Mk. 2:18–22 we have the passage connecting the non-fasting of the disciples of Jesus with the new dispensation (new cloth, new wine). Our two main features are present: the graphic presentation of the new element in the old situation, and its relation to a feature of the law: fasting. The disciples with their Master are pictured as a wedding party, and the joyful announcement of the Kingdom is set over against the old dispensation in sharp contrast.[4] The point of the parables of the new wine and the new cloth is the incompatibility of old and new. The new power to fulfil the law, as evident in Jesus and those he teaches, this power that evidences the time of salvation, means that for such a feature of the law as fasting there is no present occasion.

Still more significant is the Q passage in which Jesus comments on the Baptist, and goes on,

---

[3] Cf. the temptation account, also Lk. 10:18–19 and 13:10–17, cf. Bultmann, *Jesus*, pp. 29–30; *Jesus and the Word*, p. 28.

[4] "It is then really true! The promise of the prophets is fulfilled.

> The blind see, and the lame walk,
> The lepers are cleansed, and the deaf hear—

The time of joy is dawning; sorrowing and fasting are over; it is festival time, and who would fast in the days of the wedding season?" Bultmann, *Jesus*, p. 29; *Jesus and the Word*, p. 28. Cf. the music and dancing at the return of the prodigal son.

And from the days of John the Baptist until now the kingdom of heaven suffereth violence, and the violent take it by force. For all the prophets and the law prophesied until John. Mt. 11:12–13.[5]

The understanding here is that with the coming of the Baptist was ended the period of anticipation. From the time of the Baptist on (though Mt. distinguishes the period of John when the forces of evil stormed the Kingdom and the period of Jesus and the church when these forces were conquered) the actual thing prophesied was present, i.e., the Kingdom of God.[6] For the subject of prophecy was understood to be the messianic age. "All the prophets prophesied on one subject alone, namely, the Days of the Messiah."[7] John's preaching of the Kingdom set him in a higher place than any of the prophets. With him the time of the new age begins.

Bacon thus paraphrases the answer made by Jesus to the disciples

[5] A persuasive reading of this passage and its Lukan parallel is given by C. H. Kraeling in a ms. note:

"In both Mt. and Lk. the word surveys an historical development. In Lk. that development is presented in the form of two major periods, 1) Μέχρι Ἰωάνου, 2) ἀπὸ τότε (including John *and* Jesus). In Mt. I seem to see three periods, 1) ἕως Ἰωάνου (prophets and law), 2) ἀπὸ Ἰωάνου . . . ἕως ἄρτι (John's period), 3) [ἀπὸ τοῦ νῦν] (consummation = Jesus' period), implied by ἕως ἄρτι. The ἕως ἄρτι seems to me to imply that upon the period of violence there follows through Jesus' conquest of the forces of evil a period of supremacy of the Kingdom over the stormers . . ."

Thus the Lukan and Matthean forms both evidence the view of Jesus that the Kingdom is present from the time of John on (for then the prophets and the law reached their term), though for a time under duress.

This view matches closely the one presented by Dibelius, *Die Urchristliche Ueberlieferung von Johannes dem Täufer* (Göttingen, 1911, pp. 24–29), who deals with the passage in a detailed study that keeps in mind the opposing interpretation as argued by Harnack. Here again the stormers are the evil spiritual powers, Paul's "rulers of this age," who since the time of John have hindered and handicapped the Kingdom. But now with the coming of the Kingdom, signalized for Dibelius not by Jesus' activity or death, but by the eschatological event, a third period begins in which the powers of evil are overcome and the Kingdom attains its unhindered fulfilment. We prefer the view that the third stage was thought of as beginning with the signs and powers wrought by Jesus, which testify to the binding of the strong man, Satan. That this interpretation is not incompatible with that of Dibelius is apparent from a note of his recognizing the fluctuation of the eschatological mood which now assigns its goal to the future and now in part to the present.

[6] Schlatter, *Der Evangelist Matthäus*, pp. 369–70.

[7] Spoken by R. Chijja b. Abba (c. A.D. 280).

of John, bringing out the significance of his work: " 'Yes,' says the Nazarene, 'it [your work] is being carried on, and more. The great Repentance has begun. The lost sheep are being rallied to the standard of the Kingdom; and not only so, but God's "finger" has been stretched forth to heal, an assurance "from heaven and not from men" that the power of the Strong Man is already breaking before the Stronger than he. Satan is being cast out. But not by Beelzebub. Not by any human power. The God of Israel has Himself drawn near to open blind eyes, to unstop deaf ears, to cleanse the lepers and make the lame to walk.' "[8] Again, "The rule of 'book-religion' had been 'until John'; since then the kingdom of God had been preached. . . ."[9]

The justification of the plucking and eating of grain on the Sabbath by the examples of David and the priests[10] points to a correspondingly exceptional situation and all-important function of Jesus and his disciples. They are thereby privileged with regard to the law. Again, this entirely exceptional epoch is pointed out in the saying,

But blessed are your eyes, for they see; and your ears, for they hear. For verily I say unto you, that many prophets and righteous men desired to see the things which ye see, and saw them not; and to hear the things which ye hear, and heard them not. Mt. 13:16–17.[11]

The allusion is to the wonderful signs and deeds of the time of salvation.[12] A similar assumption lies behind the misunderstood words,

Lo, a greater matter than the preaching of Jonah is here at issue . . . lo, a greater matter than the wisdom of Solomon is here concerned. Mt. 12:41, 42.[13]

[8] Bacon, *Studies in Matthew*, p. 392.
[9] *Ibid.*, p. 342.
[10] Mt. alone includes the precedent of the priests, 12:5. Bacon, as we have seen above, finds no abolition of the law by Jesus in such passages as these, but demonstration that certain aspects of the law are justifiably waived in view of the circumstances.
[11] Cf. Lk. 10:23–24, Jn. 8:56, Heb. 11:13, 1 Pet. 1:10 f. for N. T. passages illuminating the passage.
[12] Cf. Bultmann, *Jesus*, p. 28; *Jesus and the Word*, pp. 27, 28. Bacon, *op. cit.*, p. 394.
[13] Translation, Bacon, *op. cit.*, p. 395.

This indicates that the situation is unparalleled, and that the teaching, and this includes the ethical teaching, is of greater moment and authority than that of Jonah or Solomon. Again, the saying concerning the scribes discipled to the Kingdom (Mt. 13:52) envisages a sharp distinction between the old scribes and their instruction and loyalty, and the new scribes (cf. Mt. 23:34). For the latter, the old teaching, including ethics, will show new meanings and content. To the old teaching, still drawn upon, will be added new.[14] In effect, the new situation, with the present preaching of the Kingdom, has new ethical aspects. The same truth is reflected, finally, in the parable of a certain man, who made a great supper.[15] By the Baptist and by Jesus, God is represented as extending his general invitation to the imminent supper or marriage feast of the Kingdom. But this is evidently, then, a new and extraordinary situation and one involving corresponding special responsibilities.

2. *Jesus out of his unique sense of mission has authority to rule freely on ethical issues.*

We have seen that Jesus looked upon his day as one in which the conditions of the ethical life were changed. The law and prophets were until John. Now the Kingdom comes. Now Satan is bound. God is evidently drawing near to soften the hearts of publicans and sinners. These were the days that many wise men and prophets had longed to see.

Can we say more than this? Can we go on and say that not only is the situation as regards ethics changed but that Jesus gives a new content to the will of God? Not merely over against the prevailing ethics of the scribes, but over against the law itself, the written law? We believe that this can be claimed. Jesus out of his fuller and deeper understanding of God and man and their relation by word and action fulfilled and corrected the law. With sovereign originality and insight he gave a new expression to the will of God and related it in a new way to the religious life.

The evidence for this is apt to be obscured if we turn only to the

[14] Cf., incidentally, Mk. 1:27. "What is this? a new teaching!"
[15] Lk. 14:16–24 (Mt. 22:1–10).

well-known passages where Jesus deals with the law, the Sabbath, ablutions, etc., and the debate here is endless. The more conclusive evidence is drawn from the total picture, from Jesus' sense of vocation, from what we have seen of his ultimate appeal to moral discernment rather than to authority, from his approach to the "sinners," his declaration of the forgiveness of sins, and some of his great statements, the implications of which were revolutionary.

Let us, however, consider the evidence in the gospels for his attitude to the law at the debated points. Examination of Mt. is of special value, here. What, according to Mt., is Jesus' relation to the law, written and oral? A simple answer cannot be given to this question. There are contradictions in Jesus' words and actions bearing on this subject. He is represented in some instances as ascribing great authority to the law in all its details. "For verily I say unto you, Till heaven and earth pass away, one jot or one tittle shall in no wise pass away from the law, till all things be accomplished" (5:18). "The scribes and Pharisees sit on Moses' seat: all things therefore whatsoever they bid you, these do and observe . . ." (23:2–3). But in other instances Jesus is represented as overriding or directly contradicting the law, and as transgressing it in action. Any interpretation of his attitude as Mt. gives it which tries to reduce it to a simple principle will be unsatisfactory.

The fact is that the evangelist has included in his gospel sayings from different traditions and from different points of view. Students often conceive of the editorial role in the gospels in a mistaken way. The compiler did not pursue a deliberate dogmatic and tendentious aim in such matters, nor did he have the highly perspicacious attention we attribute to him in these issues. He was assembling materials and ordering them in a given situation, indeed. But the "tendencies" natural to that situation would be rather unconscious than deliberate. And the shaping process would lack much of our modern logical preoccupation.

At the bottom of the discrepancies, moreover, we may reasonably assume a genuine variety of expression in the case of Jesus himself. Recognition of the place of overstatement in his pedagogical method, and of the diversity of situation to which he spoke, would sufficiently account for considerable variation in reports of his attitudes and actions.

However, it still remains possible to generalize as to Jesus' relation to the law and to reach a conclusion as to the sayings which should be deemed most indicative. We hold that amidst the diversity of representations of Mt.'s Jesus, those that show him ruling and over-ruling freely and authoritatively on matters concerning the law are most significant, and best fit the total picture of the gospel.

Examination of this conclusion can most profitably be carried out by reference to interpretations by two scholars, with criticism of their treatment.

Schlatter proceeds thus in reconciling the contradictions. The disciples thought that the presence of the Messiah carried with it, according to prophecy, the denial of the law.[16] Jesus demurs, but retains the assumption that his presence involves a new situation, the time of salvation. "Think not that I came to destroy the law or the prophets: I came not to destroy, but to fulfil." The time of salvation is characterized in prophecy by *the carrying out into performance* (so πληρῶσαι)[17] of the law and the prophets. Jesus will not, like the scribes in the case of "corban" and of the weightier matters of the law, loose men from the law's responsibilities. Yet for him the law *is* a burden in another aspect, and now, "in the Heilszeit, under the lead of Christ, that necessity that had bowed men under the law was ended."[18] Therefore Jesus in his sense of his mission enables men to "fulfil" the law; stresses even with peculiar emphasis the responsibility of it in contrast to the general search for ways to avoid it; and then in the following section (Mt. 5:20 ff.) transcends and annuls it. There is no contradiction in Jesus' words once it is plain that in loosing from the law he is not giving opportunity to the sinner. Jesus is placing himself at a higher point of view, and therefrom criticizes and contradicts the law. "The law retains for him uncompromised the holiness of a divine demand, and is only replaced by the new law because it has not yet expressed what now the will of

[16] Just as in Mt. 10:34 they thought, according to Zech. 9:10 that it carried with it the establishment of peace.

[17] *Op. cit.*, pp. 153-54. Windisch, *op. cit.*, p. 46.

[18] Schlatter, *Der Evangelist Matthäus*, p. 152.

God had assigned as duty to Jesus and his disciples. Jesus is the first to state what must be done now that God's reign is near, and what can be done since it is present. The law of the Kingdom of heaven and that of Moses are not the same."[19] Schlatter seems to us to make out a convincing case for the essential supersession of the law in the time of salvation by the "law of the Kingdom." But his effort to reconcile this with the words stressing the obligation of the detail of the law seems hopeless. He is even here on safe ground where he interprets these as referring to what Jesus called "the weightier matters of the law." There is no incompatibility between the strongest insistence on the carrying out into performance of the weightier matters (justice, mercy, truth) and the new ethics of the Kingdom. But there *is* incompatibility between insistence on the literal law of Moses (jot and tittle) and the new ethics. And in Mt.'s representation the emphasis on the literal law of Moses here and in 5:19 and 23:2–3 is inescapable. We must just recognize it. But we can still assign priority in significance to the other emphasis.

Again, we can consider and criticize the different conception of Bacon. Bacon's conclusions are that Jesus did not innovate nor condemn the law. He played the role that had been played by the prophets in distinguishing between the word of God and the precepts of men. He distinguished in the law the divine and the human element. But like the scribes he never thought of impeaching the law but rather recognized it as the abiding expression of the will of God. Proof of this is found in the fact that Paul and the early Christians found no support for their setting aside of the law in the records of Jesus' life that they knew.[20] Now according to Bacon, Mk. flagrantly distorts Jesus' position here in such matters as his "making all meats clean," divorce, etc., and in Mt. we see, on the other hand, the judicious restoration, correction of Mk.'s error. So that the effect of Mt.'s work is to place Jesus "within the law." Jesus, indeed, exercises great freedom in the prophetic role of discrimination; he with the Baptist falls back on the great prophetic insight into righteousness

[19] Schlatter, *op. cit.*, p. 154.
[20] *Studies in Matthew*, p. 355, 357. Contrast B. S. Easton, *Christ in the Gospels* (New York, 1930), pp. 123–25, also B. H. Branscomb, *Jesus and the Law of Moses*, pp. 278–79.

and with it confronts the scribes and their book-religion, but Jesus does not teach a new ethics or a new law. Not only do we note Mt.'s words in defense of the law, but we note in particular that the Markan accounts are corrected to hold Jesus within the role of a son of the law.[21]

"To quote the Decalogue *seriatim* accompanying each citation with a more searching requirement under the rubric 'But I say' was to admit that mere 'law-righteousness' was not enough," and to accept "the distinction between a divine and a human element in the law," but this need not imply imperfection in the law, only that "not all parts of it have the same object in view."[22]

Let us consider Bacon's view more closely. In the issue raised with regard to the ablutions omitted by the disciples[23] we have a very illuminating case. The narrative in Mk. shows us Jesus condemning the Pharisees for leaving the commandment of God and holding fast the tradition of men. This he further illustrates by the evasion of the duty to parents by the "corban" pretext. Then,

And he called to him the multitude again, and said unto them, Hear me all of you, and understand: there is nothing from without the man, that going into him can defile him; but the things which proceed out of the man are those that defile the man. 7:14–15.

In further explanation Mk. comments, "This he said, making all meats clean." The central issue in Mk.'s account is the issue of clean and unclean meats, though the original occasion for this teaching was the question of the washing of the hands. In the narrative in Mt., however, changes are introduced which indicate that the issue throughout for Jesus is that of ablutions. Note especially the conclusion peculiar to Mt., "but to eat with unwashed hands defileth not the man."[24] Thus Mk. represents Jesus as overruling the all-important provisions of the written law bearing on clean and unclean meats. Even abstracting his own interpretation to this effect quoted above,

[21] Mt. "has adjusted the Markan radicalism to an attitude of entire loyalty to the eternal and divine commandment of Moses." *Op. cit.*, p. 350.

[22] *Ibid.*, p. 353.

[23] Mt. 15:1–20. See Markan narrative for differences, Mk. 7:1-23.

[24] 15:20b. See Bacon's discussion, *op. cit.*, pp. 352–53.

in his narrative of Jesus' words this impression is given. The charge of "precepts of men" is leveled at the distinctions of clean and unclean in the law. But in Mt. this charge is leveled only at the scribal (oral) rules of ablutions. Thus Bacon shows that Mk. betrays a very advanced Gentile-Christian scorn for the law, evident especially in 7:1–4 and elsewhere, and gives us a very untrue picture of Jesus' relation to it. Here as elsewhere Mt. is truer to the original situation. In this case Jesus condemns the scribal oral tradition, justifies his disciples' negligence and says nothing against the provisions of the law that deal with meats. Here Bacon recognizes, however, that Mt. does have in mind the later annulling of the distinctions of clean and unclean by Peter.[25] Bacon's conclusion is that Jesus, as Mt. portrays him, does not overrule the law. By his attack on the oral tradition ("every plant which my heavenly Father planted not, shall be rooted up," 15:13) and by his generalization with regard to defilement, he stands in the role of the prophet who points men from the outer to the inner, subordinating, not abolishing the outer.

Here we have a test case where it is possible to question Bacon's whole conclusion as to Jesus and the law. It appears to us that he overlooks the shattering import of Jesus' saying on defilement, which transcends its immediate occasion.

Hear me all of you, and understand: there is nothing from without the man, that going into him can defile him; but the things which proceed out of the man are those that defile the man. Mk. 7:14–15.

Mk. was no doubt wrong in interpreting this as immediately and forthwith "cleansing all meats," but Mk. is closer to the truth than Mt. in revealing the radical and revolutionary character of Jesus' approach to such matters. For such a saying by implication subjects to an empirical test not only the scribal rulings but any legislation that may stand in its way. It is true that this saying was not an explicit contradiction of the law. But it would be too much to say that the earliest church did not seek warrant for its setting aside of the law in this and similar sayings. One may object that the scribes sometimes said similar things about the Sabbath, about defilement, about

[25] See the substitution of Peter as the inquirer for the disciples, 15:15.

the summary of the law as love. But it is always quite evident in such cases that the scribe never dreams of disallowing the law. It remains a commandment for him. But for Jesus, his whole teaching and conduct demonstrate that in the last analysis the ultimate purpose of the law must overrule any particular statute of it, that is, "he had need" must overrule the prohibition or the requirement.

In the matter of divorce Bacon sees the matter as follows. Mt. errs in representing Jesus in the role of judge and legislator here. Behind the accounts in the gospels Bacon sees Jesus making a "prophetic" protest against a mere righteousness of the letter on the part of the husband who divorces, and not making a criticism of the law. Jesus looks on Moses' prescription of the bill of divorcement as a lawmaker's provision in view of the hardness of men's hearts. Jesus calls on men not merely for such legal correctness but for the inner goodness which does not cruelly put the wife away, and names him an adulterer who thus having divorced remarries. Thus Jesus does not, according to Bacon, alter the law. Yet it seems clear that the written law sanctioned divorce and remarriage, and that Jesus held it adultery! We are led to feel that Bacon's conception of a prophetic interpretation of the law does not differ much from an overruling of the law. Here again Jesus appeals beyond the law to a higher principle, buttressed indeed, in this case, by a citation from the law.

Professor B. S. Easton deals tellingly with the basic issue here.[26] He shows how Jesus makes "man" the master of the Sabbath and thence interprets the sense in which Jesus said that the whole law hangs on the two great commandments. "The Law had as its purpose the total good of God's people . . . Under normal conditions the separate precepts all contributed to the general end, but under exceptional circumstances the final purpose of the legislation must override individual precepts."[27] But, we are told by contemporary Jewish scholars, Pharisaic circles in Christ's time would have assented widely to Jesus' summary of the law.

"Assent in general principle, however, is by no means the question. The real problem was the application of the general principle when

---

[26] *Christ in the Gospels*, pp. 116–23.
[27] *Ibid.*, p. 119.

laws conflicted, and it was here that Jesus and the Pharisees clashed. The difference finds its perfect expression in a saying of no less a Rabbi than the great Jochanan ben Zakkai who declared: 'Death does not defile, nor does water cleanse,'[28] a saying that reminds us irresistibly of Jesus' pronouncement that food cannot make unclean. But while Jesus was content to emphasize his saying by repeating it in the positive form, 'the things that proceed out of the mouth are those that defile a man,' R. Jochanan felt obliged to continue, '(Obedience to the rule for clean and unclean is necessary) because it is an ordinance of the King of kings: God has said: I have made a statute, I have commanded an ordinance; no man is justified to transgress my ordinance, for it is written, this is the statute of the law which the Lord has commanded.'[29] In other words: 'We must obey the law of cleanness solely because it is commanded, and even though we know that "clean" and "unclean" do not really mean anything.' "[30]

For the scribes, for the Jew, the law was valid because it was commanded, as G. F. Moore has stressed. Jesus looked beyond the commandment to the ultimate purpose of the commandment. This was to overthrow the law as law. Bacon characterizes what Jesus did as "a new prophetic expression in Israel," within the law. We feel that he fails thus to do justice to the novelty of Jesus' attitudes, but that it is mainly a matter of words perhaps. For a great prophetic statement of the will of God was always a revision of the national covenant implicitly. But Bacon's characterization does not go far enough to bring out sufficiently the radical nature of Jesus' teaching. Jesus feels conscious not only of a vocation to call men back to the weightier matters of the law and to enact a role over against the synagogue standards analogous to that of Amos or Micah over against the priestly. He feels more than that, that the hour of Jeremiah's New Covenant is here, it is the time of the anticipated "restoration" and of the supersession of the period of "hard-heartedness." The heart of flesh is given for the heart of stone and therefore the

[28] Pesiq. 40b and elsewhere; cf. Strack-Billerbeck on Mt. 15:11.
[29] Num. 19:2.
[30] Easton, *op. cit.*, pp. 120–21.

relations of God and man are new and different and involve different obligations.[31]

Jesus' sense of authority over against the law comes out further in his attitude to the sinners of his time. It is true that the scribes and Pharisees were peculiarly censorious as regards this group. But more than that, in view of the character of the law itself, the publicans and sinners were debtors and offenders. For though grace lay behind the Torah yet the will of God for ethical and ceremonial practice was set forth in the law in the form of a commandment. Restoration to the favor of God and pardon depended therefore emphatically on the initial repentance of the sinner. In the period with which we are concerned the prevailing attitude to the law reinforced this expectation. But Jesus breaks with this situation by not waiting for the repentance of the unrighteous. In his parable of the two debtors this understanding of the matter is illustrated by the words: "And when they had not wherewith to pay, he forgave them both."[32]

Jesus approaches ethical issues, then, with a sovereign independence arising out of his own prophetic insights, but also in immediate relation to the dawning of the new age. "Jesus then assigned himself an especial authority and brought his own person into such immediate relation to the eschatological situation as no other prophet before him had done. Jesus' sense of vocation is responsible for his giving his ethical teaching so sharp and decisive a form and for his having broken so radically with the Judaism of his time."

These words of Sevenster[33] following an independent survey would appear warranted. We know that Jesus spoke with great authority and independence in the matter of ethics. We know that

[31] How near Bacon, perhaps inconsistently, comes to this view is seen in the following quotation. Jesus "surely did offer to his followers another 'yoke' than that of the scribes. He surely did give a 'new commandment' as even Paul bears witness (Rom. 13:8–10) . . . Jesus surely did offer a new ethic to his followers, contrasting it with that which others (including their former teachers of the synagogue) might offer. He congratulated them on the Kingdom in store for them as 'sons and daughters of the Highest.' He made this principle basic for the entire conduct of life." *Op. cit.*, p. 341.

[32] Lk. 7:42.

[33] *Op. cit.*, p. 212.

he looked upon his day as the expected time of salvation. We know
that he spoke and acted out of a sense of vocation whose messianic
character he could not, perhaps, finally deny. We conclude that we
have evidence here then, which indicates how the differentia of his
ethics is determined by an eschatological factor: the presence of the
Kingdom.

3. *The ethics determined by the new situation can best be characterized not as interim ethics but as ethics of the time of salvation or
new-covenant ethics.*

We have said that the new situation determines a new ethic. We
have said that Jesus rules freely on ethics and the law. What characterizes the new ethic that results?

We take it that it is not an interim ethic. The new situation is
not *essentially* characterized by the fact that it is a respite before the
terrors of the Judgment. The new situation is rather the anticipated
time of salvation in which men are no longer hard-hearted, in which
they become God's sons in a full sense, receive forgiveness on the
occasion of the Great Repentance, know the Spirit, and recognize
the overthrow of Satan and the demons. It is the time in which God
is enacting his great deliverance, and in which he is drawing near
to men in a way he had not done since the time of Moses, and is
making a new covenant with them, not as the covenant which he
made with them in the time of Moses, which they had broken. The
feature that Jesus is present as herald of this gospel, and as central
evidence of this new situation, is subsidiary to the main fact of God's
action.

Thus the ethic is not an interim ethic. It is not even a repentance
ethic in the sense of an extreme renunciation or asceticism as penance
for the emergency. It *is* a repentance ethic in the sense that it calls
for "fruits worthy of repentance," i.e., conduct evidencing the
changed disposition. Rather, it can be best designated as an ethic of
the present Kingdom of God or a new-covenant ethic. It is not primarily an ethic for the relations and conduct of the future transcendental Kingdom. Nor is it a Kingdom ethic in the sense that its
practice would admit to the Kingdom nor that it would "build" the

Kingdom. It is a Kingdom ethic in the sense that it represents the righteousness of those living in the days of the new covenant and empowered and qualified by the reconciliation and redemption of that age.[34]

But what of the transcendental Kingdom? It is true that Jesus taught that the new era is to have its all-important manifestation in a supernatural way: advent of the Son of Man, Judgment and the miraculously instituted Kingdom. And it is true that Jesus cast his ethic, with the repentance it involves, in the form of entrance conditions to that Kingdom. The point is, *the conception of that eschatological culmination so partook of the nature of myth or poetry that it did not other than formally determine the ethic.* The conception of the Judgment and the supernatural rewards, including the Kingdom, stand to Jesus and to the community as *representations,* with full validity and credibility, indeed, of the unprophesiable, unimaginable but certain, God-determined future. This future and God's action in it lend immense weight and urgency to their present moral responsibility. Yet this temporal imminence of God is but a function of his spiritual imminence, and it is this latter which really determines conduct. It is not a dualistic other-worldliness that meets us in Jesus' inattention to property, family ties and citizenship, but a selective valuation and a particular focus of concern consequent upon immediate confrontation with God. The sense of the divinely determined future, however apocalyptically it may be formulated, does not in actual fact put an end to the this-worldly concern of Jesus and the church. Reserves may be made for the evidences of true interim phenomena of the early church, but these are not typical. The radical character of Jesus' ethics does not spring from the shortness of the time but from the new relation to God in the time of salvation. The sanction for it is not the sanction of imminent supernatural retributions—except formally—but the appeal to the God-enlightened moral discernment recognizing the nature and will of God and inferring consequences (thence eschatologically dramatized).

[34] We can see how easily and naturally the ethics so understood would be taken over by the church of the time of the evangelist as basic guide for its code, both in relation to the law and in relation to the conduct of life generally. Thus the church was thought of more and more as itself the Kingdom of God.

What these ethics were we can only suggest. Jesus virtually super-sedes the law by the lengths he goes in appealing to its deeper prin-ciples. We can see that the dispute as to whether he did or did not overthrow the law is ambiguous. Many scribes exercised their judg-ment in discriminating the weightier or more central demands of the law; and it can well be said that Jesus upheld by saying and act the word of God in the law. But we are satisfied to rest the case for his *virtual setting aside of the law on the degree of independent interpretation he exercises. He goes so far beyond such scribes in matters of emphasis and spirit that the difference in degree becomes a difference in kind,* and confirmation of this is found in the attitude to him of the scribes and Pharisees.

Going on we note further as to the ethics that Jesus goes back to the great principles of the prophets, judgment, mercy and truth, but he sees these in a religious background different from that of the prophets, namely, his new portrayal of the nature of God. The ethics are conceived as responses to the nature of God, along emphatically positive lines. God's generosity, his forgiveness become determinative. Purity, sincerity and unreserved devotion answer all to another main aspect of his religious conception, the fact of such full sonship as implies immediate relation of obedience and response. The full per-sonal will of the individual is therefore in play. This is a point that Bultmann makes much of. Ethics is now unqualifiedly the relation of the heart to God, person to Person, and this is ever present and controlling in the relation of man to man.

We must bear in mind a group of the most drastic summons of Jesus as in a class by themselves. Those sayings we mean that have seemed most inhuman and that have led men to think of Jesus' ethics as interim ethics, as determined by the imminent end of all earthly relations. We come to these in the next chapter, and can only forecast the conclusion that these imperatives grow out of the demand above for complete loyalty to God's will, but have their special urgency not in the thought of the end, but in the emergency of Jesus' own career and in the struggle of the Kingdom in this interim period when the powers of evil are opposing it.

CHAPTER NINE

The Claims of Discipleship in the
Crisis of the Kingdom

THE ethic of Jesus is what it is first of all because the time of
salvation has come and the time of law and prophets is drawing to a close. Thus eschatology conditions it. But the advent
of the new age in the midst of the old constitutes a crisis. A period
of conflict calling for devotion, witness and sacrifice, lays heavy demands upon the sons and heirs of the Kingdom. These were the
throes of the end-time in which men were living, and the claims
made on the faithful were therefore eschatologically conditioned.
These claims are often formulated by Jesus in terms of discipleship
to himself or of "following" or confessing him. In particular, the
most exigent requirements of Jesus have to do with following him in
the crisis of the Kingdom when its fortunes are so closely linked
with his own.

We can recognize, however, that the tendency to emphasize the
theme of confession of Christ and to identify the ethic of the Kingdom with discipleship was one that grew with time, and we can
distinguish examples of this in our gospels. The more clearly Jesus
was thought of in the tradition as the self-confessed Messiah in the
days of his flesh, the greater the tendency was to view his Kingdom-
ethic as a discipleship-ethic. Yet even if we conclude that Jesus was
actually very reticent as to his person, yet his sense of vocation did
play a considerable part in the formulation of his ethical demands.

Here too eschatology conditions the ethic, for Jesus saw his person and work in significant relation to the coming of the Kingdom.

1. *We note first that Jesus identifies himself closely with the coming Kingdom so that its meaning is represented in his person.*

In him it is arriving. The Kingdom has come upon men in his words and cures. He is the touchstone, attitude to whom determines admission to the Kingdom. We recall the various evidence indicating that in Jesus, his overthrow of Satan in the temptation and the exorcisms, and his cures and gospel, the Kingdom of God has come upon men, and then we note the final words with which he answers the Baptist. "And blessed is he, whosoever shall find no occasion of stumbling in me." Jesus is the representative of the wisdom of God in calling men to receive the promises. The close connection of Jesus with the Kingdom is most clearly marked in that Jesus relates himself immediately to the future Son of Man-Judge of the parousia. This meant that in dealing with Jesus in the villages of Galilee, men were in some sense dealing with him who should rule on their admission to the Kingdom at the Day of Judgment.

Jesus then identifies himself very closely with the Kingdom. "He is so absorbed in the Kingdom and its coming that it amounts practically to an identification, to a loss of self-identity in the commanding conviction of a cause to be championed."[1] The point becomes clearer as we go on to show how as a result the *demands* of that Kingdom are represented in his own person.

2. *The Kingdom makes extraordinary claims in the present crisis.*

It is possible to distinguish between the ethics of the Kingdom, the new-covenant ethics, which we have dealt with above, and the special claims made upon disciples in the short period when the Kingdom is still struggling with the present evil age. Jesus' exposition of the higher righteousness is the essential matter. That new ethic in its new religious setting, that new way of life of the sons of the Father, is the basic claim. But for the present it has to make its way against opposition. The word falls on stony ground. There

[1] W. E. Bundy, *The Religion of Jesus* (Indianapolis, 1928), p. 129.

are tares in the wheat. There are those that appear to have been predestined to reject it. The cities are impenitent. The evil and adulterous generation has responded neither to the warning of the Baptist nor to the invitation of Jesus. Those responsible for the oracles of God and their keeping, those that sit on Moses' seat, have called good evil and light darkness. The Kingdom is stormed by the hosts of evil, the world-rulers of darkness, Satan and his hierarchy of demons. In such circumstances the member of the Kingdom is subject to special vocation. There is no difference in his essential motive or responsibility of single-mindedness and total abandonment to God. But in such circumstances this will find expression in particular ways.

We find an analogy to this whenever a new order is breaking in upon an old. The new order has its own new and unique way of life, scale of values, social pattern. These can be advocated and partially practiced before that order has superseded the old order. But in that period of transition special and temporary demands are made upon the disciples of the new order, demands which we can summarize as those we associate with witness, missionary and martyr.

So in the time of Jesus those who had repented and taken upon themselves the yoke of the Kingdom were subject further to the special claims of witnessing, and liable to special sacrifices of this time of travail. The children of the Kingdom for the present time of crisis are as lambs in the midst of wolves. It is at this point that we find many sayings of Jesus bearing on renunciation and denial of the world which have a special bearing. More than the teachings considered in the previous section they are relative to their occasion, though corresponding occasions in history may recur to make them specially pertinent. It is the characteristically drastic demands of Jesus in this category that have misled students into thinking that Jesus' ethic was an interim ethic. For such world-renouncing teachings plausibly suggested that their occasion must have been the expectation of the imminent Judgment. But a more convincing explanation of them can be given.

Further, these extraordinary claims of the Kingdom in the present crisis are inseparable from discipleship to Jesus. His call to confession of the Kingdom in this time of division must necessarily be the call to *follow him* in witness and in mission. The disciple is, naturally, to be as his Master.

3. *Therefore the claims of the Kingdom take the form of claims of discipleship to Jesus in the accomplishment of his errand.*

Jesus' unique sense of mission underlies his assertion of authority where conduct is concerned, whether in his boldness to fulfil the law or in his relating of the claims of the Kingdom to discipleship to himself. He himself bears such a responsibility for the mediation of the Kingdom and its preparation, that it is natural for him to call on men for adhesion, confession, discipleship. His unique prophetic vocation in the end-time means more than that he has authority to teach and to rule on ethical issues. It means more in two respects. It means first that he himself is so peculiarly the embodiment of the Kingdom, the touchstone of the Kingdom, that men cannot reject him without rejecting it, or accept it without accepting him. And it means secondly that the supremely important work of ushering in the Kingdom is his responsibility, and that therefore he may well call on particular men for drastic sacrifices in the pursuit of that work in its various phases and crises. This last point we would further emphasize. Central with Jesus was his work, his errand. He was driven by a prodigious sense of vocation. This was the meat that others knew not of, to do the will of Him that had sent him. This was *his* work and in a sense his alone. It was the supreme act of God to which the whole experience of the people of God had been leading. Its successful accomplishment was so immense an issue (greater than those in which Jonah or Solomon were concerned), and its success so hung upon the person and career of Jesus himself, that no demand for devotion to it and to him or renunciation for it and for him was too great. The forms such demands would take would vary with the situation and the individual. But the only way in which significant contribution to the grandiose deed of God could be made was by adherence to Jesus, following him, confession of him, obedience to him. Obedience to the Golden Rule, fulfilment of the law in the way the rich young man had recognized the will of

God, obedience to the double great commandment, these missed the chief point, because they overlooked the supreme issue of history in the present offering of the Kingdom of God in the person and destiny of Jesus.

We shall see how the call to repentance and to the higher right-eousness is associated with the summons to follow Jesus, yes, to confess him. Confession or denial of the prophet of the Kingdom was decisive in the great crisis of the new order, and those that denied him in his lowly hour of humiliation and costly witness would be denied before the angels of God. From this angle, those not with him were against him. The self-assertion of Jesus at this point cannot raise objection. He never failed to connect his pre-rogative with his humiliation and he related his prerogative to the triumph of God's cause. The centrality of the person of Jesus, however accented in the tradition of the gospels, goes back to the beginnings.

We cannot then distinguish between the general ethical principles of Jesus, as represented for instance in the Sermon on the Mount, and the drastic summons to personal discipleship. They have the same root. The alleged general ethical principles are the ethics of a new covenant and a radicalized religious insight and relation, which carry with them inexorable demands of separation and witness. Wholehearted devotion to God, single-mindedness, thorough-going love and forgiveness, abandon of oneself without anxiety to the will of God, these came from Jesus together with the faith that motivated them and the growing new household that encouraged them, and these would find their expression in costly confession of him during the birth pangs of the Kingdom. Such discipleship might take the form of the mission in its narrow sense at his appointment, but in any case it involved unreserved adhesion to his cause.

Certainly, one great object with Jesus for the urgent form in which he spoke his demands was to make clear to his hearers the issues of their *own* salvation. The sacrifice of eye or hand, the need of striving in view of the straitness of the gate, the renunciation of the lower self—these summons had in view the fateful responsibility of men for their own fate. But an equally pressing object, and one that determines many of the drastic sayings, and one also that lies back of the more general preaching, is the imperative need of support in the successful prosecution of his own role. His claims are here determined by the practical exigencies of his work, that is, by his need of devoted followers in the vicissitudes and uncertainties of his career. The drastic element often grows out of this, not out of the nearness of the end as such, though the latter is a formal expression of the vast issues of his career. We have in this aspect of it discipleship ethics or mission ethics rather than interim ethics.

The special claims growing out of the crisis of the Kingdom and the emergency of Jesus' work (and these go together) come out in various sayings. The Q passage on witness that bids the disciples be fearless of those that kill the body assures those that confess Jesus of confession before the angels of God.[2] Mt. precedes this with the saying that associates the lot and the sacrifices of the disciple with those of the teacher. The latter theme is found in the assurance to the sons of Zebedee that they shall drink the cup of their Master.

The point comes out best perhaps in Jesus' saying,

He that is not with me is against me: and he that gathereth not with me scattereth. Mt. 12:30 = Lk. 11:23.

The contrary saying does not appear in Mt. Bacon explains the omission by the bitterness of the evangelist and the community against the Hellenistic false prophets of "lawlessness" in the church. The author of Mt. would not admit that such were "for" Christ, even though they were not against him. In the above passage Jesus teaches that any "gathering" (exorcisms by the sons of the Pharisees) apart from his own harvesting leads to a confusion of the great issue. "In this last hour, the hour of decision, he is sent with the final crucial word. Happy is he that understands it, that finds no occasion for stumbling in him! The occasion calls for decision for him or against him."[3] According to this word those not with Jesus

[2] Mt. 10:28–33. Bultmann gives this message, in its Lukan form, 12:8–9, a central place in presenting his conception of the *Entscheidungzeit*: receiving or denying of Jesus and his gospel are offered as an ultimate and fatal choice. *Jesus*, p. 31; *Jesus and the Word*, pp. 30, 31.

[3] *Ibid.*

in personal espousal are against him. For his person so represents the Kingdom and its righteousness that in that hour none can espouse it without espousing him, or reject him without rejecting it. It is to be noted that in the apparently contrary saying of Jesus, the individual whose cures apart from the disciples he encourages works them in the name of Jesus.[4]

It is true that Jesus repudiates those that say Lord, Lord, but this is a condemnation of superficial discipleship, not of true confession. More pertinent is Jesus' recognition that forgiveness will be accorded those who speak a word against the Son of Man, but not to those who speak a word against the Holy Spirit. The saying shows that Jesus attached importance to himself only in so far as he was the representative of a cause, that of the divine purpose. But the whole context, condemning blindness to the Holy Spirit, refers to the manifestation of that Spirit in the overcoming of Satan through Jesus and his disciples.

Such passages evidence the close relation of the new ethic with confession of Jesus. What confession might involve comes out in various cases. It is clear that Jesus expected thorough-going and radical change of disposition and life on the part of all who repented at his preaching. They thereby became disciples whether they followed in his personal company for a long or a short time. Zacchaeus who continued in his own calling but with a revolutionized life, the healed paralytic or leper of whom we do not further hear in Jesus' immediate following, were disciples under as exacting demands of allegiance as the Twelve themselves.

The call to take up one's cross and follow Jesus as a disciple is the supreme expression of his appeal to his generation. This is not directed only to an inner circle. The Lukan narrative represents him as speaking to the great multitudes that followed him without realizing the importance of sitting down and considering the cost, and adjoins the saying about the uselessness of salt that has lost its savor. Mt., though he includes the saying in his discourse of Jesus to the Twelve as they go out, shows by the context, with its references to the sword of division in families that Jesus brings,

[4] Mk. 9:38–40.

that it envisages all hearers of the word. The same summons is given by Jesus to the multitudes on the occasion of the rebuke of Peter near Caesarea Philippi.[5] Following Jesus with one's cross is here associated again with losing one's own life for the sake of Jesus. In connection with the episode of the rich young man, Peter protests, "Lo, we have left all, and followed thee," and Jesus says:

There is no man that hath left house, or brethren, or sisters, or mother, or father, or children, or lands, for my sake, and for the gospel's sake, but he shall receive a hundredfold now in this time, houses, and brethren, and sisters, and mothers, and children, and lands, with persecutions; and in the world to come eternal life. Mk. 10:29–30.

Mt. here includes the promise to the Twelve that they shall sit on thrones in the regeneration, alongside the above promise to all others that have made renunciation for the Name. For the evangelists the above passage refers both to Jesus' own followers who were persecuted for his name in his lifetime, and to those who met the persecutions of the first and second generations of the church without denying him. Ostracism, division in families, excommunication and exile are as truly referred to, as abandonment of all for missionary work, and no doubt often went together. In both cases the ethics or conduct at issue grow out of allegiance to Christ's work.

The passage in Mt.'s tenth chapter that we have referred to pictures scourgings, trials, family divisions, hatred, persecutions and death for Christ's sake, and has its climax in the summons to the cross. It is only ostensibly addressed to the twelve disciples. It is evident that this charge to the disciples for their mission is a compilation of the evangelist who borrows from the secondary apocalypse of Mk. in part. "The compilation is intended to meet the needs of the itinerant 'gospellers' who in the period of the *Didaché,* some years if not decades later than this Gospel, still bore the title 'apostle' . . . ," says Bacon of this "Second Book" of Mt. (8–11:1).[6] And with particular reference to this section in 10:15 ff., "it passes unobserved with the saying on sheep among wolves (v.

[5] Mk. 8:34–37. Mt. has "to his disciples"; Lk., to "all."
[6] *Studies in Matthew,* p. 361.

16) into a warning of persecution to be endured by Jesus' representatives in a hostile world after the death of their master."[7] From this point on the evangelist draws his picture in terms of his eschatology. He is picturing the sufferings of the church in the throes that precede the parousia. "The 'apostle' of these days . . . must go with his own cross upon his shoulders, ready to meet his Master's fate. But the time of endurance will not be long. The End is in sight. Before the persecuted Church, driven from city to city in hope of safe refuge, shall have gone over the cities of Israel, the Son of Man will have come to their deliverance."[8]

The conduct in view in this passage, still as Mt. represents it, is very evidently bound up with confession of and following of the Messiah. The theme recurs in many forms: "for my sake" (vv. 18, 22, 39); "a disciple is not above his teacher" (v. 24 f.); "confess me" (v. 32); "worthy of me" (vv. 37–38. Lk. "cannot be my disciple"); "follow after me" (v. 38); "in the name of a disciple" (v. 42. Mk.: "because ye are the Messiah's"). The ethics thus take on the form of loyalty. The supreme preoccupation is the great work with which the Messiah is identified.

We have emphasized the presentation of this material in Mt. for several reasons. It becomes clear that the interests of the church have strongly affected the sayings of Jesus in which he calls upon his hearers for renunciation and sacrifice. It is also clear that the prominence of the "confession" theme can be laid to the growing dogmatism of the church. But in both cases we have original sayings of Jesus combined with the later elaborations as appears from the earlier part of this section and the diversity of source-witness in the material treated just above.

The call to renunciation appears in more specific form in some sayings. Simon and Andrew leave their nets immediately at Jesus' call to go after him and to become fishers of men. James and John similarly leave their work in the boat and their father. In the case of the disciple Matthew (or Levi) it is likely that he being a tax-gatherer could not henceforth return to his occupation once he had

---

[7] *Ibid.*, p. 364.
[8] *Ibid.*, p. 369.

left it, as could the fishermen. As Jesus sends out the Twelve with authority to preach and heal he describes their manner of life and the possessions allowed them. The requirements expressed in connection with such calls to discipleship are not to be taken as incumbent upon all. They may be relative solely to Jesus' immediate mission.

> And he charged them that they should take nothing for their journey, save a staff only; no bread, no wallet, no money in their purse; but to go shod with sandals: and, said he, put not on two coats. Mk. 6:8–9.

This instruction of Jesus to his missioners for a particular season of work presupposes the need of haste as well as the traditional right of prophets to support. We would certainly be entirely unjustified in giving these provisions, as for instance that which bears on property, a general application.

We see from Lk. 10:2 that the object of Jesus' more specific appointments is that they may be laborers in the harvest, and that this really means the expansion of his own work, preaching the Kingdom, healing, exorcism, whether in his company or apart from him. It is the supreme urgency of his work which occasions his call upon chosen disciples for immediate and drastic renunciations and risks. The number so instructed must have been much larger than twelve.

We have striking evidence of Jesus' costly claim upon individuals outside the Twelve. Jesus tells a scribe who offers himself as a follower that he must expect to be homeless. To "another of the disciples" Jesus speaks the strong word, "Follow me and let the dead bury their dead." To another who would pause to bid farewell to them that are at his house, Jesus says:

> No man, having put his hand to the plow and looking back, is fit for the kingdom of God.

Now these sayings like that to the rich young man (Mt. 19:21) are not governed by the shortness of the time. It has been well observed that giving alms to the poor as the rich young man is to do (compare the approval of almsgiving in Mt. 6:2–4) is not in the eschatological temper. Haste is a factor in the waiving of the filial duty[9] of burial as in the equipment of the disciples for their mission, but the haste is only an aspect of the immense importance of the work, outranking all other interests. "He that loveth father or mother more than me is not worthy of me" is a more general statement of the situation, as is Jesus' own confession of his dearest ties as those that bind him to his followers who are father and mother and brother and sister to him.

Jesus' apparent disregard of the fifth commandment and of the strict duties in regard to burial[10] is very remarkable. His saying "is unthinkable for a Jewish mind, a scandalous outrage. For this very reason is the occurrence selected and placed here in the portrait of Jesus, since it bursts every custom that might bind the disciples, permits no other obligation and demands a devotion that binds the disciple completely and alone to Jesus."[11] Such an interpretation in that it generalizes the application of the saying goes too far in contradicting Mt.'s respect for the law, but the extraordinary force of the saying indicates the urgency of Jesus' errand. We are not to understand it as a general principle of ethics and a ground for Christian anarchy, but as a particular summons in the emergency of Jesus' career and the crisis of the Kingdom.

The case of the rich young man illustrates the same truth. The summons is neither a prescription for the spiritual needs of the individual in question (Zahn), nor a teaching that the "perfect" must do *opera supererogatoria* (Klostermann) nor is it a principle of universal application, nor a magnification of poverty. The call to renunciation of wealth is connected with the words, "Come follow me." No rich man can follow Jesus on the way to the cross.[12] This does not create an artificial distinction between the "perfect" and the mass of the disciples. The rich young man is one of those

[9] Note the leaving of *their* father by James and John.

[10] "He whose dead lies before him is free from the reading of the Schema and from the Eighteen Prayers and from the Thephillin." Berachoth III:1. Cf. Tobit 4:3, 6:15.

[11] Schlatter, *op. cit.*, p. 238, who thinks moreover (with Klostermann) that the "dead" who are to bury their dead are the living not followers of Jesus, an interpretation that is too ingenious.

[12] Schlatter, *op. cit.*, p. 579.

with the ten talents whom Jesus specially called to this work rather than another, and this work has as its concomitant, poverty as we have seen (Mk. 6:8).

Thus, much of the so-called absolute ethics of Jesus can be referred to specific occasions to which its immediate application is restricted. Yet this does not mean that the summons of Jesus, generally, is watered down. With each individual a particular vocation develops out of the supreme work of Jesus and the duty of confession with reference to it.

The saying concerning "eunuchs that made themselves eunuchs for the Kingdom of heaven's sake" belongs among these we are treating. The motive here is not asceticism (cf. Mt. 11:19) nor is it anticipation of the end, but special vocation. The wrong interpretation of this saying is represented by Principal A. J. Grieve in Peake's *Commentary*:[13] "We must probably interpret the praise of celibacy . . . in 12 as having an eschatological background. If the Kingdom was imminent, the best thing was to forego ordinary relationships and be ready for it." No, "Jesus is thinking of men who 'for the sake of the Kingdom of heaven' (that is, rather 'in order to work for the Kingdom' than 'in order to win it for themselves') have freely renounced the sexual life . . . Cf. T. Jebamoth 8, 4 (c.250), 'My soul hangs upon the Torah (there is therefore no time left for marriage): may the world be sustained by others!' "[14] Schlatter notes that early Christianity could both sanctify the natural condition and transcend it.[15]

Attention to all this material has been necessary in order to distinguish and relate the various kinds of claims that Jesus made on his hearers, and the various objects he had in making those claims. From the point of view of the individual's salvation at the Judgment, Jesus called on them for a total and single-minded devotion to the Kingdom of the Father as Jesus interpreted it. But in view of the present striving of the new world to be born Jesus pointed out the corollaries of that total devotion in the present emergency.

[13] P. 717.
[14] Klostermann, *Matthäusev.*, p. 155.
[15] Schlatter, *op. cit.*, p. 574.

The member of the Kingdom is called upon for costly witness, and to be missionary and martyr. But the issue of the Kingdom centers so closely in the career and destiny of Jesus himself that the extraordinary claims made for the Kingdom become claims of confession of and discipleship to himself. Jesus so identifies himself with the cause of the Kingdom that its demands merge with loyalty to his person.

CHAPTER TEN

Conclusion to Part II: Sources of the
Differentia of the Ethics

O UR study of the relation of eschatology to the content or
differentia of the ethics has led us to the following conclusions:

1. The ethical teaching of Jesus is different from that of Jewish
ethics of the time in both spirit and content.

2. This difference is not determined by the imminence of the
Judgment; that is, the ethics are not interim ethics.

3. The difference is determined by the presence of the time of
salvation or the days of the new covenant.

4. This difference is more fundamentally determined by the
deepened experience and interpretation of God as known in his
present redemptive action, and mediated especially by Jesus to his
following.

5. The markedly drastic demands arise indeed out of a condition
of crisis. That crisis, however, is not one created by the imminence
of the Judgment but by the conflict of two eras, the death throes of
the one and the birth pangs of the other; a crisis inseparable from
the errand of Jesus. This crisis is urgent in a double sense: (1) it
requires espousal of the gospel immediately by all for their own
salvation, and (2) it calls for the uttermost devotion of disciples
for its successful issue.

6. The ethical and religious elements in the gospel are so interwoven, and these again so come to focus in the person and errand

of Jesus, that the ethic commonly assumes the form of a summons to discipleship to him and confession of him.

Illumination of these conclusions can be found in consideration of the position taken by Sevenster on the whole position.[1]

Sevenster approaches his study in the main from the issue of interim ethics, and is interested in correcting J. Weiss and Schweitzer here and in going on to note the differentia of Jesus' summons as against either interim ethics on the one hand or prophetic, wisdom, and rabbinic ethics on the other. It should be noted that he finds elements in Jesus that belong to each of these groups. He begins with homage to J. Weiss and Schweitzer, and then proceeds to a criticism of the latter's view of Jesus' ethical teaching as interim ethics. The gist of the argument is that Schweitzer has made his view dependent on his thorough-going eschatological interpretation of the life of Jesus. But the reconstruction of the life of Jesus attempted by Schweitzer is sadly vitiated by various errors and neglects. Hence the interim-ethics view rests on a false foundation, and as a matter of fact it is evident that much of Jesus' teaching is not eschatologically determined. Thus Sevenster states his two main aims to be (1) to show that the interim view of Jesus' ethics is far from sufficient, and (2) to inquire what the nature of these ethics really is as against the other types.

By showing the great similarity between much of Jesus' ethics (both in respect of content and sanction) and those of the prophets, the wisdom school, and the rabbis, Sevenster feels that he has disproved the thorough-going interim view; but he holds that a reminder can well be called interim ethics because it is so evidently determined by the exceptional crisis situation (the near Judgment) and because it so resembles the ethics of the apocalypses. Such passages are the ones in which ultra-stringent demands are made: surrender of eye, hand, family ties, wealth, life itself. These have no parallel in the prophets, etc., and only partly in the apocalypses, and must be entered, he concludes, as determined by the imminence of the Judgment.

But Sevenster leaves us unsatisfied in trying to explain why the

[1] *Ethiek en Eschatologie in de Synoptische Evangeliën.*

same teacher should voice such diverse kinds or strains of ethics in the same brief career, and in trying to show how a reconciliation can be found in Jesus' mind for such divergent claims. He surrenders the attempt to explain it psychologically. He then shows how in theory the two divergent types of imperative can both go back to a radicalized conception of God as determining both drastic renunciation on the one hand, and obedience of the prophetic and wisdom preaching on the other. But this is unsatisfactory. He recognizes that to put the differences in the claims down to moods or "intermittence" of Jesus inspiration (J. Weiss) is no answer, and finds a better explanation in the greater tension of Jesus' later career (though he grants that the chronology for the sayings is uncertain as a guide here).

Sevenster has accomplished his task of disproving the interim character of most of the teaching, and he has reached significant results in relating Jesus' ethics to other types, but he has left the teaching in a wholly artificial scheme whereby part is separated as by a watertight compartment from the rest. In this he is in the same position as others who still hold the interim character of the more drastic demands. If Jesus did really so repeatedly call on men for the impossible, for the utterly exceptional, in view of the fearful tension of the interim before the Judgment, and if he did thus dissolve in such claims the standing norms of conduct, how could he possibly have preached such optimistic and long-range and sapiential and serene ethics in almost the same breath?

It is not possible to solve this dilemma on the basis of the assumptions made by Sevenster and others. The basic assumption they make is that the eschatological event was literally and prosaically conceived by Jesus. Such an assumption naturally demands interim ethics,[2] but interim ethics, even in part, clashes irreconcilably with characteristic veins of Jesus' preaching.

Sevenster only fails of reaching a fully harmonious view of Jesus' ethical teaching because of what remainder of Schweitzer's posi-

---

[2] "The apocalyptic outlook of the first Christians probably did not have either the ethical or the practical results one would logically expect of it." H. J. Cadbury, *The Making of Luke-Acts* (New York, 1927), p. 29. Because the apocalyptic outlook lacked the crassness we assign it.

tion on this point he still retains. As long as this false emphasis is thrown on the interim in even a part of the teaching it will be impossible to grasp the fundamental unity of Jesus' religious outlook and ethical demand. It is indeed just to relate the extreme demands to the "crisis" but the error arises in the meaning given to the crisis here in view. As long as the superficial and temporal aspect of the crisis is given first place of importance this same artificial conception of the interim and of interim ethics will mislead us. But give the crisis its true and fundamental meaning of the hour of decision for Israel offered in the clash of the two eras and the errand of Jesus, then the tension is assigned its natural cause, and the more urgent ethical claims their more natural occasion. The apocalyptic event in the future is secondary to and derivative from the judgment inherent in the offered time of salvation.

For the generation of Jesus faced the fulfilment of the time, an historical *kairos,* a moment charged with responsibility and fate. This was conditioned by social and political circumstances. More profoundly, the maturing of a harvest at this time was due to immanent spiritual forces that had been at work through the whole history of Israel. The signs of the time were there for those who could read them, and the preaching and success of the Baptist were the best indication of it before Jesus came on the scene. But the grace and judgment that offered themselves to Israel in this hour found their characteristic and adequate voice and vehicle in Jesus, his word and the whole drama of his career. Jesus was the bearer of the new era that pressed upon the old. The stern warnings and claims that he voiced were the fateful demands of the crisis. His sense of being the spokesman and touchstone of the crisis speaks with especial clearness through the following passage:

Think ye that I am come to give peace in the earth? I tell you, Nay; but rather division: for there shall be from henceforth five in one house divided, three against two, and two against three. They shall be divided, father against son, and son against father; mother against daughter, and daughter against her mother; mother in law against her daughter in law, and daughter in law against her mother in law. Lk. 12:51-53.

It is true that Jesus presented the in-breaking future that constituted
this crisis in terms of the Kingdom of God, usually in apocalyptic
terms. This was the inevitable language of his people for so significant an hour.

Jesus was the bearer of the new era. The issues focused upon his
soul and upon his vocation. One may say that he was the conscious
bearer of the new era. But he was to a degree its unconscious
bearer. That is, its full purport he could not, need not, grasp. To do
the will of God was enough. Yet he grasped enough of the future of
grace and judgment that pressed upon his age to proclaim it and to
live it. The threads of the great crisis were so drawn through his life
that he was its unique spokesman and embodiment. This gave him
his understanding of his special vocation. If Jesus was led as we
have shown to make personal claims and to identify himself with
the Kingdom it was inevitable. "I came to cast fire upon the earth."
"I have a baptism to be baptized with." "I came to call. . . ." "He
that denieth me in the presence of men shall be denied in the
presence of the angels of God." None can raise serious question as
to the genuineness of these sayings. For confirmation of the last
of them, a Q saying quoted from Lk. 12:9, see Mk. 8:38. Whether a
messianic claim be involved in such sayings or the general situation
need not be insisted on. If it was so involved Prof. F. C. Grant has
put it well, paraphrasing W. Bousset:[3] ". . . to the very end of
[Jesus'] life his Messiahship was a heavy burden, but one from
which he could not set himself free; a heavy burden, but an inevitable one, for it was his one clue to the understanding of himself and his mission, it gave him his inner hold upon himself."
Professor Grant goes on: "One thinks of a remote but not meaningless parallel, Emerson's words about Michael Angelo:

> 'The hand that fashioned Christian Rome
> And groined the arch of Peter's dome
> Wrought in a sad sincerity:
> Himself from God he could not free.' "[4]

[3] *Jesus* (1906), pp. 82 ff.
[4] "The Beginning of Jesus' Ministry," *Journal of Biblical Literature*, LII, Part IV
(Dec. 1933), pp. 193–94.

We could well add one of the following lines:

> "He builded better than he knew,"

in the sense, that is, that his knowledge of the character of the future of which he was the bearer was only partial.

The point at which it becomes clear that Jesus thought of himself not merely, like John, as the proclaimer of the Kingdom but as its bearer is his Passion. There is sufficient evidence to indicate that Jesus offered his death to the cause of the Kingdom with a sense of its critical significance, with a confidence that God would use it in some major way toward the coming of the Kingdom. Such a contribution toward the final overthrow of the reign of the prince of this age was only a final step in that overthrow characteristic of his whole ministry. But Jesus' interpretation of his death, anticipated as likely from the close of the Galilean ministry, helps us to understand his willingness to lay stress on discipleship to himself and confession of himself.

In the Passion the conflict of the old and the new eras—a conflict which had announced itself from the time of John—finally came to clear expression. It was here that the old era fully manifested its bankruptcy and that the proffered salvation clearly declared itself and ended the old order. In the Passion Jesus was inevitably led to take upon himself almost the sole burden of the Kingdom or the future; to become its door, if we may use that expression. But the sense of being bearer of the new age in this special responsibility had come to him at certain times earlier in his ministry as we have seen by the sayings cited. We can then understand how it came about that at least in the later part of his career Jesus presented his calls to discipleship as practically interchangeable with the call to repentance.

The interpretation of the Passion which we have given was, indeed, Paul's view. Paul writes in Col. 2:14–15 that by the cross, God (or Christ) canceled the written ordinances involving condemnation, and despoiled the principalities and powers of the spiritual world which under the old dispensation had tyrannized over men. But the same view is found in a saying of Jesus if the interpretation we have adopted on page 175 above be correct.

And from the days of John the Baptist until now the kingdom of heaven suffereth violence, and the violent take it by force. Mt. 11:12.

As Professor Kraeling says (see above): "The ἕως ἄρτι seems to me to imply that upon the period of violence (i.e., exerted by the spiritual powers of evil) there follows through Jesus' conquest of the forces of evil a period of supremacy of the Kingdom over the stormers." From the days of the Baptist, Jesus says, the Kingdom suffers duress, but only "until now." For now begins the overthrow of these powers. That is, the overthrow of the rule of Satan is assigned to the development of the situation after John, to the phase centering in the ministry of Jesus. But Jesus came to see the necessity of his Passion as the finally effective means for the overthrow of the evil powers. His allusion to the covenant in whatever form on the last evening points to this as well as the saying about the cup he must drink and the baptism with which he must be baptized.

The full purport of the future was a mystery that Jesus could only leave with God. He knew himself its bearer but we may well believe that his intimations of its character fluctuated in some respects. That future was God's and as such the only adequate language for it was the Kingdom of God transcendentally understood. Such suprahistorical terms for it spoke the faith which Jewish prophecy and eschatology had always held that God would have the final word with men. But such transcendental and ultimate categories for the outcome of the crisis did not in Jesus' mind exclude more immediate fulfilments. We have noted in our second and third chapters that he could anticipate the new era in less dualistic terms. Our conclusion here is that Jesus' demands grew out of the concrete crisis of his situation rather than out of the *interpretation* of it in apocalyptic terms. The apocalyptic event in the future is essentially of the character of myth, and the interim thus created is formal and conceptual rather than real.

These demands rose out of a much more real crisis and were justified by a much more valid occasion, namely the crucial question, would Israel recognize the message and the messenger of God and the hour of its visitation and the things that belonged to its peace, and so fulfil its age-old vocation? While the decision of the nation was still in the making, especially as the final hour of choice drew near, Jesus called on men for crisis-devotion (which was, indeed, only a particular case of the whole-souled devotion which he continually made basic). The unflinching allegiance of his disciples to himself and to the ethics of the Kingdom—connoting widely varying situations and responsibilities, indeed—would be determinative for the working out of what Paul was later to call the mystery of God's purpose. Therefore Jesus' appeal was in its general aspect a summoning of all to a total response of obedience to the Father, newly understood, in order that he might effect the restoration of all things now immediately in course in the nation, and in another respect the imposition on particular individuals of the special obligations incumbent on them.

We have thus a point of view that harmonizes the two so different moods in Jesus' summons. This summons all in all is one to a new kind of righteousness arising out of the presence of the promised times of the new covenant and the corresponding new relation to God. One aspect of this is the special renunciation called for in the crisis thus present and the conflicts thus inevitable, on the part of the adherents, renunciations varying with circumstances.

Conclusion

CHAPTER ELEVEN

The Ethics of the Kingdom and the Mission of Jesus

THERE are two sections in the study we have completed of the relation of eschatology to ethics in Jesus' teaching. The latter deals with the differentia of the ethics, the former with its sanction. Eschatology is a factor in both. The differentia of the ethics arises from the presence of the promised eschatological times. The sanction of the ethics arises from the anticipation of the culminating features of those times, the Judgment. But that Judgment is only a formal sanction; the conceptions of the parousia and the subsequent retributions and the regeneration are essentially imaginative. Therefore they do not require and involve interim ethics, and such we see, indeed, to be the case. For the ethics in themselves ignore an imminent catastrophe.[1] Their true sanction evidently is something else: whatever lies behind the symbolic picture of Judgment. This something else, the true sanction, is the fact of God and his nature and his will with men as assented to by the discernment of mind and heart. But it is this same fact which really determines the differentia of the ethics. It is the new apprehension of God and his will which compels a new ethics. In this respect the cogency of the ethics lies in their nature. In the other aspect, that of sanction, the cogency of the ethics lies in the instant perception of consequences involved in choice and in conduct where such a God is concerned. As we have seen, such perception of consequences elaborates itself step by step

[1] See especially Windisch, *Bergpredigt,* pp. 13 f.

in eschatological features, an extreme stage of this process appearing in certain strains of the gospels. The reward and penalty aspect of the ethical teaching is understood then as a natural formulation of the sense of consequences inevitably aroused by the particular conception of God.

But we reach the conclusion, then, that fundamental to the ethics, both as inspiration and sanction, is the apprehension of God and his will. Now this apprehension of God proceeds from his own grace; it is God himself who at last in this fulfilment of the time, this year of his favor, reveals himself, and who writes his law on men's hearts and therewith brings into being an order of relationships not heretofore possible. But the effective demonstration of all this falls to Jesus as his task; in fact the full disclosure of it waits upon the cross when the very resistance of the old order throws into high relief the motives of the Kingdom. The religious and ethical elements in the gospel are inextricable. Moreover, it is in the teaching and action of Jesus that the new work of God comes most plainly into view and is most effectively mediated to men. In him the thoughts of many hearts were revealed. It follows then that the ethics of the Kingdom are a footnote to the new religious situation, the time of salvation, and that the new religious situation is most clearly characterized by the teaching and fate, the word and story, of Jesus.

In the midst of his ministry this sense of responsibility for the fulfilment of the work of salvation then in course accounts for the drastic and urgent note in the ethics which has led some to the conception of interim ethics. Not the nearness of the end but the supreme significance of his errand and the resistance from the old order governs the world-renouncing claims. And this was not something which denied human relationships or led to asceticism or anarchy necessarily, but something that enriched those relationships; save that in an emergency it could require renunciation, and save that its newness had in it the possibility of cleavages. The redemption of Israel, the fulfilment of the promises, the hope of Israel's ministry to the nations, hung in the balance during this emergency.

Some such sense of the issues of his life breaks through the words of Jesus in the gospel, and some such sense of the responsibility of his followers. This activist view of Jesus' work is not incompatible with his sense of the divine disposition of events. And it follows that for the crucial few years or months or days of the career of Jesus upon which all this depended, any claim could be made upon those that had ears to hear. Hence the call to take up the cross and follow him in the supreme hour of God's action with his people.

"But then we conclude that the conceptions of 'interim ethics' and 'exceptional legislation' do not touch the essential feature. The radicalism does not depend so much on the fact of the imminence of the final revelation and on the fortuitous shortness of the term, but on the essential factor that that conjuncture for which men must prepare is the Kingdom of God, that the summons is a summons that comes from God who now through the mouth of Jesus is demanding something whole and perfect."[2] In this passage Windisch comes close to agreement with our emphasis on the crisis as consisting first of all in the preaching of the gospel by the prophet and the bearer of the Kingdom, and he in any case clearly sets aside the interim conception as of determining importance. He fails to throw the stress on the personal claim and errand of Jesus, stressing rather the Kingdom itself. The significance of both is to be maintained. It is true that the Kingdom is not the work of an individual, even though that individual be Jesus; it is a social creation of God. But Jesus is more than the proclaimer of that Kingdom. Only by his life and death are its motives fully declared and embodied in a social context, and Jesus himself perceived this and testified to it, if only by hint and parable.

Our interpretation of the drastic demands in some of the sayings appears liable to the just criticism made of any view that distinguishes between an ethics for those that are perfect and one for the rest. Jesus' claim was not thus double. He offered the Kingdom to all at the same time that he laid on all its easy yoke of complete surrender. But the specific actions called for from individuals varied with circumstances. Acknowledgment of the spirit of God manifest

[2] Windisch, *op. cit.*, p. 12. For his analysis showing absence of interim-preoccupation in the Sermon on the Mount see especially pp. 12–18.

in his works and words, together with the repentance and obedience
he demanded, might in the case of any hearer involve extreme persecutions, separations, renunciations. The purity, the truth, the mercy,
the devotion to heavenly treasure, the witness that he called for,
might well not be compatible with safety. And drastic words of Jesus as to ridding oneself of the offending member apply here, as well
as his sayings as to loving him more than father or mother. But the
other similar claims for extreme renunciations apply rather to particular cases of those whom Jesus judged able to do special tasks in the
exigencies of his ministry and passion. It is in keeping with this that
we find this type of summons more characteristic of the last period
of the ministry, when the enemies of Jesus were growing more
determined and the response of the people more ambiguous. Out of
the sharpest throes of the momentous crisis came the words that we
find most inhuman. The church even so could well apply such
sayings later to those who at that time were carrying on the great
errand of Christ in the midnight before the return of the bride-
groom; and the church ever since has found its exigencies when such
words were in season.

If one thinks of the practical issues of a mission field in our own
day one can easily recognize two types of occasion for extraordinary
and exacting demands. In the first place, the converts—especially
those with ten talents, or indicated by their freedom from various
handicaps and responsibilities—will be called upon for extraordinary
effort and devotion in view of the greatness of the opportunity and
the fewness of the laborers.[3] In the second place, over against the
old life and its ethics which may be exerting a strong pull upon those
that are leaving it, a sharp demand may well be laid upon the
vacillating disciples bidding them endure the persecutions and costly
renunciations incident to their reformation, and pointing out the
inescapable moral issues and the penalties involved. Such a twofold
aspect we see in the sterner sayings of Jesus, some addressed to
disciples calling them to the uniquely great occasion and opportunity

[3] Cf. Schweitzer's discussion of the factors that led him to turn from his academic
career and go to Equatorial Africa as a medical missionary, but which, he points out,
would *not* apply to many other Christians. *Out of My Life and Thought, An Auto-
biography* (New York, 1933), pp. 111–12.

and responsibility of the mission; some bringing home to the more general type of hearer the sacrifices he must be prepared to make and the cleavages he must be ready to accept in espousing the gospel.

One of the chief emphases we would make is on the necessity of referring the ethical teaching of Jesus just as far as possible to its occasion; not only the general occasion but the specific occasion. The fondness of interpreters like Bultmann for evaporating the factor of the situation, at all costs reducing the variety of the sayings to a unity, seems over simple. It is at this point that Windisch's protest is welcome. Historical-critical tests come first in studying the meaning of Jesus' ethics. The theologian must wait.

Bultmann, indeed, recognizes that the preaching of Jesus represents the Hour of Decision for men. "This is the last hour, make your choice; those not with me are against me; deny me and be denied before the angels of God; all things must be left for the sake of the Kingdom of God; it is a great case of either, or . . ."[4] And Bultmann recognizes that Jesus' ethics despite this are not interim ethics in the sense that Jer. 16:1–9 is, but are conditioned by the fact of God and his nature. Our criticism is that he simplifies too much a complex teaching, and that he takes a vein of Jesus' summons on particular occasions and erects it into a universal principle. Bultmann himself says in connection with Jesus' word on divorce, "To be sure he did command the foregoing of marriage *under certain circumstances.*"[5] But this qualification which we have italicized should hold for a large number of the drastic utterances, and it is this that Bultmann does not acknowledge. It is often in very specific circumstances that Jesus spoke his claims. A further criticism of Bultmann would demur, finally, at the absence in his total picture of the feature of grace, the positive aspect of the gospel. But this utterly grim and stern aspect of Bultmann's whole picture rises out of the essential error that we have noted above. He has eclipsed the easy yoke with the stern challenge of a specific hour. One notes that he ends up with the position that it is the sacrifice that is the essential thing, or the obedience itself, rather than the generosity to man or the impulse of

---

[4] *Jesus,* p. 31 (paraphrase); *Jesus and the Word,* p. 31.
[5] *Ibid.,* p. 93; *Jesus and the Word,* pp. 99–100.

gratitude and response to God. What is pleasing to God, he says rightly, is not poverty itself but sacrifice. But, we say, neither is sacrifice for itself pleasing to God. Jesus called for sacrifice with his eye not on the obedience of his hearer, but on the precarious and great cause to be served, and the reward of the hearer incident to it.

We have gone a long step farther, however, than Windisch himself in finding the key of the ethics in the factor of the situation. It is true that this scholar and others agree to the diversity of situation, complexity of the strands of ethical teaching, Jesus' readiness to speak as sage as well as prophet, and finally to the changed mood of the later career. But we would go farther in holding that most of the drastic ethics has its origin in the personal situation of Jesus in the ministry; that is, that its original occasion and reference should be sought in the exigencies of his work. These desperate summons to discipleship with their denial of every human tie were least of all general principles of universal application. They were in the strictest sense occasional, limited, specific, in their utterance, though belonging indeed to a supreme occasion. Jesus' main concern was with his work from hour to hour, and his greatest task as his way grew narrower and the future more enigmatic, was to hold at least some other human beings besides himself to the calling he had received. We must remember that to him in the midst of the uncompleted drama there was no assurance beyond faith that his course would have any more success than that of John. We recover, then, an historical, a biographical setting for the so-called ethical absolutes. Their generality of application vanishes, the interim aspect vanishes. They are occasional utterances to particular persons which the sacred records have lifted out of the obscurity of their original moment. Religious faith *can* generalize them, as every great occasional utterance or act can have wider significance, but such is the work of the preacher not the historian.

This characterization of the more drastic sayings applies in a lesser degree to the ethics we are accustomed to think of as in a more serene mood. Certainly large elements of it are occasional in the different sense of being occasional to particular questions asked, controversy, incidents. But much on the other hand is a plea for such attitudes, concerns, outlook, as are prerequisite for discipleship and confession. That is, Jesus is not, or not only, laying down general tests but is preparing disciples for his own campaign.

Correlatives for our time for the urgency of the ethics of Jesus are indicated by our conclusions. Our appeal should not be to an anachronistic and literal Second Coming or forensic Judgment viewed as impending in our day. Yet we can properly appeal to rewards and penalties, eschatological and otherwise, as a legitimate way of making clear the fateful character of conduct. Nor should our appeal be to the injunctions of Jesus in any wooden or legalistic way which fails to take account of the circumstances of his utterance and the changes that have taken place in the life-situation of the believer and the church.

What is above all imperative is that we should continually recapture a dynamic vision of God in his historical activity of such a compelling kind that we are thereby continually redirected and animated along the line of his purpose. This vision in any clarity carries with it a divination of the consequences of choice, individual and social, which match in their way the eschatological rewards and penalties of the gospel. Likewise, we should continually renew our grasp and discernment of the supreme significance of Jesus' person, errand and witness as affording us our decisive and incomparable disclosure of the meaning of history and of the sources of moral power and abundant life. Such emphasis on the person of Christ involves corresponding renewed recognition of the church, where it is true to itself, as similarly commanding allegiance as in a unique way the redemptive agent of God.

CHAPTER TWELVE

The Kingdom of God and the Moral Life

OUR conclusions as to the character of Jesus' ethic can be illuminated and corroborated if we approach the matter from a somewhat different angle from that we have followed in our exposition hitherto. We have seen that this ethic is conditioned by eschatology. Not only is its urgency determined by the near approach of the Kingdom, but its very content is qualified by the dawn of the new age. The nature and purpose of God, and these exhibited in historical action, determine the ethic. It is clear that the ethic of the gospel is a religious ethic. The moral life of the believer or the church must never be thought of or ordered as though it were an independent sphere. We must go further and say that while love and righteousness are essential tests of the Christian, we fail of a just grasp of the gospel if we define it first of all in ethical terms. Here we have the danger of moralism, a danger which is commonly recognized where it takes the form of legalism or of what is called Puritanism, but which often takes more subtle and more noble forms. Contemporary theology and piety are not free of this misunderstanding and a full grasp of the Christian faith is thereby handicapped.

Our aim in this chapter is, accordingly, to define more exactly the religious character of the gospel ethic. To this end we propose to introduce new considerations not prominent in our main argument, and to relate the discussion to contemporary issues. We shall raise the question whether there may not be a true sense in which the Kingdom of God is above good and evil and in which it transcends moral preoccupation. The eschatological formulation of the gospel by Jesus and his ultimate sanction of ethics in the glory of God would appear to point this way. Moreover, the genesis of ethics in the Old Testament as well as the New would seem to derive from a level of experience of God in which the ethical and the religious relation are inseparable; at a creative level, indeed, which is misrepresented if the ethical aspect is exaggerated. It is here that the category of mysticism needs to be taken seriously, though it is a category which is generally suspect in contemporary interpretation of the Old Testament and of Jesus. Our chief departure, then, in this chapter from our approach hitherto will lie in our consideration of the category of mysticism rather than that of eschatology in examining the religious context of the ethic of the gospel. It is to be remembered in this connection that, as Albert Schweitzer has argued, there is such a thing as an eschatological mysticism. The experience of the present sovereignty of God has much of the psychological and religious content which we ordinarily assign to mysticism properly understood. It is of course important to safeguard the recognized distinction between prophetic religion and mysticism, but the distinction can be exaggerated. Rejection of mystical aspects of the primitive gospel seems too often to accompany a moralistic interpretation of the faith. If the term mysticism be suspect here either on account of its vagueness or its associations with non-biblical religion it is in any case important to insist that the Christian experience in its height and depth should not be misconceived.

The teaching of Jesus, if his positive message of grace and "realized" salvation is stressed, can be construed as justifying a kind of antinomianism if only in the sense that the life of the Kingdom ultimately transcends good and evil and raises the new man to a state in which the toils of conscience are for the time being left behind. It is here that the congeniality of mysticism to Christian faith and piety is suggested. The gospel should not be thought of as limiting man's relation to God to an ethical encounter. It can also understand this relation as a substantial participation in God. Reactions today against Romanticism and allied religious types lead many theologians to condemn even those Hellenistic mystical elements which admittedly found their way into the later New Testament and subsequent Christian theology. This anti-mystical tendency can go so far as to end in a quasi-moralistic or voluntaristic interpretation on the one hand, or an existential interpretation in terms of crisis and "decision" on the other, one which is also voluntaristic in its own way.

But all such views fail to come to terms with the doctrine of the Kingdom and that of the Spirit in the gospel, and it is here that the general conclusions of our main study become relevant. There is an eschatological mysticism in the message of Jesus resting on the sense of the glory of God and reflected in the endowment of Jesus' person. This eschatological mysticism furnishes the precedent and justification for the development of later quite different types of mystical Christianity. It is because the ethic of Jesus is an eschatological ethic that it should never be transformed into a moralism. On the other hand, such an ethic runs the risk of antinomianism. One of the chief services that biblical theology can render today to show how moralism can be avoided without a lapse into ethical irresponsibility.

There is a recurrent impulse of men long tormented by the problems of conscience to seek a salvation beyond good and evil:

> Outworn heart, in a time outworn,
> Come clear of the nets of wrong and right.

Sometimes it takes the form of a frank paganism or return to an age of innocence in some South Sea island where the spontaneity of life is allegedly unmarred either by the conventions of a civilized society or the inner toils of introspection. Sometimes it is rather an insistence of the self on its own integrity, on self-reliance, against all heteronomy, the insistence on being true to one's own nature irrespective of dwarfing or distorting patterns from the outside. Sometimes it is a plea for an attainment of the spirit that escapes the tests of utility of whatever kind, that passes beyond practical considerations even the most lofty into sheer enjoyment or contemplation. Thus Allen

Tate protests: "The fusion of human success and human error in a vision of the whole of life, *the vision itself being its own goal,* has almost disappeared from the world of the spirit."

How far does Christianity justify such an impulse to rise beyond the moral level? This is all the more pertinent a question in view of the tendencies noted among recent Christian thinkers to define the gospel largely in terms of the moral will, obedience, decision or the I-Thou personal relation. The suspect character of all *eros* as well as the sharp distinction made by Heiler between mysticism and prophetic religion, and the preference for the latter as only truly Christian in certain continental writers, among them Fernand Ménégoz and Robert Will of Strasburg, all this raises the question whether there will be any place for mysticism in essential Christianity.

We have, further, new expressions in our day of the tendency sharply to distinguish religion from ethics, and from this point of view to depreciate the Jewish-Christian tradition because of its intense ethical preoccupation. "The content of the specifically religious experience," writes Professor Benjamin Miller, "is without moral nature or implication, and its aesthetic character is unrelated in kind to social vision or its imperative. . . . Morality does not depend upon the authority or sanction of a more-than-human imperative."[1] This writer presents religion as a "sensuous, mystical rapport with the cosmic phase of [man's] natural environment," and illustrates his theses with quotations from the poetry of Robinson Jeffers. Dr. Friederich Spiegelberg similarly takes a view that would seem to contradict the Jewish-Christian conception of a religiously motivated ethic. In his view the only approach to ethics from religious experience is *via* the value judgment of selflessness inspired by it. Anything else is moralism, and moralism is a disease if it has grown up out of blindness to that "beyond" which requires us to be selfless (not, "unselfish"). To say that God is good is a rationalistic projection.[2]

[1] "The Demands of the Religious Consciousness," in *The Review of Religion,* vol. IV, no. 4 (May, 1940), pp. 407–8.

[2] Position as summarized in the report of the "Week of Work" of the National Council on Religion in Higher Education, 1939. Prof. George F. Thomas in this same discussion is quoted as saying that it was a strength of the Jewish tradition

In examining Christianity at its fountainhead with these issues in mind we meet the following questions. Can we define the point in Christian experience at which a moral preoccupation or the moral phenomenon arises? Is it derivative and if so what exactly is the character of its derivation? Or is it inseparable from the religious experience proper and simultaneous with it? Even if the biblical view naïvely reads it into the very nature of God, may there not be grounds for distinguishing the numinous experience itself and the ethical attributes that become identified with it? Again, recognizing that the Christian religion assigns a primordial significance to the ethical domain, what is the real structure of the religious and ethical elements in its make-up? In particular, if salvation is achieved in connection with moral activity, how far does this exclude mystical elements from the Christian life, elements which have so large a part in other religions? To what degree, and how legitimately, has Christianity in some forms assimilated mystical elements originally absent?

1. *Numinous versus Moral Elements in the Jewish Conception of God*

The roots of the New Testament conception of God and of the religious life being in the Jewish heritage, we turn to ask first what exactly the place is of the moral factor in Judaism. We are confronted immediately with the unique testimony of this faith to the righteousness of God and his demands of righteousness as of his very being. His moral aspects are not merely attributes or manifestations in his relations with men but involved in his very nature as personal. This appears for instance in the rabbinic tradition that even before the creation the Law was among those things that already existed in heaven. The Scriptures are by no means lacking in vivid report of the numinous character of the deity. Israel was cognizant of his non-moral or supra-moral aspects. But these are always inseparably related to his righteousness.

Without denying the basic insight of Israel at this point, it is yet

that it did not separate the "eternal-temporal" dualism from the "holy-unholy," and that a moral dualism might at least be viewed as a functional revelation.

possible for us to discern in the sources two moments of religious experience, the numinous and the ethical, which unreflective piety was not inclined to separate. Study of the concept of holiness as applied to the deity is illuminating. Its older content of "separateness" shades off into a moral connotation. Yet as far back into primitive experience as one wishes to press the inquiry, the holiness of Jahveh is related to his covenants and has, therefore, a moral aspect. It stood as a sanction of the peculiar mores of his favored tribes. But, conversely, however far down we come in the period of the full moralization of the idea, the numinous aspect is not surrendered in the least. In the fully developed stage the vision of Isaiah remains typical of the content of the Jewish experience of God. He is seen in his numinous aspect as conveyed by the details of the seraphim, the *trisagion,* the smoke that filled the Temple. But the immediate reaction of the prophet was: "Woe is me for I am a man of unclean lips." A similar classic passage is the account of the giving of the decalogue in a setting of volcanic activity and numinous horror. A very interesting narrative at a more primitive stage is that which describes the God's covenant epiphany to Abraham in Genesis 15. After Abraham had set out the divided sacrifices and driven away the birds of prey, we read:

And when the sun was going down, a deep sleep [*ecstasis* in the LXX] fell upon Abraham; and, lo, a horror of great darkness fell upon him. . . . And it came to pass, that, when the sun went down, and it was dark, behold, a smoking furnace and a flaming torch that passed between these pieces. In that day Jehovah made a covenant with Abram . . .

Similarly in Job 4 we have the hair-raising numinous experience and then "a voice saying, Shall man be more just than God!" Thus we have characteristically the two moments, closely related, of numinous and ethical. Yet one would go too far to say that God is never viewed in abstraction from his aspect of righteousness. The creation of a world good in the non-ethical sense, and of man as a creature, king over the other creatures and in innocent enjoyment of the creation, is told in Genesis 1–2:3. It is only at 2:9 that the moral preoccupation appears in the Bible with the mention of the tree of good and evil.

The same double aspect appears if we examine the motivation of Jewish ethics. Apart from the motives involved in seeking reward or in the fear or love of God, the imitation of God is specially significant. "Ye shall be holy, for I, the Lord your God, am holy." G. F. Moore writes of this with a somewhat remarkable guardedness of expression, "This injunction suggests a likeness between the holiness of God by nature and the holiness of character which men are to strive after." A further and even more significant sanction of Jewish ethics is found in that of the sanctification of God's name, "the most characteristic feature of Jewish ethics both as principle and as motive" (Moore). The meaning of this motive is that the action of the faithful should be such as to bring honor and glory to the God of Israel. The New Testament expressions "Hallowed be thy name" and "glorify your Father who is in heaven," are exact expressions of this. The conception rests really upon the vivid sense of the holiness of God especially in a numinous and then in an ethical sense. Both these motives for ethics, that of the holiness of God and that which evokes his sanctity or glory, presuppose on the one hand an overwhelming sense of the *mysterium tremendum,* of the numinous itself, and then, bound up with it, certain objective aspects of God's character susceptible of imitation, such as his holiness in the ethical sense, his justice and his mercy. These are attributes derived from the religious experience itself yet distinguishable from it.

In Jesus' outlook we find these same features. The *Abba* apostrophe in his prayers appears to have made no distinction between God's majesty and his attributes of goodness and righteousness. The Jewish motive of the imitation of God is echoed in his words, "that ye may be sons of your Father who is in heaven," and "Be ye merciful even as your Father is merciful." The sanctification of the name of God is echoed in Jesus' words as we have seen and is immediately related to ethics as a motive. We are face to face with the fact that the grounding of ethics in the gospel is religious. This inseparability of religion and ethics appears nowhere more clearly than in the eschatology. Both the imminence and the ethical character of the Kingdom of God derive from the experience of God as holy. As has been said earlier: the same sensitive moral and spiritual discernment that beholds with Isaiah the glory of God also recognizes the inevitability and urgency of judgment and the inevitability of salvation. To know the Father in his inconceivable glory is to know that he acts and will act to the ends of righteousness.

We may, however, claim to distinguish in Jesus' case also the two elements of the numinous and the ethical. In the Lord's Prayer the closing doxology is secondary, but it merely makes explicit the ethics-transcending acknowledgment: Hallowed be thy name. The glory of the Father, indeed, is evoked by Jesus as we have seen in connection with the motivation of ethics. Ethics is also transcended in a sense in the first of the two great commandments. But Jesus' sense of the divine majesty appears with particular force in two sayings with regard to oaths:

But I say unto you, Swear not at all; neither by the heaven, for it is the throne of God; nor by the earth, for it is the footstool of his feet; nor by Jerusalem, for it is the city of the great King. Mt. 5:34–35

He that sweareth by the temple, sweareth by it, and by him that dwelleth therein. And he that sweareth by the heaven, sweareth by the throne of God, and by him that sitteth thereon. Mt. 23:21–22

It is true that ethical claims are immediately implied in connection with these words exalting the reality of God. But the two aspects are evidently distinguishable. No better example of this can be found than in the juxtaposition in the Lord's Prayer of the two phrases,

Thy kingdom come,
Thy will be done, as in heaven, so on earth.

The second phrase brings out the ethical implications of the coming of the Kingdom, but it is not equivalent. One may again distinguish the same elements in the basic announcement of Jesus: Repent, for the kingdom of heaven is at hand.

Thus we may conclude that the Jewish conception of God always had numinous features that underlay or crowned the ethical features, and that the same holds with Jesus. To restrict worship to acknowledgment of the ethical or consciously personal aspects of God—for instance to the suggested "I-Thou" relation—would be to impoverish it. It is sufficient to recall such a passage in the Psalter as the following that portrays the voice of Jahweh in the storm:

> The voice of the Lord shaketh the wilderness;
> The Lord shaketh the wilderness of Kadesh.
> The voice of the Lord maketh the hinds to calve,
> And strippeth the forests bare:
> And in his temple everything saith, Glory!
>
> Ps. 29:8–9

In what sense such worship may be called mystical will appear below.

2. *Charismatic versus Moral Elements in the Person of Jesus*

Persuasive considerations have led scholars to set aside as suspect most of the passages in the Synoptic Gospels in which ecstatic experiences are assigned to Jesus, or experiences of visions or voices. This judgment has not been altogether unwelcome to a widespread school of interpreters who for plausible motives tend to identify prophecy at its best with sobriety. Outstanding passages thus questioned are: the Baptism; the Temptation; the Transfiguration; the visionary pronouncement, "I beheld Satan as lightning fallen . . . "; and finally the so-called Johannine saying, which voices an esoteric revelation to Jesus, Lk. 10:21–22 (cf. Mt. 11:25–27). Moreover, even the few apparently trustworthy passages in which he connects the Spirit with his work and with that of the disciples are generally discounted as an importation into the situation from the outlook of the church. The effect of such exclusions is to deny to Jesus any features of supra-normal experience such as are clearly present in the case of Paul. The argument that the narratives of the Baptism, Temptation, and Transfiguration cannot go back to actuality in anything like their present form has been convincingly argued.[3] All these experiences of the Nazarene or his disciples represent assurances to the reader of Mark that despite appearances of a humble ministry there were nevertheless for Jesus and an inner circle divine attestations. The character of these incidents as typical Jewish midrash has been

[3] For example: H. Windisch, "Jesus und der Geist," in S. J. Case, *Studies in Early Christianity* (New York, 1928), pp. 209 ff.; H. J. Cadbury, *The Peril of Modernizing Jesus* (New York, 1937), pp. 177 ff.

most effectively demonstrated by B. W. Bacon. "The vision of Jesus, the *bath-qol* which declares his divine vocation, the temptation of Satan, these are poetic forms under which some unknown, primitive evangelist has set forth his conception of the true significance of the Lord's career."[4] As for the utterance with regard to Satan's fall, W. E. Bundy, granted its genuiness, sees in it no more than picturesque language rather than evidence of a visionary experience. The well-supported sayings of Jesus about the operation of the Spirit in his work reduce themselves to only two or three, and it is easy to conclude that this was not a characteristic feature of his thinking. When we add to this our current explanation of his healings and exorcisms in terms of contemporary faith cures, we can see how plausible is the exclusion of supra-normal psychical phenomena in the case of Jesus, especially when we remember the diminishing place they seem to have held in the later prophets. "In his religious experience we see a practical, if not a complete, elimination of the ecstatic element in prophecy," says Bundy. And again, "His experience of God is intimate, intense, simple, but in the main too prosaic and practically personal to admit of true mysticism."[5] Even admission of his dualistic eschatology does not seem to have led to hesitation in this conclusion.

Here, however, we meet the view of Otto, supported independently by Windisch and D. B. MacDonald, the Islamic specialist. They recognize in one way or another in the whole Semitic tradition what Otto calls the charismatic type. With the latter it is closely related to the eschatological outlook. Charismatic gifts, according to him, do not effect miracles in the sense of the *portentum* and the *prodigium,* but they involve (1) capacity for the spiritual and psychic experiences of a distinctive kind; (2) heightened talents such as *kubernesis* (guidance) and *diakrisis* (discernment); (3) operations of the soul and of psychic powers upon other souls.[6] Certain Greek terms taken in their strict religious significance, *exousia, dynamis, pneuma, charisma,* indicate the type. Moreover, the Scriptures convey it still more clearly in the recognized role of the *Ish Elohim* or man of God.

[4] *The Story of Jesus* (New York, 1927), p. 145; also in E. H. Sneath, ed., *Religion and the Future Life* (New York, 1922), pp. 268 ff.

[5] *Our Recovery of Jesus* (Indianapolis, 1929), pp. 102, 145, 295.

[6] *The Kingdom of God and the Son of Man,* p. 340.

In Paul's case, who because of his firsthand testimony becomes a criterion, we have special manifestations such as *glossolalia, horasis,* exorcism, *gnosis,* and transport into the third heaven.

Otto argues that Jesus belonged to this charismatic or numinous type, other examples of which he finds in Zoroaster and Mohammed. He agrees with Windisch who holds that the gospel of Mark gives us evidence that Jesus' hearers acknowledged him as such and responded with the emotions of wonder and excitement that would naturally follow. The characterization of him as one with *exousia,* says Windisch, is "a pre-dogmatic interpretation of Jesus and it reproduces the impression made by his appearance."[7] Otto is satisfied that Jesus traced his own charismatic gifts to the Spirit as Paul did. The force of Otto's argument lies especially in the light it throws on various aspects of the activity of Jesus and the coherence of all this with Semitic religious conceptions. For instance, one of the most startling features of charismatic activity, widely attested at least as a belief of the age, is confidence in ability to work effects at a distance. Paul gives us in I Cor. 5:3-5 an example of it. The gospels may then rightly ascribe to Jesus confidence in his power to effect cures at a distance. It is of interest that MacDonald reached a belief in telepathy through his observation of charismatic phenomena in Islam. Another example of the unexpected in Otto's view is his exposition of the charismatic gift of the discernment of spirits, a gift acknowledged by Paul, and one assigned to Jesus in the tradition. It is a capacity closely related to that of second sight as well as to exorcism in that it includes power to look into another person's soul or to read his inner state. Otto illustrates amply from the usage of Arabic *walis* and *sufis* and from that of early Christian monasticism, and makes allusion to mediumistic phenomena. Thus he scrutinizes a wide range of the activities of Jesus. He concludes that he belonged to the type of seer, *Ish Elohim,* prophet, endowed in a very concrete sense with the Spirit, and this in particular reference to the eschatological fulness of the times.

Windisch does not use the term "charismatic" but is concerned to bring out the role of the Spirit in Jesus' work and in his self-con-

[7] "Jesus und der Geist," in Case, *op. cit.,* p. 226.

sciousness, arguing the possibility of ecstatic experience in his case. He admits the midrashic character of the Baptism and similar narratives. But he points out that the character of Jesus as spiritistic does not rest only upon these passages but on much additional evidence: (1) his claim of *exousia* in the post-prophetic era, and the spontaneous recognition of it by the people; (2) the extraordinary presuppositions conveyed by the expression, *elthon,* "I am come . . . "; (3) his view of the "mighty works" or *dynameis,* i.e., exorcism, etc., as given by the Spirit, and transmissible to the disciples. With this and other evidence before him Windisch returns to the passages in dispute, especially the Baptism, and insists that there must have been some charismatic experience of an extraordinary kind lying back of the *exousia* with which Jesus felt himself clothed. We note that Edwyn Bevan writes as follows in his *Sibyls and Seers,* "If one may with reverence make any conjecture regarding that which took place in the inner life of Jesus, one might suppose that the voice heard at the Baptism took the form of [such] an audition."

In spite of unconvincing details in Otto's literary criticism, the evidence presented by him and Windisch is very persuasive. In his *Idea of the Holy* the former had persuasively stated the features of the numinous in Jesus' person as experienced by his hearers. No doubt this is always to a considerable degree a social product rather than an individual's own quality. The power of the "king's touch" lies rather in his sovereignty than in his person. So the *exousia* of Jesus, that is, his prestige for the populace, was partly socially conditioned. But so was his self-consciousness. Both were closely related to the eschatological situation. The value of Otto's emphasis lies in his reminder to us of the categories in which men of that time and place would view the emergence of religious leadership in a crisis of social tension and religious susceptibility. The multitudes of Israel in those decades had reached a point of high inflammability, not only to political incitement, but far more important, to religious suggestion. In fact, as Jesus declared, the Kingdom of God was at hand, i.e., nascent in the age, and this moral situation vastly extended the ordinary ranges of faith and all emotional and spiritual possibilities. In these conditions one who sensed deeply the obscure forces of the occasion and articulated them would inevitably be viewed (and view himself) in prophetic terms as one endowed with numinous authority. Such an objective not to say magical view of religious authority was, however, decisively safeguarded by the personal terms in which Jesus viewed divine action and in which he viewed human responsibility. On the one hand Jesus felt that he was empowered by the Spirit to dispossess the household of Satan and borne along by the powers of the inbreaking new *aeon*. On the other hand it was in the spiritual and psychic experiences of this situation that he yet truly personalized the religious relation to a further degree than even before, fulfiling the anticipations of the new covenent of Jeremiah.

This means that a definite mystical element must be recognized in Jesus' self-consciousness.[8] It is not different in kind from the similar endowment of the prophets, but the prominence of the charismatic gifts of healing and exorcism, and the framework of eschatological intensity and of demonism and Satanism in which it is set to give it a special character. The personal-ethical aspects of Jesus' consciousness are not to be under-estimated, but they are found in a charismatic matrix, as in the case of Isaiah, Paul and St. Francis. Are we not confronted with the fact that personal life is complex and lived at various levels psychologically? At one level (the highest?) its relationships are conscious, rational, responsible, voluntary. At other levels, not necessarily inferior in the ethical sense, the relationships of personality are unconscious, sacramental, charismatic, and may be conceived in terms of substance rather than rationality. The most scrupulous personalist in religion, anxious to interpret religion strictly as personal faith, and to worship "in spirit and in truth," falls into the danger of a merely cerebral piety unless he admits impersonal aspects of the religious life, i.e., in sacrament and in such impersonal elements as "spirit" and "power." Denial of over-

---

[8] "The child-like confidence of Jesus towards God the Father always remains a personal communion; it never has its issue in a mystical union." (Heiler) This is true, but Heiler fails to inquire whether it may not issue in a mystical *participation*. The word "union" evades the question. "His goal is not a mystical union with the divine, but a moral harmony of life with the divine will." (Bundy) This is true, but again extreme alternatives alone are considered. "Le mysticisme de Jesus ne connaît qu'une union personnaliste de la volunté de l'homme avec la volunté transcendante de Dieu . . ." (Ménégoz)

whelming supra-personal experiences of a mystical character in prophetic religion results from an impoverished moralism, or a dogmatic emphasis on transcendence, or an arbitrary absolutizing of the distinction between *eros* and *agape,* too probably dictated by a false obsequiousness on the part of the creature. We know too little of Jesus' self-consciousness to deny that he had supra-normal experience. It is arbitrary to deny of him what is so universal in the religious life and especially in the religious life of the ancient world. So extraordinary a prophetic and eschatological vocation as that of Jesus can hardly have arisen or continued without the usual concomitants of psychical experience. It is only the prepossessions of a certain type of liberal Protestantism, confining the dynamics of the religious consciousness to a prosaic voluntarism, which could ever have questioned it.

3. *Supra-moral versus Moral Elements in Jesus' Conception of the Kingdom*

One cannot be too careful in defining the place of the moral factor and the role of the ethical life in Jesus' preaching and outlook. We are here face to face with a paradox which reappears in Paul and all later Christianity. It is this paradox which has given ground for the charges of antinomianism always raised against Christianity whenever it has remained true to its evangelical doctrine of grace. For the gospel despite the prominence of the ethical claims appears to approach the sinner with indulgence, to waive the law, to confound all human standards of justice as in the parable of the eleventh hour workers in the market place, and to make salvation ultimately a matter of divine grace. "The publicans and the harlots go into the kingdom of God before you." This issue confronts us with the fact of supra-moral elements in Christianity that go back to Jesus himself. The solution of the paradox itself lies beyond any satisfactory formulation in the essential mystery of personality.

There is no question that Jesus appeals to his hearers for moral repentance with every assumption that freedom to repent and to choose is theirs. We should insist on this point, obscured by dogmatic interpreters: it is one of the glories of Jesus' position that he relied on the native discernment and responsibility of his hearers. His confidence in the persuasive power of truth and in the ultimate moral discernment of common men took precedence with him over all other considerations in his ethical appeal. The simplest illustration of this is his frequent use of unanswerable rhetorical questions. "How much then is a man of more value than a sheep!" Also with regard to the ethical life of disciples after the initial act of repentance, Jesus views this too in terms of responsible freedom. Moreover, membership even in the future transcendent Kingdom itself is never described as a condition to which humility and love are unrelated. The ethical disposition that conditions membership holds for the Kingdom whether present or future. Those anxious to secure escape for the Christian from the "nets of wrong and right" may not do it by confining moral activity to this world in contradistinction to the next. Nevertheless, the Christian is relieved of moralism, and that in both worlds.

The point is, that from the very beginning the moral phenomenon takes on a special character in the gospel. Moral qualification is paradoxically viewed as given rather than as required. For Jesus relied on other factors than the free voluntary consent of the individual, and here we have the role of non-moral and in a sense mystical elements in salvation. The faithful benefit by eschatological factors; they participate in the powers of the age to come. Yet the responsibility of the individual remains. This peculiarity of Christian ethics runs through the whole of Christianity, notably in Paul and the reformers. The paradox posed in Paul's doctrine of justification and in Luther's *sola fides* appears in the fact that in actuality both these men think and preach in terms of moral freedom and responsibility.

Jesus appealed to the free consent of men: "Repent!" "Thou wouldest not!" "And that servant, who knew his lord's will, and made not ready, nor did according to his will, shall be beaten with many stripes; but he that knew not . . . with few stripes." *But Jesus saw men's free responsiveness as stimulated by the eschatological situation.* For this reason, though the demands of the Kingdom were harder than those of the law they could be easier. But this eschatological situation meant a great deal more than heightened moral capacity. The advent of the Kingdom, already present in one aspect, meant salvation in the widest sense, and Jesus' cures and the interpretation he put on them are symbolic of this more-than-ethical significance of the good news. Even when Paul defines the gospel, that is, the operation of God in Christ, as the revelation of the "righteousness" of God, he had much more than an ethical revelation in mind, as we know by the associations of the word "righteousness" in the Psalter and in Isaiah. Jesus saw himself as part of a great redemption-transaction being carried through to its climax in his generation, a work of God in community terms, forecast by the prophecies of the age of the Spirit and of the New Covenant. In this transaction which meant the overthrow of Satan's household, the Spirit and the *dynamis* of God were manifest, and particularly in himself as a Spirit-endowed or charismatic figure. The parables of the Kingdom point to the irresistible and irreversible operation of God. The idea of predestination in Jesus' thought as well as later arises primarily from this aspect of the time of salvation as proceeding from the sole initiative of God, and only secondarily from astonishment at the obduracy of the non-repentant.

In Jesus' situation the solution of the antinomy of the moral responsibility of the disciples and the antinomianism of the gospel lies in the following consideration. The proclamation of the Kingdom by Jesus in word and act, taken in connection with the anticipation of the time—the apperception mass of the hearers—occasioned a profound deepening of the terms of personal existence. The sinner who hears the preaching of the Kingdom is carried out of the comparatively shallow moorings of his habitual moral life into the new depths implied and promised in the gospel. In this moment of creative personal crisis the role of moral autonomy appears as follows. He may repent and surrender himself to the Kingdom and the new dimensions of personal existence of which he has become aware. Such surrender is, indeed, his free choice, but it is the choice of a greatly modified self, since it is a self profoundly altered by the situation into which it has been plunged by the impact of the gospel. Therefore it is true to say that the old self was not free to accept salvation. It was the new self that accepted it, and the new self came into being from the creative impact of the powers of the Kingdom. We have thus a solution of the antinomy of freedom and grace in the process of justification, or of the antinomy of moralism and grace in Jesus' work. This principle should by no means be confined to Christianity. The message of one of the Jewish prophets, for example, would have the same effect in deepening the terms of personal existence and offering the opportunity of a new level of the moral life. We note here also that Luther's denial of all personal co-operation in the process of justification with his doctrine of the enslaved will is perfectly true to the facts, for the old self needs to be excited and thrown into solution as it were by new stimuli before it is able to desire or to choose new values. It is at this point that Erasmus' view was far more superficial.

The crux of the matter, then, is this. Any access of moral vigor must wait upon a prior emancipating act of God. There must be successive acts of divine creativity as antecedents to increased personal autonomy in the moral realm. It is only because the Kingdom of God represents such supra-moral values that it has such significance for moral attainment.

The fact is, that for Jesus the Kingdom of God represented as it always did in the faith of Israel something far more than a condition characterized by moral attainment and moral relations. It was a state in which men would participate directly in the glory of God, would see his face. This is not to say that the Kingdom of God is beyond good and evil in every sense. It is beyond good and evil in the sense that the paroxysms of the divided self are overcome and that the life of personal relations is sustained spontaneously rather than voluntarily. There is no moralism, no law, no calculation of duty, nothing mechanical, no bondage of the conscience, no seal placed on the springs of individuality. As Luther says in a passage in which he exults at the transcendence of Christian liberty over all bondage and all moralism: "The Christian rises above all that one can wish or hope. He lives like Adam in Paradise." But in a higher sense ethics still characterizes the fellowship of the Kingdom in that it is a kingdom of personality, a communion of selves, whose peculiar beatitude is made possible by the combination of liberty and loyalty.

Such beatitude requires a certain disposition of the members of the Kingdom, i.e., a moral activity. But the moral activity is not itself the life of the Kingdom. The life of the Kingdom is divine operation, which, availing itself of such a disposition, brings to pass through the members its own incalculable and unimagined creations. This is the sense of the statement in the Westminister Catechism that men exist to glorify God and enjoy him forever.

The gospel in its message to sinning men inevitably gives large place to the moral demand upon them. But it is to be noted that what ultimately characterizes it—the more-than-ethical of the Kingdom of God—runs through it from the beginning. God is numinous as well as righteous. Jesus is a charismatic figure as well as a prophet in the ethical sense. The step of repentance or justification takes place in a crisis created not only by moral demand (as with law) but by eschatological deepening of the terms of personal existence. The Christian life is lived to the glory of God, that is in participation in his creativity, and this is far beyond all moralism.

Granted then that the conception of the Kingdom of God outruns moralism and that the conception of the glory of God finally subordinates and silences the moral preoccupation altogether, in what sense can the life of the believer at this stage be called mystical? And note that we are talking about the believer here and now and not only in the perfected Kingdom, since he already participates in it. His experience may be called mystical first in view of the eschatological outlook. As Schweitzer says, eschatology is an attempt to transcend dualism. The eschatologist like the mystic is conscious of being at the meeting place of two worlds not only in the moral sense but also in the metaphysical, and of participating in the eternal world partially and proleptically present.[9] He is conscious of living already by the power of the *aeon* to come. One very searching test of mysticism is the value set on history; indeed, Heiler recognizes that the contrast between prophetic and mystical religion nowhere appears so clearly. But on this test Jewish-Christian eschatology satisfies the requirements of mysticism. Apocalyptic eschatology dissolves history, and it does so because it is conscious of transcending the

[9] *The Mysticism of Paul the Apostle* (New York, 1931), p. 37.

distinction between the temporal and the eternal. The experience of the disciple of the Kingdom may be called mystical, secondly, because his type of piety satisfies Leipoldt's definition of mysticism as a "piety that seeks to secure the presence of God with man in a manner that alters the normal human consciousness." The doctrine of the Spirit in Christianity, the characteristic feature of what we may call New Testament psychology, tacitly and even expressly acknowledged in the outlook of Jesus, is a doctrine of the alteration of the human consciousness in consequences of the presence of God. If any refuse to accept as genuine Jesus' references to the operation of the Spirit in his work and that of his disciples a corresponding recognition of present divine power is self-evident in his view of the Kingdom as having a present phase.

Students have hesitated to acknowledge the mystical aspects of Judaism and of the primitive gospel because they have thought of mysticism in terms of union rather than of participation. But mysticism in its extreme form of complete union and of complete monism is exceptional. Our object should be not to deny the mystical aspect of Christianity but to characterize and differentiate it.

In both prophetic religion and in mysticism we meet with similar psychological features, for the same psycho-physical mechanisms are brought into play, though by different symbols and stimuli. The presence or absence of visions and voices, beatitude and ecstasy, is determined by cultural and temperamental factors and is not specially significant. The quality of the religious satisfactions is, however, different. In prophetic religion the visions and mystical states have a greater richness because they are associated with the triumph of personal values and fellowship. The realization or proleptic realization of the Kingdom of God has this meaning. These experiences and insights presuppose full recognition of personal and social frustration. They are never purchased at the expense of a *reduction* of the area of evil as in the case of many forms of mysticism. The mysticism and ecstasy of the Christian subject is therefore mixed with grief and is in this respect unique in tone or quality. The classic formulas are: "Sorrowing but always rejoicing;" "Blessed are they that mourn;" or Luther's expression, *Kreuzseligkeit.* It is said of Luther that even in his mystical period, "his flights never dissolved his anguish." He was true to his prophetism when he said: "Do not even attend to Christ in glory until you have seen him crucified." In the usual mystic, on the other hand, while there is also consciousness of victory over evil, only part of the gamut of evil is involved since there is less sensitivity to the realm of personal values. Evil tends to restrict itself for him to bodily and material bondage.

To put it another way, the ecstasy of the mystic proper is based on deliberate and methodical excitation of selected psychic areas, by a process of abstraction from or real reduction of the field of human consciousness and relations. It is an effort to "return to the original fountains" or to an "unstated being"—that is to the supposed irrational ground of being, the abyss, or pre-personal stage or level. By contrast, the emotion and ecstasy of prophetic religion make no such reduction of the field of experience and responsibility, but draw on the same primordial energies to articulate them through the whole range of personal life. Its concentration in prayer and devotion is not a real reduction but an act of the whole self in relation to the whole of reality. Of course most religious types represent shades and combinations of these widely differing extremes. The Christian mystic often borrows from the method of the mystic proper, and sometimes, to his loss, from his irresponsibility. The pagan or aesthetic mystic, on the other hand, is often influenced by the prophetic type. It thus often comes about that actual mysticism as we know it in East and West has a great deal in common with prophetic religion or "faith mysticism" in the Jewish Christian tradition. The concern for personal fulfilment in the true sense of person may be present in both. Likewise the disinterested contemplation and enjoyment of God transcending moralism may be present in both, though in terms of quite different symbols.

Life in the Kingdom of God constantly points to and approximates to an experience beyond good and evil. This is what is implied in the New Testament conception of the Spirit, or its assurance to the believer even in this age of the "first fruits" or of an "earnest" of eternal life. To "taste the powers of the age to come," or to behold even here the glory of God, similarly suggests a transcendence of the tormenting moral antinomies and preoccupations which still commonly characterize our human condition. Life has its hours of transfiguration, and nature and art offer their reflections and analogies of that new Eden in which indeed love abides, but as a free gift and not a duty.

Bibliography

ALTHAUS, PAUL. *Die letzten Dinge: Entwurf einer christlichen Eschatologie*. 4th ed. Gütersloh, 1933.

BACON, B. W. *Studies in Matthew*. New York, 1930.

BARTSCH, H. W., (ed.) *Kerygma und Mythos: Ein theologisches Gespräch*. ("Theologische Forschung" 1) Hamburg, 1948.

BIETENHARD, HANS. *Die Reichgottes-Erwartung im Neuen Testament*. Bern, 1946.

BOUSSET, WILHELM. *Die Religion des Judentums im späthellenistischen Zeitalter*. 3d ed. Tübingen, 1926.

BOWMAN, J. W. *The Intention of Jesus*. Philadelphia, 1943.

BULTMANN, RUDOLF. *Jesus*. Berlin, 1929; English ed., *Jesus the Word*. New York, 1934.

———. "Die Eschatologie des Johannes-Evangelium," in *Glauben und Verstehen*. Tübingen, 1933.

———. *Offenbarung und Heilsgeschehen*. ("Beiträge zur evangelischen Theologie," Band 9.) Munich, 1941. See here, "Neues Testament und Mythologie: Das Problem der Entmythologisierung der neutestamentlichen Verkündigung," pp. 27–69; also reprinted in Bartsch volume indicated above, pp. 15–53, with discussion by various writers.

———. "Heilsgeschichte und Geschichte," *Theologische Literaturzeitung*, 73 (1948), 659–66.

———. *Theologie des Neuen Testaments*, I Lieferung. Tübingen, 1948.

BURI, F. *Die Bedeutung der neutestamentlichen Eschatologie für die neuere protestantische Theologie*. Bern, 1934.

BURKITT, F. C. *Jewish and Christian Apocalypses*. London, 1914.

BURNET, ADAM W. *The Lord Reigneth: A Popular Explanation of the Book of Revelation*. New York, 1947.

CADOUX, C. J. *The Historic Mission of Jesus: A Constructive Re-examination of the Eschatological Teaching in the Synoptic Gospels*. New York, 1943.

CAMPBELL, J. Y. "The Kingdom of God Has Come," *Expository Times,* XLVIII (1936–37), 91–94.

CHARLES, R. H. *The Apocrypha and Pseudepigrapha of the Old Testament in English.* Oxford, 1913.

CLARK, K. W. "Realized Eschatology," *Journal of Biblical Literature,* LIX (1940), 367–83.

COLWELL, E. C. *An Approach to the Teaching of Jesus,* chaps. v, vi. New York, 1946.

CRAIG, C. T. "Realized Eschatology," *Journal of Biblical Literature,* LVI (March, 1937), 17–26.

CULLMANN, OSCAR. "La Pensée eschatologique . . ." (a discussion of Holmström), *Revue d'histoire et de philosophie religieuses,* XVIII (1938), 347–55.

———. *Le retour du Christ, espérance de l'Eglise, selon le Nouveau Testament.* Neuchatel, 1945.

———. *Christus und die Ziet: Die urchristliche Zeit- und Geschichtsauffassung.* Zürich, 1946.

DAVIES, PAUL E. "The Relevance of Apocalyptic for Ancient and Modern Situations," in H. R. WILLOUGHBY (ed.), *The Study of the Bible Today and Tomorrow,* pp. 279–97. Chicago, 1947.

DIBELIUS, MARTIN. *Geschichtliche und übergeschichtliche Religion im Christentum.* Göttingen, 1925. 2d ed. (*Evangelium und Welt*). Göttingen, 1929.

———. *The Sermon on the Mount.* New York, 1940.

DOBSCHÜTZ, ERNST VON. *The Eschatology of the Gospels.* London, 1910.

DODD, C. H. *The Parables of the Kingdom.* New York, 1936.

———. "The Kingdom of God Has Come," *Expository Times,* XLVIII (1936–37), 138–42.

———. *The Apostolic Preaching and Its Developments.* Chicago, 1937.

———. *History and the Gospel.* New York, 1938.

———. "The Kingdom of God and History," chap. ii in the volume of the same title in the series, "Church, Community and State," Vol. III. London, 1938.

EASTON, B. S. *Christ in the Gospels.* New York, 1930.

GILMOUR, S. MACLEAN. "Interpreting the Sermon on the Mount," *Crozer Quarterly,* XXIV, No. 1 (January, 1947), 47–56. (A useful summary of parts of WINDISCH, *Der Sinn der Bergpredigt.*)

GLOEGE, G. *Das Reich Gottes und Kirche im Neuen Testament* ("Neutestamentliche Forschungen," 2 Reihe, iv). Gütersloh, 1929.

GOGUEL, MAURICE. *The Life of Jesus.* New York, 1933.

GRANT, F. C. *The Gospel of the Kingdom.* New York, 1940.

————. "Ethics and Eschatology in the Teaching of Jesus," *Journal of Religion,* XXII, No. 4 (October, 1942), 359–70.

HÉRING, JEAN. *Le Royaume de Dieu et sa venue: Objet de l'espérance de Jésus et de S. Paul.* Paris, 1937.

HOLMSTRÖM, FOLKE. *Det Eskatologiska Motivet I Nutida Teologi.* Stockholm, 1933. German trans., *Das eschatologische Denken der Gegenwart,* Gütersloh, 1936.

HÜGEL, FRIEDRICH VON. "The Apocalyptic Element in the Teaching of Jesus," in *Essays and Addresses in the Philosophy of Religion,* chap. v. London, 1921.

KEPLER, T. S. *Contemporary Thinking about Jesus: An Anthology.* New York, 1944.

KLAUSNER, JOSEPH. *Die messianischen Forstellungen des jüdisches Volkes im Zeitalter der Tannaiten.* Berlin, 1904.

KNOX, JOHN. *The Man Christ Jesus,* esp. chap. ii. Chicago, 1941.

————. *Christ the Lord,* chap. ii. Chicago, 1945.

KÜMMEL, W. G. "Die Eschatologie der Evangelien," *Theologische Blätter,* XV (1936), 225–41 (reprint, Nos. 9–10).

————. *Kirchenbegriff und Geschichtsbewusstsein in der Urgemeinde und bei Jesus.* Uppsala, 1943.

————. *Verheissung und Erfüllung: Untersuchungen zur eschatologischen Verkündigung Jesu.* Basel, 1945.

————. "Mythische Rede und Heilsgeschehen im Neuen Testament," in *Coniectanea Neotestamentica* XI (Lund, 1947), pp. 109–131.

KÜNNETH, WALTER. *Theologie der Auferstehung.* 2d ed. Munich, 1934.

LÖWITH, KARL. *Meaning in History: the Theological Implications of the Philosophy of History.* Chicago, 1949.

McCOWN, C. C. "The Eschatology of Jesus Reconsidered," *Journal of Religion,* XVI (1936), 30–46.

————. *The Search for the Real Jesus.* New York, 1940.

————. "In History or beyond History," *Harvard Theological Review,* XXXVIII, No. 3 (July, 1945), 151–75.

————. "Jesus, Son of Man: A Survey of Recent Discussion," *Journal of Religion,* XXVIII, No. 1 (January, 1948), 1–12.

MANSON, WILLIAM. *Jesus the Messiah.* Philadelphia, 1946.

MASSON, CH. "Christ et le temps," *Revue de théologie et de philosophie,*

XXXIV (1946), 75–88. (An examination of CULLMANN, *Christus und die Zeit*.)

MICHAELIS, W. *Täufer, Jesus, Urgemeinde: Die Predigt vom Reiche Gottes vor und nach Pfingsten.* 1928.

———. *Der Herr verzieht nicht seine Verheissung: Die Aussagen Jesu über die Nähe des jüngsten Tages.* 1942.

MINEAR, PAUL S. "The Relevance of the Message for Our Day," *Journal of Bible and Religion,* X, No. 2 (May, 1942), 88–92.

———. "The Conception of History in Jesus and the Prophets," *ibid.,* XI, No. 3 (August, 1943), 156–61.

———. "Time and the Kingdom," *Journal of Religion,* XXIV, No. 2 (April, 1944), 77–88.

———. *Eyes of Faith.* Philadelphia, 1946.

MOORE, G. F. *Judaism in the First Centuries of the Christian Era: The Age of the Tannaim,* Vols. I–III. Cambridge, 1927–30.

MOULD, E. W. K. *The World View of Jesus.* New York, 1941.

OTTO, RUDOLF. *Reich Gottes und Menschensohn.* Munich, 1934. English ed., *The Kingdom of God and the Son of Man,* trans. from the rev. German ed. by F. V. FILSON and B. L. WOOLF. London, 1938.

PORTER, F. C. *The Messages of the Apocalyptical Writers.* New York, 1905.

———. "Judaism in New Testament Times," *Journal of Religion,* VII, No. 1 (January 1928), 30–62.

PREISKER, HERBERT. *Die Ethik der Evangelien und die jüdische Apokalyptik.* Breslau, 1915.

PRENTER, H. "Mythe et évangile," *Revue de théologie et de philosophie,* XXXV (1947), 49–67.

ROWLEY, H. H. *The Relevance of Apocalyptic: A Study of Jewish and Christian Apocalypses from Daniel to the Revelation.* London and Redhill, 1944.

RUST, E. C. *The Christian Understanding of History.* London, 1947.

SCHWEITZER, ALBERT. *Das Messianitäts und Leidensgeheimnis: Eine Skizze des Lebens Jesu.* 1901. English ed., *The Mystery of the Kingdom of God,* translated with an Introduction by WALTER LOWRIE. London, 1925.

———. *Von Reimarus zu Wrede: Eine Geschichte der Leben-Jesu-Forschung.* Tübingen, 1906; 2d ed., 1913. English ed., *The Quest of the Historical Jesus: A Critical Study of Its Progress from Reimarus to Wrede,* trans. W. MONTGOMERY. London, 1910, 1948.

Scott, E. F. *The Kingdom and the Messiah*. Edinburgh, 1911.

———. *The New Testament Idea of Revelation*. New York, 1935.

Sevenster, Gerhard. *Ethiek en Eschatologie in de Synoptische Evangelien: Een Studie over het Typische in Jezus' Zedeleer*. Leiden, 1929.

Sharman, H. B. *Son of Man and Kingdom of God: A Critical Study*. New York, 1943.

Sneath, E. H. (ed.) *Religion and the Future Life*. New York, 1922.

Stauffer, Ethelbert. *Die Theologie des Neuen Testaments*. Geneva, 1945.

Strack, H. L., and Billerbeck, P. *Kommentar zum Neuen Testament aus Talmud und Midrasch*. Munich, 1922–28.

Troeltsch, Ernest. "Eschatologie: Dogmatisch" in *Die Religion in Geschichte und Gegenwart*, II, 622 ff. 1st ed. 1910.

Weber, H. E. *"Eschatologie" und "Mystik" im Neuen Testament*. Gütersloh, 1930.

Weiss, Johannes. *Die Predigt Jesu vom Reiche Gottes*. Göttingen, 1900.

Wendland, H.-D. *Die Eschatologie des Reiches Gottes bei Jesus: Eine Studie über den Zusammenhang von Eschatologie, Ethik und Kirchenproblem*. Gütersloh, 1931.

Werner, Martin. *Die Entstehung des christlichen Dogmas, problemgeschichtlich dargestellt*. Bern and Leipzig, 1941. (See especially chap. ii on consistent eschatology and present-day New Testament scholarship.)

Windisch, Hans. *Der Sinn der Bergpredigt: Ein Beitrag zum Problem der richtigen Exegese*. Leipzig, 1929.

———. *The Meaning of the Sermon on the Mount*, trans. S. M. Gilmour. Chicago (prospective).

A Symposium on Eschatology. By Members of the Society of Biblical Literature and Exegesis. New Haven, 1923.

The Kingdom of God and History. ("Church, Community, and State Series.") Papers by Wood, Dodd, Bevan, etc. London, 1938.

Index

Althaus, P., 47
Anesaki, M., 33 n.

Bacon, B. W., 78, 101 f., 149 f., etc.; on Jesus and the law, 131, 154–59
Berdiaeff, N., 23
Bevan, E., 205
Boisen, A., 50 n.
Bowman, J. W., 15
Branscomb, B. H., 132 n., 154 n.
Bultmann, R., 12 f., 14, 45, 62, 133 n.; criticism of his *Jesus and the Word*, 138 ff., 191 f.; on his "Entmythologisierung" of the New Testament, 47, 64–66
Bundy, W. E., 164, 203, 206 n.

Cadbury, H. J., 178 n.
Cadoux, C. J., 15
Carlyle, T., 33
Cullmann, O., 74 n., 48 f.

Daniel, Book of, 44, 54
Dante, 23
Dibelius, M., 14, 45
Dodd, C. H., 15, 43 f., 54 ff., 62

Easton, B. H., 154 n., 157 f.
Emerson, R. W., 180 f.
Eschatology, as myth, 21 ff., 134, 161; of the Puritans, 22, 24 f.; of Nicheren (Japanese), 33 n.; of the American Indians (Paviatso), 33 n.; as dramatization of value, 32 ff.; *see* Jewish eschatology
Ethics, Jewish; motives of, 87, 90, 120 f., 125, 200 f.; moral attributes of God, 198 ff.

Ethics of Jesus, modern validity of, 9 f.; appeal to reason, 116–19, 138 f., 207 f.; their ground in the nature of God, 119, 200 f.; and the new ethical situation, 147 ff., 158 f., 208 ff.; new covenant character, 160 ff.; relation to discipleship, 166–75, 188, 192; emergency claims, 164 f., 167 ff., 182 f., 190 f.; on defilement, 155–58; on divorce, 157; the rich youth, 173 f.; *see* Jesus and the law; *also,* Rewards and penalties

God, his nature as sanction, 119–29; Jesus' conception of, *ibid.;* Jewish conception of, 198–202; sanctification of the name, 123–29
Goguel, M., 40 f.
Grant, F. C., 15, 48 f., 180
Green, J. R., 25 n.

Harnack, 13, 44
Heiler, 197, 206 n., 211
Heilsgeschichte, 48, 65, 67
Héring, J., 48 f., 68 f.
Hocking, W. E., 134 n.
Holmström, F., 44 ff., 49
Hooker, Thomas, 25 n.

Inge, W. R., 29 n., 33 n.
Interim ethics, 38; denied, 160 f., 178 f., 182, 189

Jesus, self-interpretation, 57, 166, 169, 179 ff.; Schweitzer's view of, 37 ff.; charismatic character, 202–7; symbolic character of his eschatological teaching, 34 ff., 56, 134 f., 161; significance of the Passion, 58, 181 ff.; authority as

221